AQA Physics for Combined Science: Trilogy

Third edition

GCSE

Teacher Handbook

Darren Forbes
Editor: Lawrie Ryan

OXFORD
UNIVERSITY PRESS

OXFORD
UNIVERSITY PRESS

Great Clarendon Street, Oxford, OX2 6DP, United Kingdom

Oxford University Press is a department of the University of Oxford.
It furthers the University's objective of excellence in research,
scholarship, and education by publishing worldwide. Oxford is a
registered trade mark of Oxford University Press in the UK and in
certain other countries

© Oxford University Press 2016

The moral rights of the authors have been asserted

First published in 2016

All rights reserved. No part of this publication may be reproduced,
stored in a retrieval system, or transmitted, in any form or by any
means, without the prior permission in writing of Oxford University
Press, or as expressly permitted by law, by licence or under terms agreed
with the appropriate reprographics rights organization. Enquiries
concerning reproduction outside the scope of the above should be sent
to the Rights Department, Oxford University Press,
at the address above.

You must not circulate this work in any other form and you must
impose this same condition on any acquirer

British Library Cataloguing in Publication Data
Data available

978 0 19 839589 8

10 9 8 7 6 5 4 3 2 1

Paper used in the production of this book is a natural, recyclable
product made from wood grown in sustainable forests.
The manufacturing process conforms to the environmental regulations
of the country of origin.

Printed in Great Britain

Darren Forbes would like to give huge thanks to his wife Samantha and
daughter Emma for their love and patience and to first mate Pliny Harris
for his wise words.

Lawrie would like to thank the following people for their help and
support in producing this teacher handbook. Each one has added value
to my initial efforts: Annie Hamblin, Sadie Garratt, Emma-Leigh Craig,
Amie Hewish, Andy Chandler-Grevatt.

Index compiled by INDEXING SPECIALISTS (UK) Ltd., Indexing house,
306A Portland Road, Hove, East Sussex, BN3 5LP United Kingdom.

COVER: Johnér / Offset

Contents

Required practicals		v
Introduction		vi
Assessment and progress		viii
Differentiation and skills		x
Kerboodle		xii

1 Energy and energy resources — 2

Chapter P1 Conservation and dissipation of energy — 4
- P1.1 Changes in energy stores — 4
- P1.2 Conservation of energy — 6
- P1.3 Energy and work — 8
- P1.4 Gravitational potential energy stores — 10
- P1.5 Kinetic energy and elastic energy stores — 12
- P1.6 Energy dissipation — 14
- P1.7 Energy and efficiency — 16
- P1.8 Electrical appliances — 18
- P1.9 Energy and power — 20
- P1 Checkpoint — 22

Chapter P2 Energy transfer by heating — 24
- P2.1 Energy transfer by conduction — 24
- P2.2 Specific heat capacity — 26
- P2.3 Heating and insulating buildings — 28
- P2 Checkpoint — 30

Chapter P3 Energy resources — 32
- P3.1 Energy demands — 32
- P3.2 Energy from wind and water — 34
- P3.3 Power from the Sun and the Earth — 36
- P3.4 Energy and the environment — 38
- P3.5 Big energy issues — 40
- P3 Checkpoint — 42

2 Particles at work — 44

Chapter P4 Electric circuits — 46
- P4.1 Current and charge — 46
- P4.2 Potential difference and resistance — 48
- P4.3 Component characteristics — 50
- P4.4 Series circuits — 52
- P4.5 Parallel circuits — 54
- P4 Checkpoint — 56

Chapter P5 Electricity in the home — 58
- P5.1 Alternating current — 58
- P5.2 Cables and plugs — 60
- P5.3 Electrical power and potential difference — 62
- P5.4 Electrical currents and energy transfer — 64
- P5.5 Appliances and efficiency — 66
- P5 Checkpoint — 68

Chapter P6 Molecules and matter — 70
- P6.1 Density — 70
- P6.2 States of matter — 72
- P6.3 Changes of state — 74
- P6.4 Internal energy — 76
- P6.5 Specific latent heat — 78
- P6.6 Gas pressure and temperature — 80
- P6 Checkpoint — 82

Chapter P7 Radioactivity — 84
- P7.1 Atoms and radiation — 84
- P7.2 The discovery of the nucleus — 86
- P7.3 Changes in the nucleus — 88
- P7.4 More about alpha, beta, and gamma radiation — 90
- P7.5 Activity and half-life — 92
- P7 Checkpoint — 94

3 Forces in action — 96

Chapter P8 Forces in balance — 98
- P8.1 Vectors and scalars — 98
- P8.2 Forces between objects — 100
- P8.3 Resultant forces — 102
- P8.4 Centre of mass — 104
- P8.5 The parallelogram of forces — 106
- P8.6 Resolution of forces — 108
- P8 Checkpoint — 110

Chapter P9 Motion — 112
- P9.1 Speed and distance–time graphs — 112
- P9.2 Velocity and acceleration — 114
- P9.3 More about velocity–time graphs — 116
- P9.4 Analysing motion graphs — 118
- P9 Checkpoint — 120

Chapter P10 Force and motion — 122
- P10.1 Forces and acceleration — 122
- P10.2 Weight and terminal velocity — 124
- P10.3 Forces and braking — 126
- P10.4 Momentum — 128
- P10.5 Forces and elasticity — 130
- P10 Checkpoint — 132

4 Waves and electromagnetism	134
Chapter P11 Wave properties	**136**
P11.1 The nature of waves	136
P11.2 The properties of waves	138
P11.3 Reflection and refraction	140
P11.4 More about waves	142
P11 Checkpoint	144
Chapter P12 Electromagnetic waves	**146**
P12.1 The electromagnetic spectrum	146
P12.2 Light, infrared, microwaves, and radio waves	146
P12.3 Communications	150
P12.4 Ultraviolet waves, X-rays, and gamma rays	152
P12.5 X-rays in medicine	154
P12 Checkpoint	156
Chapter P13 Electromagnetism	**158**
P13.1 Magnetic fields	158
P13.2 Magnetic fields of electric currents	160
P13.3 The motor effect	162
P13 Checkpoint	164
Answers	**165**
Index	**177**

Required practicals

Practical work is a vital part of physics, helping to support and apply your scientific knowledge, and develop your investigative and practical skills. In this Physics part of your AQA Combined Science: Trilogy course, there are eight required practicals that you must carry out. Questions in your exams could draw on any of the knowledge and skills you have developed in carrying out these practicals.

A Required practical feature box has been included in this student book for each of your required practicals. Further support is available on Kerboodle.

Required practicals		Topic
14	**Determining specific heat capacity.** Determine the specific heat capacity of a metal block of known mass by measuring the energy transferred to the block and its temperature rise, and using the equation for specific heat capacity.	P2.2
15	**Investigating resistance.** Set up circuits and investigate the resistance of a wire, and of resistors in series and parallel.	P4.2 P4.5
16	**Investigating electrical components.** Correctly assemble a circuit and investigate the potential difference–current characteristics of circuit components.	P4.3
17	**Calculating densities.** Measure the mass and volume of objects and liquids and calculate their densities using the density equation.	P6.1
18	**Investigate the relationship between force and extension for a spring.** Hang weights of known mass from a spring and, using the correct apparatus, measure the resulting extension. Use the results to plot a force-extension graph.	P10.5
19	**Investigate the relationship between force and acceleration.** Using a newton-metre, investigate the effect on the acceleration of an object of varying the force on it and of varying its mass.	P10.1
20	**Investigating plane waves in a ripple tank and waves in a solid.** Determine which apparatus are the most suitable for measuring the frequency, speed, and wavelength of waves in a ripple tank, and investigate waves on a stretched string.	P11.4
21	**Investigating infrared radiation.** Determine how the properties of a surface affect the amount of infrared radiation absorbed or radiated by the surface.	P12.2

Introduction

About the series

This is the third edition of the UK's number 1 course for GCSE Science. The student books have been approved by AQA, and our author teams and experts have been working closely with AQA to develop a blended suite of resources to support the new specifications.

All resources in this series have been carefully designed to support students of all abilities on their journey through GCSE Science. The demands of the new specifications are fully supported, with maths, practicals, and synoptic skills developed throughout, and all new subject content fully covered.

The series is designed to be flexible, enabling you to co-teach Foundation and Higher tiers, and Combined and Separate Sciences. Content is clearly flagged throughout the resources, helping you to identify the relevant content for your students.

Assessment is an important feature of the series, and is supported by our unique assessment framework, helping students to track and make progress.

The series is edited by Lawrie Ryan. Building on his vast experience as an author for much-loved titles such as Spotlight Science and the Chemistry for You Lawrie has become one of the best-known authors and editors of educational science books both nationally and internationally. A former Head of Science, Science Advisor, and Ofsted Inspector, he understands the demands of modern education and draws on his experience to deliver this new and innovative course that builds upon the legacy of previous editions

Your Teacher Handbook

This Teacher Handbook aims to save you time and effort by offering lesson plans, differentiation suggestions, and assessment guidance on a page-by-page basis that is a direct match to the Student Book.

With learning outcomes differentiated you can tailor the lessons and activities to suit your students and provide progression opportunities to students of all abilities.

Lesson plans are written for 55-minute lessons but are flexible and fully adaptable so you can choose the activities that suit your class best.

Section opener

The Section opener provides an overview of the parts of the specification, required practicals, and maths skills covered in the section.

Lesson
Specification links

Specification links

This table provides an overview of the specification topics covered in the chapters of the section. It also gives an indication of which Paper each specification topic will be mainly assessed in.

Required practicals

This table indicates which required practicals are covered within this section. It also gives a list of Apparatus and techniques that could be assessed by that practical.

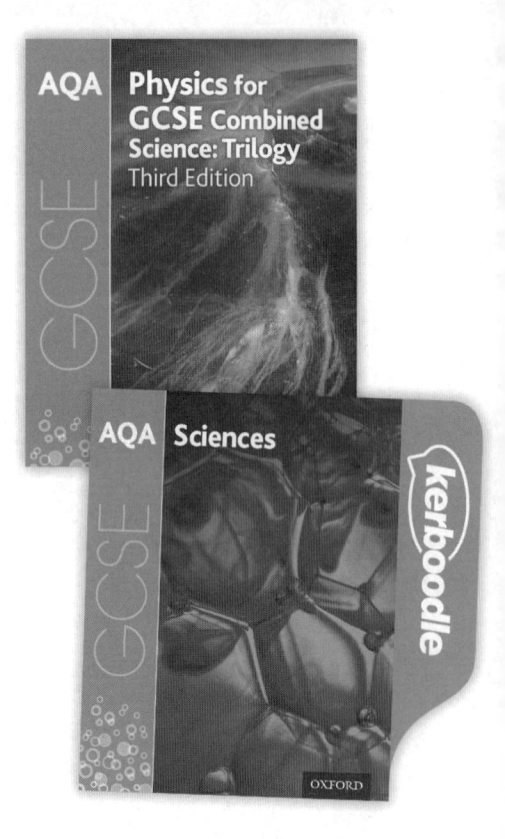

Key Stage 3 and GCSE Catch-up

This table outlines Key Stage 3 knowledge that is a pre-requisite for this section. Later Section Openers will also include GCSE knowledge from earlier in the course. Quick checkpoint activities, to assess students understanding of each statement, are provided

For each statement, a suggestion for how you can help students catch up is also provided, as well as an index of which topic each statement links to.

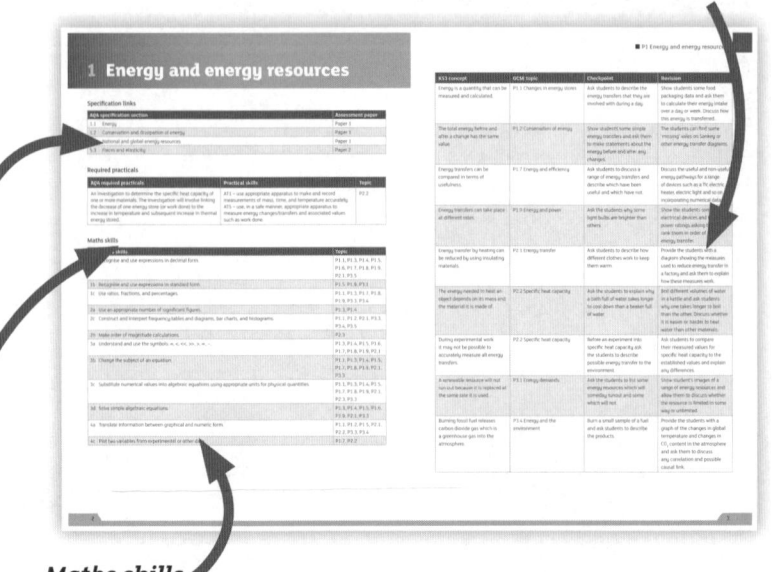

Maths skills

This table provides an overview of the maths skills covered in the chapters of the section.

This indicated the area of the *AQA GCSE Combined science: Trilogy (9–1)* 2016 specification this lesson covers. Relevant Working scientifically and Mathematical requirements links are also provided.

Differentiated outcomes

This table summarises the possible lesson outcomes. They are ramped and divided into three ability bands. The three ability bands are explained in the Assessment and progress section. Each ability band has two to three outcomes defined, designed to cover the specification content for different ability levels

An index of questions and activities is given for each learning outcome, helping you to assess your students informally as you progress through each lesson

Maths and literacy

These boxes provide suggestions of how Maths and Literacy skills can be developed in the lesson. Where relevant, the Maths skills are linked to the Mathematical requirements of the specification.

Practicals

These boxes provide equipment lists, an outline method, and safety requirements for any practicals in the lesson. Required practicals are flagged with the Required practical icon.

Although safety requirements are given, a fully-comprehensive risk assessment should be carried out before any practical activity is undergone.

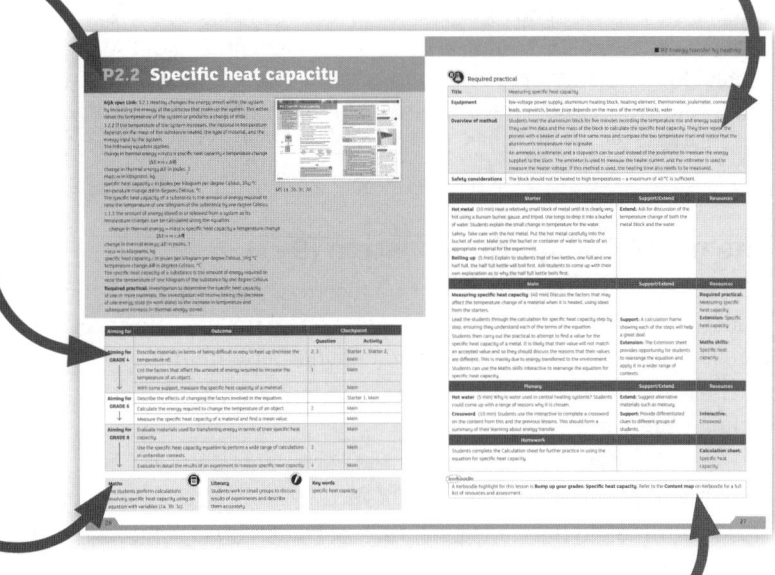

Suggested lesson plan

A suggested route through the lesson is provided, including ideas for support, extension, and homework. The right-hand column indicated where Kerboodle resources are available.

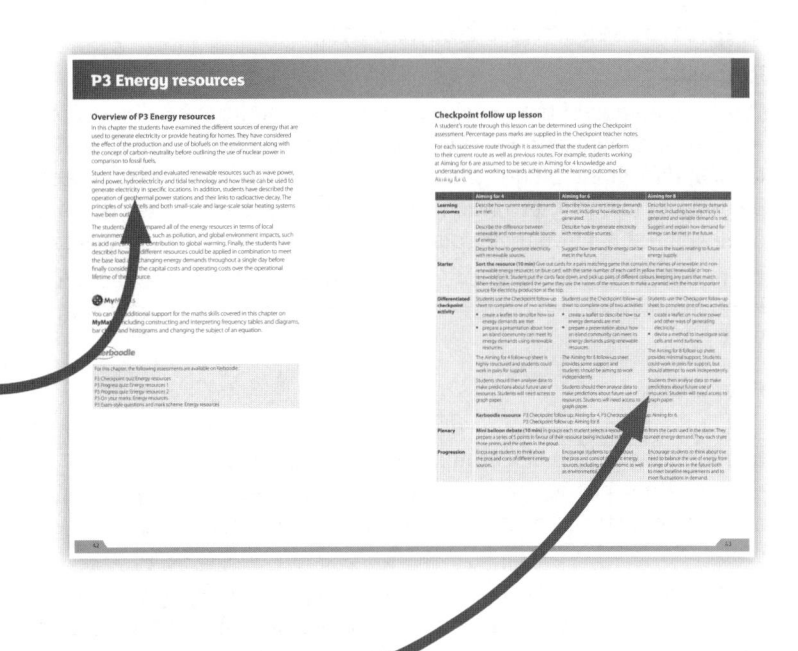

Checkpoint lesson

Overview

The Checkpoint Lesson is a suggested follow-up lesson after students have completed the automarked Checkpoint Assessment on Kerboodle. There are three routes through the lesson, with the route for each student being determined by their mark in the assessment. Each route aims to support students with progressing up an assessment band.

Checkpoint overview

This text provides a brief overview of the chapter, including the key concepts students should be confident with.

Checkpoint lesson plan

This table provides a differentiated lesson plan for the checkpoint follow-up lesson. This includes learning outcomes, starters and plenaries, supporting information for the follow-up worksheets (including any descriptions of relevant practicals), and progression suggestions to support students with progressing up a band.

vii

Assessment and progress

Dr Andrew Chandler-Grevatt

To ensure students are fully supported to make progress through the new linear exams, AQA GCSE *Sciences Third Edition* was developed in consultation with assessment consultant, Dr Andrew Chandler-Grevatt. Andrew worked with the team to develop an assessment framework that supports students and teachers in tracking and promoting progress through Key Stage 3 and GCSE.

Andrew is has a doctorate in school assessment, and a real passion for science teaching and learning. Having worked as a science teacher for ten years, of which five were spent as an AST, Andrew has a real understanding of the pressures and joys of teaching in the classroom. His most recent projects include *Activate for KS3 Science*, for which he developed a unique assessment framework to support schools in the transition away from levels.

The new GCSE grading system (9–1)

With the new specifications and criteria comes a new grading system. The old system of grades A*–G, is being replaced with a numerical system with grades 9–1. Grade 9 is the highest, and is designed to award exceptional performance.

The new grades are not directly equivalent to the old A*–C system, although some comparisons can be drawn:

- Approximately the same proportion of students will achieve a grade 4 or above as currently achieve a grade C or above.
- Approximately the same proportion of students will achieve a grade 7 as above as currently achieve an A or above.
- The bottom of grade 1 will be aligned with the bottom of grade G.

A 'good pass' is considered to be a grade 5 or above.

Throughout the course, resources and assessments have been designed to help students working at different grades to make progress.

5-year assessment framework

Purpose

The combination of the removal of levels, new performance measures, a new grading system, and more demanding GCSEs makes it more important than ever to be able to track and facilitate progress from Year 7 and all the way through secondary. Assessment plays a key role in intervention and extension, and these are both vital in helping students of all abilities achieve their potential, and add value to their projected GCSE grade.

In the absence of levels, and as we learn more about the new GCSE grades, it is important that a framework is in place in order to inform learning, teaching, and assessment from Y7-Y11.

Framework

Throughout the 5 years, it is useful to define three ability bands, which can be used to inform the design of learning outcomes, learning resources, and assessments. By defining three bands, realistic and valuable intervention and extension can be designed and implemented to help students of all abilities make progress, and improve their grade projection.

At KS3, the model is designed with the aim of encouraging every student to gain a 'secure' grasp of each concept and topic, so that they are ready to progress. These students will be on track to secure a 'good pass' (grade 5 or above) at GCSE.

In the KS3 course Activate three bands have been defined:

- **Developing**, in which students are able to know and understand a concept, and demonstrate their knowledge in simple and familiar situations.
- **Secure**, in which students are able to apply their knowledge and skills to familiar

and some unfamiliar situations, undertake analysis, and understand more complex concepts.
- **Extending**, in which students are able to evaluate and create, apply their knowledge to complex and unfamiliar situations, and demonstrate advanced use of skills.

Using the framework throughout KS3 helps you to identify which students are ready to progress, and approximately what GCSE grades they should be aiming for.

At GCSE, students can then be differentiated into three bands, aiming for different grades.
- **Aiming for 4** is for students working at the lower grades 1–3, who would have been Developing at KS3, and aspiring to a Grade 4 at GCSE. Resources and assessments for these students are supportive, and focus on developing understanding of core concepts.
- **Aiming for 6** is for students working at grades 4–6, who would have been Secure at KS3. Resources and assessments for these students help to embed core concepts, by encouraging application and analysis, and beginning to explore more complex ideas and situations.
- **Aiming for 8** provides extension for students working at grades 7–9, who are able to grasp complex concepts, and demonstrate higher order skills, such as evaluation and creation in complex and unfamiliar situations.

The framework is summarised in the table below.

Key stage 3	Band	Developing		Secure		Extending	
	Level	3	4	5	6	7	8
GCSE	Band	Aiming for 4			Aiming for 6		Aiming for 8		
	Grades	1	2	3	4	5	6	7	8	9
	Demand	Low			Standard			High		

Informing learning outcomes

The assessment framework has informed the design of the learning outcomes throughout the course. Learning outcomes are differentiated, and there is a set of learning outcomes for every lesson for each ability band.

The checkpoint assessment system

This series includes a checkpoint assessment system for intervention and extension, designed to help students of all abilities make continuous progress through the course. The system also helps you and your students to monitor achievement, and ensure all students are on-track and monitored through the new linear assessments.

Checkpoint assessments are provided in Kerboodle. These are Automarked objective tests with diagnostic feedback. Once students have completed their assessment, depending on their results they will complete one of three follow up activities, designed for intervention and extension. Students are supported with activity sheets, and lesson plans and overviews are provided for the teacher. The three follow-up routes are:

1. **Aiming for 4** is for students who achieved low score. These resources support students by helping to develop and embed core concepts.
2. **Aiming for 6** is for students who achieved a medium score. These resources encourage students to embed and extend core concepts, and begin to apply their knowledge in more complex or unfamiliar situations.
3. **Aiming for 8** is for students who have achieved a high score. These resources encourage extensive use of more complex skills, in more complex and unfamiliar situations, helping them to reach for the top grades.

Differentiation and Skills

Maths skills and MyMaths

With the introduction of the introduction of the new GCSE competence in maths, the support and development of maths skills in a scientific context will be vital for success.

The Student Books contain a maths skills reference section that covers all the maths required for the specification, explained in a scientific context and with a worked example for reference. Where maths skills are embedded within the scientific content, the maths is demonstrated in a Using Maths feature providing a worked example and an opportunity for students to have a go themselves.

In Kerboodle you will find maths skills interactives that are automarked and provide formative feedback. Calculation sheets provide opportunities for practice of the maths skills and links to MyMaths are shown in the Lesson Player and Teacher Handbook where additional resources exist that can be used to reinforce the maths skill. These include practice sheets and Invisi-pen worked examples.

Literacy skills

Literacy skills enable students to effectively communicate their ideas about science and access the information they need. Though the marks allocated for QWC are no longer present in the new specifications, a good degree of literacy is required to read and answer longer, structured exam questions, to access the more difficult concepts introduced in the new GCSE Programme of Study, to be able to effectively interpret and answer questions.

The student books flag opportunities to develop and practice literacy skills through the use of the pen icon. Key words are identified in the text and a glossary helps students get to grips with new scientific terms.

In Kerboodle, you will find Literacy Skills Interactives that help assess literacy skills, including the spelling of key words. Additional Literacy worksheets are available to reinforce skills learnt and provide practice opportunities.

The Teacher Handbook flags literacy suggestions and opportunities relating to the lesson. All of these features will help to develop well-rounded scientists able to access information and communicate their ideas effectively.

Working Scientifically

Working Scientifically is new to the 2016 GCSE criteria. It is divided up into four areas and is integrated into the teaching and learning of Biology, Chemistry, and Physics. The four areas are:

1. Development of scientific thinking in which students need to be able to demonstrate understanding of scientific methods and the scientific process and how these may develop over time and their associated limitations
2. Experimental skills and strategies in which students ask scientific questions based on observations, make predictions using scientific knowledge and understanding, carry out investigations to test predictions, make and record measurements and evaluate methods
3. Analysis and evaluation in which students apply mathematical concepts and calculate results, present and interpret data using tables and graphs, draw conclusions and evaluate data, and are comment on the accuracy, precision, repeatability and reproducibility of data
4. Scientific vocabulary, quantities, units, symbols and nomenclature in which students calculate results and manipulate data using scientific formulae using basic analysis, SI units, and IUPAC chemical nomenclature where appropriate.

Working Scientifically is integrated throughout the Student Book with flagged Practical boxes, flagged Required Practical boxes, questions. A dedicated Working Scientifically reference chapter is also provided at the back of the Student Book to refer to during investigations, when answering Working Scientifically questions and to enable investigative skills to be developed.

In Kerboodle there are Practicals and Activities resources with their own Working Scientifically objectives, additional targeted Working Scientifically skills sheets as well as other resources such as simulations and Webquests to target specific skills areas. Questions are ramped in difficulty and opportunity to build up to and practise the practical based questions for the exam are provided.

For the required practicals the guidance provided to students acknowledges the differing degrees of support and independence required, with targeted support sheets to the key grade descriptors of Grade 4, 6, and 8, with a view to moving the students over that Grade point onwards.

In the Teacher Handbook lessons will often have a working scientifically focus in mind for the activities in that lesson. Working Scientifically Learning Outcomes, where specified, are differentiated to show the expectations for the differing ability levels.

For the purpose of the practical based questions in the examination, required practicals are flagged and practice opportunities are provided through out the Student Book in the summary questions and exam-style questions.

Differentiation

Building upon the principles of *Activate* at Key Stage 3.

Differentiation using the checkpoint system

The end of chapter Checkpoint lessons will help you to progress students of every ability, targeting the key Grade boundaries of 4, 6, and 8 to enable students to review, consolidate and extend their understanding at each of the grade lesson points.

The tasks focused at students to become secure at Grades 4 and 6 are designed to help them become more secure in their understanding and consolidate the chapter. Teacher input will help them grasp important concepts from the chapter with the opportunity for some extension for Grade 6 students.

The tasks focused at students to become secure and to extend at Grade 8 are designed to develop and challenge. Students will work more independently on these tasks to free up the teacher to be able to focus on those that found the chapter more challenging.

Teacher Handbook

Lesson outcomes are differentiated and suggestions for activities throughout the lesson plans are accompanied by support and extension opportunities.

Student Book

Summary questions per lesson are ramped with a darker shading indicating a more challenging question. In the end of chapter summary questions and exam style questions, ramping occurs within the question (as would be seen in a typical exam question).

Practicals and Activities

All practicals and activities are differentiated. Where more complex areas are covered, additional support sheets may be provided to allow lower attaining students to access the activity.

For all required practicals (compulsory practicals) that may be assessed in an exam, specific support sheets are provided targeting the progression of students across the key Grades 4, 6, and 8.

Additional skills sheets may be used in conjunction with practicals to provide additional support in generic competencies such as constructing a graph etc.

Interactive Assessments

All interactive assessments are ramped in difficulty and support is provided in the feedback directing students where they can improve. In chapters with both levels of content, Higher and Foundation versions of assessment are available.

Written assessments

End of section tests and end of year tests have Foundation and Higher versions.

Kerboodle

AQA GCSE Sciences Kerboodle is packed full of guided support and ideas for running and creating effective GCSE Science lessons, and for assessing and facilitating students' progress. It is intuitive to use and customisable.

Kerboodle is online, allowing you and your students to access the course anytime, anywhere.

AQA GCSE Sciences Kerboodle consists of:
- lessons, resources, and assessment
- access to *AQA GCSE Science* Student books for both teachers and students.

Lessons, Resources, and Assessment

AQA GCSE Sciences Kerboodle offers new, engaging lesson resources, as well as a fully comprehensive assessment package, written to match the *AQA GCSE Science (9–1)* specifications.

Kerboodle offers comprehensive and flexible support for the *AQA GCSE Science (9–1)* specifications, enabling you to follow our suggested lessons and schemes of work or to create your own lessons and schemes and share them with other members of your department.

You can **adapt** many of the resources to suit your students' needs, with all non-interactive activities available as editable Word documents. You can also **upload** your own resources so that everything is accessed from one location.

Set homework and assessments through the Assessment system and **track** progress using the Markbook.

Lessons

Click on the **Lessons tab** to access the *AQA GCSE Sciences* lesson presentations and notes.

Ready-to-play lesson presentations complement every spread in the Teacher Handbook and Student Book. Each lesson presentation is easy to launch and features lesson objectives, starters, activity guidance, key diagrams, plenaries, and homework suggestions. The lesson presentations and accompanying note sections are 100% customisable. You can personalise the lessons by adding your own resources and notes, or build your own lesson plans using your own resources.

Your lessons and notes can be accessed by your whole department and they are ideal for use in cover lessons.

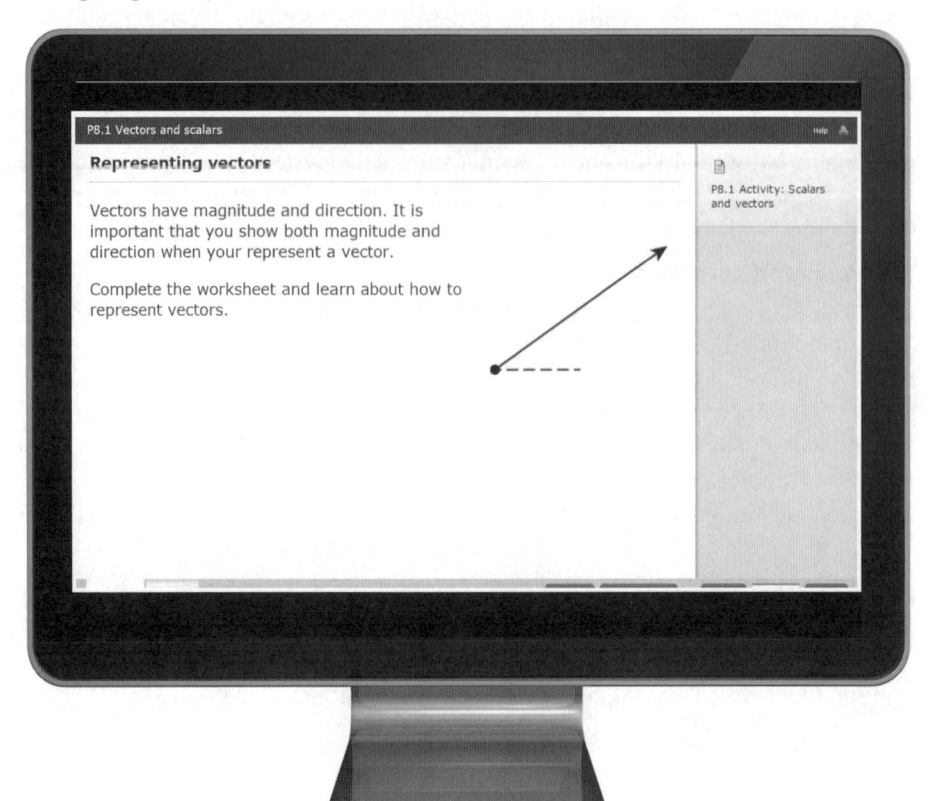

Resources

Click on the Resources tab to access the full list of AQA GCSE Sciences resources. Use the navigation panel on the left hand side to find resources for any lesson, chapter, or topic.

Navigation panel and search bar allow for easy navigation between resources by course and chapter.

Fully customisable content to cater to all your classes. Resources can be created using the create button.

Existing resources can be uploaded on to the platform using the upload button.

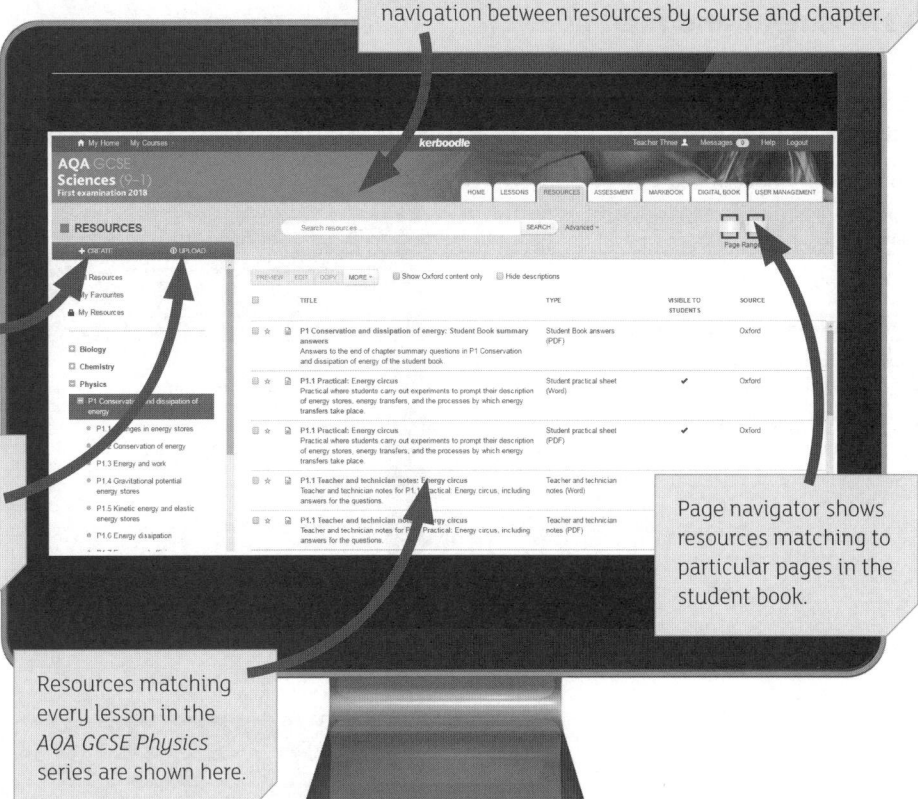

Page navigator shows resources matching to particular pages in the student book.

Resources matching every lesson in the *AQA GCSE Physics* series are shown here.

Practicals and activities Fully-editable resources provided for every lesson to guide students through a practical or activity with fully integrated Working Scientifically skills. Teacher and Technician notes are provided for all practicals and activities to give further ideas on differentiation, answers, example data where appropriate, and a list of resources required by technicians.

Interactive starters or plenaries Accompany each lesson, and can be used front-of-class to maximise student participation.

Skills sheets Editable worksheets that target Maths, Literacy, and Working Scientifically skills. They provide guidance and examples to help students whenever they need to use a particular skill.

Skills interactives Auto-marked interactive activities with formative feedback that focus on key maths and literacy skills. You can use these activities in your class to help consolidate core skills relevant to the lesson, or they can be assigned as homework by accessing them through the Assessment tab.

Animations and videos Help students to visualise difficult concepts or to learn about real-life contexts, with engaging visuals and narration. They are structured to clearly address a set of learning objectives and are followed by interactive question screens to help consolidate key points and to provide formative feedback.

Simulations Allow students to control variables and look at outcomes for experiments that are difficult to carry out in the classroom or focus on tricky concepts.

Podcasts Available for every chapter to help review and consolidate key points. The podcast presents an audio summary with transcript, followed by a series of ramped questions and answers to assist students in their revision.

Targeted support sheets Available for the full ability range and are provided to help students progress as they complete their GCSE. **Bump up your Grades** target common misconceptions and difficult topics to securely move students over the key boundaries of Grades 4, 6, and 8. Extensions activities provide opportunities for higher-ability students to apply their knowledge and understanding to new contexts, whilst **Go Further** worksheets aim to inspire students to consider the subject at A Level and beyond.

WebQuests Research-based activities set in a real-life context. WebQuests are fun and engaging activities that can be carried out individually or within a group and are ideal for peer-review.

Checklists and chapter maps Self-assessment checklists for students of the key learning points from each chapter to aid consolidation and revision. For teachers there is an additional chapter-map resource that provides an overview of the chapter, specific opportunities to support and extend, and information on tackling common misconceptions.

Assessment and markbook

All of the assessment material in Kerboodle has been quality assured by our expert Assessment Advisor. Click on the **Assessment tab** to find the wide range of assessment materials to help you deliver a varied, motivating, and effective assessment programme.

Once your classes are set up in Kerboodle, you can assign them assessments to do at home or in class individually or as a group.

A **Markbook** with reporting function helps you to keep track of your students' results. This includes both auto-marked assessments and work marked by you.

Practice or test?

Many of the auto-marked assessment in the AQA GCSE Sciences Kerboodle is available in formative or summative versions.

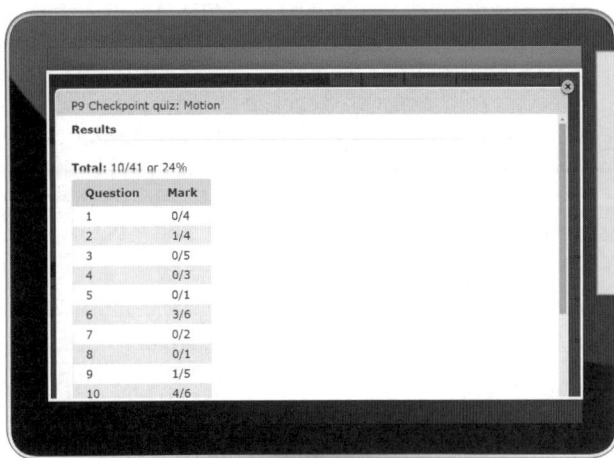

Test versions of the assessment provide feedback on performance at the end of the test. Students are only given one attempt at each screen but can review them and see which answers they get wrong after completing the activity. Marks are reported to the markbook.

Practice versions of the assessment provide screen-by-screen feedback, focusing on misconceptions, and provide hints for the students to help them revise their answers. Students are given the opportunity to try again. Marks are reported to the Markbook.

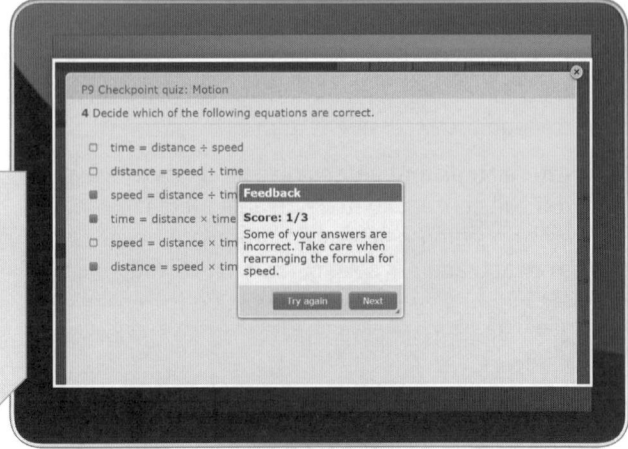

Assessment per chapter

Through each chapter there are many opportunities for assessment and determining/monitoring progress.

Progress quizzes Auto-marked assessments that focus on the content of the chapters. They are quick, engaging quizzes designed to be taken throughout the course to monitor progress and to focus revision.

Checkpoint assessments Auto-marked assessments designed to determine whether students have a secure grasp of concepts from the chapter. These assessments are ramped in difficulty and can be followed up by the differentiated Checkpoint Lesson activities.

On Your Marks Improve students' exam skills by analysing questions, looking at other students' responses, interpreting mark schemes, and answering exam-style questions.

Homework activities Auto-marked quizzes with ramped questions targeting the key Grades 4, 6, and 8 boundaries designed to help students apply and embed their knowledge and understanding from the classroom.

Formal testing

End-of-chapter tests Provide students with the opportunity to practise answering exam-style questions in a written format. There are differentiated Foundation and Higher versions, with separate options for the combined sciences and the separate sciences. Accompanied by a fully comprehensive mark scheme, data can be entered manually into the Markbook.

Mid-point and end-of-course written tests Provide students with the opportunity to practise answering exam-style questions in a full-length paper. There are differentiated Foundation and Higher versions, with separate options for the combined sciences and the separate sciences. Accompanied by a fully comprehensive mark scheme, data can be entered manually into the Markbook.

Kerboodle Book

The *AQA GCSE Sciences* Kerboodle Books are digital versions of the Student Books for you to use at the front of the classroom.

Access to the Kerboodle Book is automatically available as part of the Lessons, Resources, and Assessment package for both you and your students.

A set of tools is available with the Kerboodle Book so that you can personalise your book and make notes. Like all resources offered on Kerboodle, the Kerboodle Book can also be accessed using a range of devices.

1 Energy and energy resources

Specification links

AQA specification section	Assessment paper
1.1 Energy	Paper 1
1.2 Conservation and dissipation of energy	Paper 1
1.3 National and global energy resources	Paper 1
5.3 Forces and elasticity	Paper 2

Required practicals

AQA required practicals	Practical skills	Topic
An investigation to determine the specific heat capacity of one or more materials. The investigation will involve linking the decrease of one energy store (or work done) to the increase in temperature and subsequent increase in thermal energy stored.	AT1 – use appropriate apparatus to make and record measurements of mass, time, and temperature accurately. AT5 – use, in a safe manner, appropriate apparatus to measure energy changes/transfers and associated values such as work done.	P2.2

Maths skills

AQA maths skills	Topic
1a Recognise and use expressions in decimal form.	P1.1, P1.3, P1.4, P1.5, P1.6, P1.7, P1.8, P1.9, P2.1, P3.5
1b Recognise and use expressions in standard form.	P1.5, P1.9, P3.1
1c Use ratios, fractions, and percentages.	P1.1, P1.3, P1.7, P1.8, P1.9, P3.3, P3.4
2a Use an appropriate number of significant figures.	P1.3, P1.4
2c Construct and interpret frequency tables and diagrams, bar charts, and histograms.	P1.1, P1.2, P2.1, P3.3, P3.4, P3.5
2h Make order of magnitude calculations.	P2.3
3a Understand and use the symbols: =, <, <<, >>, >, ∝, ~.	P1.3, P1.4, P1.5, P1.6, P1.7, P1.8, P1.9, P2.1
3b Change the subject of an equation.	P1.1, P1.3, P1.4, P1.5, P1.7, P1.8, P1.9, P2.1, P3.3
3c Substitute numerical values into algebraic equations using appropriate units for physical quantities.	P1.1, P1.3, P1.4, P1.5, P1.7, P1.8, P1.9, P2.1, P2.3, P3.3
3d Solve simple algebraic equations.	P1.3, P1.4, P1.5, P1.6, P1.9, P2.1, P3.3
4a Translate information between graphical and numeric form.	P1.1, P1.2, P1.5, P2.1, P2.2, P3.3, P3.4
4c Plot two variables from experimental or other data.	P1.7, P2.2

P1 Energy and energy resources

KS3 concept	GCSE topic	Checkpoint	Revision
Energy is a quantity that can be measured and calculated.	P1.1 Changes in energy stores	Ask students to describe the energy transfers that they are involved with during a day.	Show students some food packaging data and ask them to calculate their energy intake over a day or week. Discuss how this energy is transferred.
The total energy before and after a change has the same value.	P1.2 Conservation of energy	Show students some simple energy transfers and ask them to make statements about the energy before and after any changes.	The students can find some 'missing' values on Sankey or other energy transfer diagrams.
Energy transfers can be compared in terms of usefulness.	P1.7 Energy and efficiency	Ask students to discuss a range of energy transfers and describe which have been useful and which have not.	Discuss the useful and non-useful energy pathways for a range of devices such as a TV, electric heater, electric light and so on incorporating numerical data.
Energy transfers can take place at different rates.	P1.9 Energy and power	Ask the students why some light bulbs are brighter than others.	Show the students some electrical devices and their power ratings asking them to rank them in order of rate of energy transfer.
Energy transfer by heating can be reduced by using insulating materials.	P2.1 Energy transfer	Ask students to describe how different clothes work to keep them warm.	Provide the students with a diagram showing the measures used to reduce the rate of energy transfer in a factory and ask them to explain how these measures work.
The energy needed to heat an object depends on its mass and the material it is made of.	P2.2 Specific heat capacity	Ask the students to explain why a bath full of water takes longer to cool down than a beaker full of water.	Boil different volumes of water in a kettle and ask students why one takes longer to boil than the other. Discuss whether it is easier or harder to heat water than other materials.
During experimental work it may not be possible to accurately measure all energy transfers.	P2.2 Specific heat capacity	Before an experiment into specific heat capacity ask the students to describe possible energy transfers to the environment.	Ask students to compare their measured values for specific heat capacity to the established values and explain any differences.
A renewable resource will not run out because it is replaced at the same rate it is used.	P3.1 Energy demands	Ask the students to list some energy resources which will someday runout and some which will not.	Show student's images of a range of energy resources and allow them to discuss whether the resource is limited in some way or unlimited.
Burning fossil fuel releases carbon dioxide gas which is a greenhouse gas into the atmosphere.	P3.4 Energy and the environment	Burn a small sample of a fuel and ask students to describe the products.	Provide the students with a graph of the changes in global temperature and changes in CO_2 content in the atmosphere and ask them to discuss any correlation and possible causal link.

P1 Conservation and dissipation of energy
1.1 Changes in energy stores

AQA spec Link: 1.1.1 A system is an object or group of objects.

There are changes in the way energy is stored when a system changes.

Students should be able to describe all the changes involved in the way energy is stored when a system changes, for common situations. For example:

- an object projected upwards
- a moving object hitting an obstacle
- an object accelerated by a constant force
- a vehicle slowing down
- bringing water to a boil in an electric kettle.

Throughout this section on energy students should be able to calculate the changes in energy involved when a system is changed by:

- heating
- work done by forces
- work done when a current flows
- use calculations to show on a common scale how the overall energy in a system is redistributed when the system is changed.

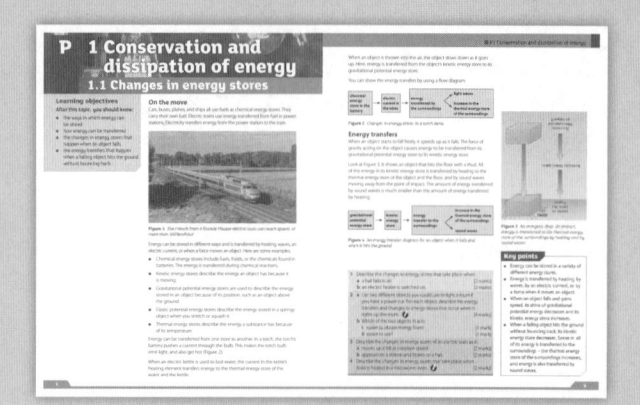

WS 1.2
MS 1a, 1c, 2c, 3b, 3c, 4a

Aiming for	Outcome	Checkpoint	
		Question	Activity
Aiming for GRADE 4 ↓	Describe some examples of energy stores.	1	Starter 2, Main 1, Main 2, Plenary 2
	State the processes that can transfer energy from one store to another.	2, 3, 4	Starter 2, Main 1, Main 2, Plenary 2
	Identify changes in some energy stores using simple examples.	2, 3	Main 1, Main 2, Plenary 2
Aiming for GRADE 6 ↓	Describe a wide range of energy stores in different contexts.	2, 3, 4	Starter 2, Main 1, Plenary 2
	Describe changes in energy stores in terms of the process that causes the change.	2, 3, 4, End of chapter 2	Main 1, Plenary 2
	Use quantitative descriptions of changes in energy stores.		Main 2
Aiming for GRADE 8 ↓	Describe the nature of energy stores in detail including the relationship between objects.	2, 4	Main 1, Plenary 2
	Explain factors that affect the size of changes in energy stores.	3	Main 1
	Represent energy transfers graphically, accounting for changes in all stores.		Main 2

Maths

Energy stores can be represented graphically using bar charts to show how full or empty they are (2c, 4a).

Literacy

The focus should be on language used to describe energy transfers. Pairs of students can describe the changes to each other and make corrections with constructive feedback.

P1 Conservation and dissipation of energy

Practical

Title	Energy circus
Equipment	yo-yo, wind-up toy, portable radio, electric torch, electric motor, MP3 player, steel ball bearing, wooden block, candle or spirit burner, matches, remote-control car
Overview of method	Set each piece of equipment up in a different place around the classroom, and label each station. In small groups, students rotate around the stations, investigating the transfers in each station and describing the process that causes changes to the energy stores.
Safety considerations	Take care with the naked flame of the candle or spirit burner, stand them in a sand tray.

Starter	Support/Extend	Resources
Off like a rocket (5 min) Show students a video of a firework. Ask them to draw an energy transfer diagram of what they see happening. Check through their diagrams to discuss the different energy stores. **What is energy?** (10 min) Ask students to express their ideas about what the word energy means. They could produce a visual summary to show their prior knowledge.	**Support:** Produce a partially completed visual summary on the board for students to copy and add additional details to.	

Main	Support/Extend	Resources
Energy stores and transfers (15 min) Introduce the concept of energy stores and how they can be filled and emptied by energy transfers. Focus on the mechanisms (forces, current, and heating) that cause these changes, avoiding the idea that the energy itself is the cause. Analyse the energy transfers of a falling object, discussing the forces acting at different stages. Remind students that it is the action of unbalanced forces that causes the changes in the energy stores. **Energy circus** (25 min) Allow students to investigate some changes in energy stores using the practical. They should identify which stores are filling and emptying and the process that causes these changes. Ask the students to be specific about the forces – is a frictional or gravitational force acting?	**Extend:** Discuss the effect of air resistance, which causes heating during the fall. **Support:** Provide the names of the relevant energy stores for each station. **Extend:** The students should discuss all of the stores, including dissipation to the surroundings.	**Practical:** Energy circus

Plenary	Support/Extend	Resources
What's the transfer? (5 min) Provide students with some examples of simple energy transfers they may encounter regularly (e.g., the ticking of a clock, the growth of a plant, or the ringing of the bell marking the end of the lesson). Students use the interactive to complete a description of what energy transfers are occurring. **Energy links** (10 min) Ask students to draw a large circle with all the different stores of energy listed around the outside. They must then link the stores of energy together with an arrow, labelled with a description of the process that can transfer the energy from one store to another.		**Interactive:** What's the transfer?

Homework		
Ask students to make a list of the energy transfers that take place in devices at home.	**Extend:** Students should produce energy transfer diagrams and find appropriate numerical values.	

kerboodle

A Kerboodle highlight for this lesson is **Working scientifically: Energy analogies**. Refer to the **Content map** on Kerboodle for a full list of resources and assessment.

P1.2 Conservation of energy

AQA spec Link: 1.2.1 Energy can be transferred usefully, stored or dissipated, but cannot be created or destroyed.

Students should be able to describe with examples where there are energy transfers in a closed system, that there is no net change to the total energy.

Students should be able to describe, with examples, how in all system changes energy is dissipated, so that it stored in less useful ways. This energy is often described as being 'wasted'.

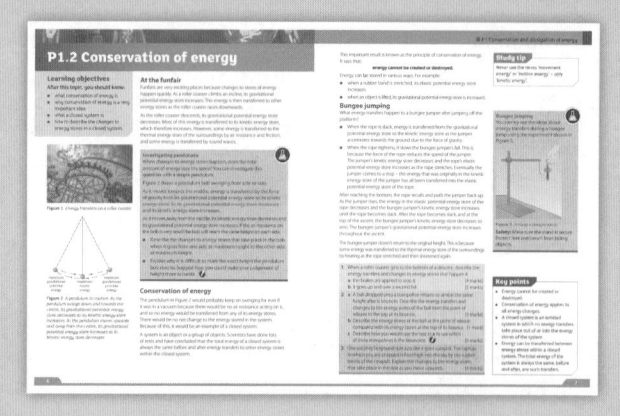

MS 2c, 4a

Aiming for	Outcome	Checkpoint	
		Question	Activity
Aiming for GRADE 4	State that energy is conserved in any transfer.	1, 2	Starter 1, Main 1
	State that energy is dissipated (is no longer useful) when it heats the environment.	2	Main 1
	Investigate the energy transfers in a pendulum and bungee.		Main 1, Main 2
Aiming for GRADE 6	Apply the law of conservation of energy in straightforward situations.	1, 2, 3	Main 1, Main 2
	Describe changes in energy stores, explaining why energy ceases to be useful.		Starter 1, Main 1
	Describe the energy transfers in a range of experiments and account for energy dissipation to the surroundings.		Main 1, Main 2
Aiming for GRADE 8	Apply the law of conservation of energy to explain why forces cause heating effects.	1, 2, 3	Starter 2, Main 1, Main 2
	Describe closed systems and the changes to energy stores within them using the principle of conservation of energy.	2	Main 1, Main 2
	Evaluate in detail experiments to investigate energy transfers.	4	Main 2

Maths
Numerical values for quantities of energy can be introduced to allow for discussion of conservation. Bar charts showing energy stores can also be used (2c, 4a).

Literacy
Pairs of students should write detailed descriptions of the processes involved in each of the experiments.

Practical

Title	Investigating pendulums
Equipment	retort stand, G-clamp, two small wooden blocks, string with bob (or 50 g mass tied to end), nail (or rod or dowel), graph or squared paper and some reusable adhesive to mount it, torch or lamp (optional)
Overview of method	Students release the pendulum from a fixed height and measure the height it reaches at the end of its swing. They repeat this using a nail to interrupt the pendulum's swing, and observe whether energy is still conserved despite the change in the shape of the swing.
Safety considerations	Only use small pendulum bobs, and restrict swing sizes. Ensure that there is adequate space.

■ P1 Conservation and dissipation of energy

Practical

Title	Bungee jumping
Equipment	retort stand, elastic with mass (or toy tied to end), graph paper and some reusable adhesive to mount it, torch
Overview of method	Students examine the motion of the bungee jumper. A bright light source can be used to cast a shadow onto the graph paper, allowing clearer measurements. Video logging may also be used.
Safety considerations	Do not touch hot filament lamps.

Starter	Support/Extend	Resources
Where does it all go? (5 min) Light a candle with a match and ask students to describe what happens to the chemical store of energy in the wax and the changes in the match. **A plane journey** (10 min) Students use the interactive to describe the changes in energy stores at each stage of an aeroplane journey, where the aeroplane lands back at the same place it took off. Ask them what has happened to the energy. Use the ideas that they produce here later in the lesson to discuss the idea that energy cannot 'go away' – it is all accounted for.	**Extend:** Expect the students to explain that the store is associated with the wax and the oxygen in the air.	**Interactive:** A plane journey

Main	Support/Extend	Resources
Investigating pendulums (20 min) After a brief recap of changes in energy stores, students should investigate the pendulum. As well as thinking about the processes that remove energy from the system (frictional forces) to explain why the pendulum slows, they will investigate whether energy is roughly conserved over the course of one swing. This allows discussion of energy transfers within a closed system. Discuss the concept of energy dissipation to the surroundings in the initial experiment and emphasise that the total energy is the same at all points in the process. The students must be able to state the law of conservation of energy.	**Support:** Provide some descriptions of the energy transfers for the students to discuss whilst observing the pendulum.	**Practical:** Investigating pendulums
Bungee jumping (20 min) Discuss the energy transfers in a bungee jump and use the experiment to look at the forces, gravitational and tension, and reinforce the idea that energy is always conserved. Make sure that the heating effect in the bungee rope is discussed.	**Extend:** Students should discuss the difficulties in measuring energy transfers quantitatively.	**Practical:** Bungee jumping

Plenary	Support/Extend	Resources
Measuring the energy in food (5 min) Ask students, as a class or in groups, to discuss some of the issues around designing an experiment to measure the energy in a food sample. Students should aim to minimise energy dissipation to the surroundings. **Evaluate and improve** (10 min) Students evaluate the results of their experiments and then design improvements to the experiment.	**Support:** Provide a checklist of energy dissipation that needs to be accounted for, for example, waste gases are hot and the energy in them needs to be measured. **Support:** Provide a list of possible improvements and ask the students to explain why they would improve the results.	

Homework		
Students find out how aeroplanes are slowed down on landing, or drag racers stop, and make a booklet or short presentation. Explanations should be in terms of forces and changes in kinetic stores.		

kerboodle
A Kerboodle highlight for this lesson is **Working scientifically: Falling cake cups**. Refer to the **Content map** on Kerboodle for a full list of resources and assessment.

P1.3 Energy and work

AQA spec Link: 5.2 When a force causes an object to move through a distance work is done on the object. So a force does work on an object when the force causes a displacement of the object.

The work done by a force on an object can be calculated using the equation:

work done = force × distance (moved along the line of action of the force)

$$[W = F\,s]$$

work done W in joules, J

force F in newtons, N

distance s in metres, m

One joule of work is done when a force of one newton causes a displacement of one metre. 1 joule = 1 newton-metre.

Students should be able to describe the energy transfer involved when work is done.

Students should be able to convert between newton-metres and joules.

Work done against the frictional forces acting on an object causes a rise in the temperature of the object.

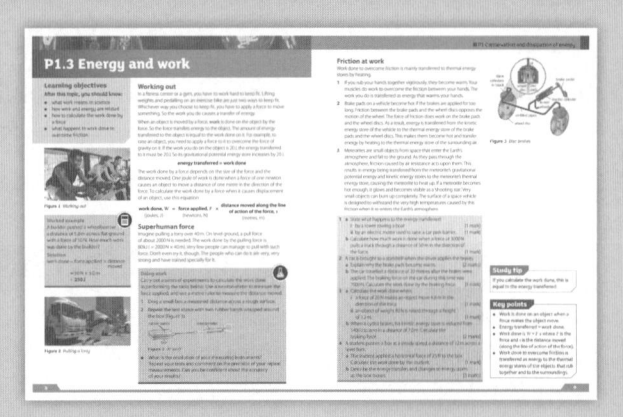

MS 1c, 3a, 3b, 3c

Aiming for	Outcome	Checkpoint	
		Question	Activity
Aiming for GRADE 4 ↓	State that energy is measured in joules (J).		Starter 1, Main
	Calculate the work done by a force.	2	Main
	Measure the work done by a force experimentally.		Main
Aiming for GRADE 6 ↓	Describe the action of frictional forces on objects and the associated heating effect.	1, 2	Main
	Use the equation for work done to calculate distances or size of forces.	2, 3	Main, Plenary 2
	Use repeat values to measure the work done by a force experimentally.		Main
Aiming for GRADE 8 ↓	Use the principle of conservation of energy and forces to explain why objects become heated by frictional forces.	1	Main
	Apply the equation for work done in a wide range of contexts.	3, 4	Main, Plenary 2
	Evaluate in detail an experiment to measure work done, explaining why there is variation in the measurements.		Main

Maths
Students perform calculations on work done (3a), including rearrangement of the equations (3b).

Literacy
Descriptions of the action of forces in doing work need to be precise. Students should focus on describing which object is increasing in energy due to work being done on it.

Key words
work

8

P1 Conservation and dissipation of energy

Practical

Title	Doing work
Equipment	newton-meter, small wooden block, elastic bands, metre rule
Overview of method	Students drag the block carefully to measure the force required for both situations and the distance travelled. There will be considerable error involved in these measurements, and so several runs and mean values should be used.
Safety considerations	Ensure that there is adequate space to perform the task. Students should not move the block very quickly, or pull it off the edge of the bench.

Starter	Support/Extend	Resources
Defining work (5 min) Students define the terms work and working as used in common language. Lead them to the idea of a force being involved in working. **Forces and energy** (10 min) Ask students to describe some situations where forces cause changes in energy stores. They should explain what factors would affect the size of changes in these stores.	**Support:** Provide some example sentences containing the terms. **Extend:** Ask the students to suggest a mathematical relationship between the changes in the stores and the size of forces and distances involved.	

Main	Support/Extend	Resources
Doing work (40 min) Build on the previous idea of forces causing changes in energy stores to introduce the idea of doing work on something. Be careful with the definition here – it is very specific as opposed to the general term work, with which the students will be familiar. Students should perform a few calculations to embed the equation. Students then carry out the practical, including supporting calculations. There will be considerable errors in the experiments, which the students should discuss. Discuss the heating effect of frictional forces using the examples. These can be supported by practical demonstrations such as hand rubbing, bicycle brakes, and so on.	**Support:** Provide a calculation frame and limit the calculations to the basic form of the equation ($W = Fs$). **Extend:** Differentiate the calculations to stretch the students. **Extend:** Students can use the uncertainty in the measuring instruments in their calculations to find the maximum and minimum work done.	**Practical:** Doing work

Plenary	Support/Extend	Resources
Working or not? (5 min) Hold a heavy weight but do not lift or drop it. Ask if mechanical work is being done on the weight, and if not, why energy is being transferred as you hold it. **Mathematical work out** (10 min) Students use the interactive to answer some additional questions involving the equation for work done.	**Support:** You may have to remind students that heating is an energy transfer here. **Support:** Provide a template, and restrict calculations to ones that do not require rearrangement. **Extend:** Include non-base units (e.g., grams) and rearrangement of the equation.	**Interactive:** Mathematical work out

Homework		
Students can describe scenarios where mechanical work is being done in various jobs and show example calculations of the amount of work done. As an alternative, sports can be used.	**Support:** Provide some example scenarios with suggested values for the forces and distances.	

kerboodle

A Kerboodle highlight for this lesson is **Extension sheet: Meteor fall**. Refer to the **Content map** on Kerboodle for a full list of resources and assessment.

P1.4 Gravitational potential energy stores

AQA spec Link: 1.1.1 Throughout this section on energy students should be able to calculate the changes in energy involved when a system is changed by:
- work done by forces
- use calculations to show on a common scale how the overall energy in a system is redistributed when the system is changed.

1.1.2 Students should be able to calculate the amount of energy associated with an object raised above ground level.

The amount of gravitational potential energy gained by an object raised above ground level can be calculated using the equation:

g.p.e. = mass × gravitational field strength × height

$[E_p = m\,g\,h]$

gravitational potential energy E_p in joules, J

mass m in kilograms, kg

gravitational field strength g in newtons per kilogram, N/kg (In any calculation the value of the gravitational field strength g will be given)

height h in metres, m

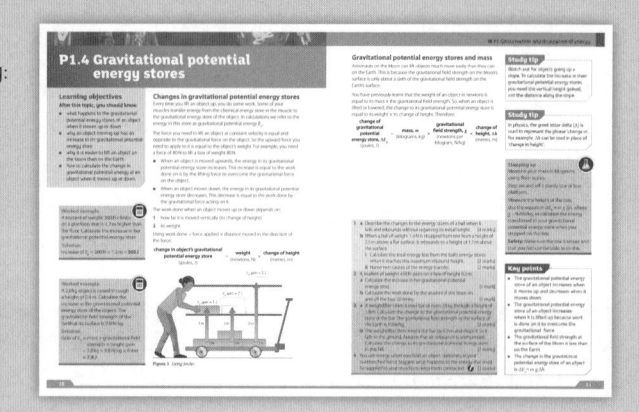

WS 1.2

MS 1a, 1c, 3b, 3c

Aiming for	Outcome	Checkpoint	
		Question	Activity
Aiming for GRADE 4	State the factors that affect the change in the gravitational potential energy store of a system.		Starter 1, Main 1
	Calculate the gravitational potential energy store of a system using the weight of an object and its height.	1, 2, End of chapter 4	Main 1
	Measure the gravitational potential energy store changes in a system with a simple practical.		Main 1
Aiming for GRADE 6	Describe the effect of a different gravitational field strength on the gravitational potential energy store changes of a system.		Main 2
	Calculate the gravitational potential energy store of a system using the mass, gravitational field strength, and height.	1, 3	Main 2
	Describe energy transfers that involve a heating effect as opposed to movement of an object.	End of chapter 4	Main 2
Aiming for GRADE 8	Perform calculations using rearrangements of the gravitational potential energy store equations.		Main 1, Main 2
	Apply the gravitational potential energy store equations in a wide range of contexts.	1	Main 2
	Account for all changes of energy during falls or increases in height, including heating effects.	4	Main 2

Maths
Students will perform a range of calculations using the gravitational potential energy store relationship (3c); some students will rearrange the equation to solve problems (3b).

Literacy
Students discuss and develop the concept of energy stores leading to specific calculations for a gravitational potential store.

P1 Conservation and dissipation of energy

Practical

Title	Stepping up
Equipment	Scales that measure weight in newtons, objects to step onto. The objects should be robust enough to pose no significant hazards; use steps or benches from the PE department.
Overview of method	The practical should only take a few minutes. Some students may be sensitive about their weight, but you could ask them to move objects onto shelves or up some stairs as an alternative task.
Safety considerations	Any tasks performed should be relatively simple and non-strenuous. Make sure that the students have no medical conditions that could be triggered by the activities.

Starter	Support/Extend	Resources
Lifting work (5 min) Remind students of the idea of work being done by a force when an object moves a distance. Demonstrate lifting things from the floor to a desk and ask them to describe changes in energy stores. Ask them to explain what factors affect the size of energy transfers. **All work** (10 min) Give students some scenarios and let them decide if mechanical work is being done. Students use the interactive to explain whether work is being done or not.	**Extend:** Move on to ask about what affects the weight (mass and the strength of gravity).	**Interactive:** All work

Main	Support/Extend	Resources
Gravitational potential energy transfers (15 min) Link the equation for work done ($W = F\,s$) to the idea of changing height as the distance. Ask the students to form a simple equation linking change in height to work done. Ask where the energy provided to the lifted object would now be stored, and lead on to the idea of gravitational potential energy stores. Define the gravitational potential energy equation. The students should then perform some simple calculations of work done and changes in gravitational potential energy stores. **Stepping up** (25 min) Introduce the idea of calculating weight from $m \times g$ and expand the original GPE equation. As before, students should perform some calculations including some set on different planets. Students can carry out the simple practical to reinforce their use of the GPE equation.	**Extend:** Rearrangement of the equation is required. **Support:** Limit the calculations to simple scenarios with no rearrangement. **Extend:** The students should try some rearrangements of the equation.	**Practical:** Stepping up

Plenary	Support/Extend	Resources
How high? (5 min) Ask students to calculate the E_p of a jumbo jet (400 000 kg) with a cruising altitude of 10 700 m. The E_p is 41 986 800 000 J (~42 GJ). **A hard day** (10 min) Students estimate the energy they transfer by climbing stairs when moving between lessons during a typical day by estimating the height changes and their weight.	**Extend:** Students should provide answers in standard form. **Support:** Provide some suitable estimates of the numbers – a weight of 500 N and travel upwards through 15 m each day.	

Homework		
Students estimate E_p for three different places they encounter regularly, for example, walking up stairs at home.		

P1.5 Kinetic and elastic stores

AQA spec Link: 1.1.2 Students should be able to calculate the amount of energy associated with a moving object, a stretched spring.

The kinetic energy of a moving object can be calculated using the equation:

kinetic energy = 0.5 × mass × (speed)² $\quad [E_k = \frac{1}{2} m v^2]$

kinetic energy E_k in joules, J

mass m in kilograms, kg

speed v in metres per second, m/s

The amount of elastic potential energy stored in a stretched spring can be calculated using the equation:

elastic potential energy = 0.5 × spring constant × (extension)²

$$[E_e = \frac{1}{2} k e^2]$$

(assuming the limit of proportionality has not been exceeded)

elastic potential energy E_e in joules, J

spring constant k in newtons per metre, N/m

extension e in metres, m

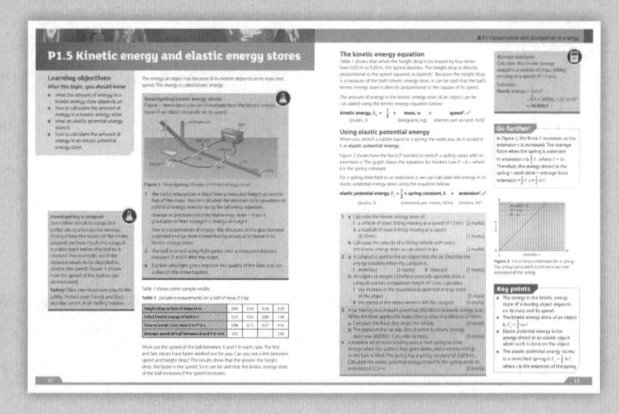

WS 1.2

MS 1a, 1c, 3b, 3c

Aiming for	Outcome	Checkpoint Question	Checkpoint Activity
Aiming for GRADE 4 ↓	State the factors that affect the size of a kinetic energy store of an object.		Main 1
	State the factors that affect the elastic potential energy store of a spring.		Main 2
	Describe energy transfers involving elastic potential energy and kinetic energy stores.	2, End of chapter 5	Main 1, Main 2
Aiming for GRADE 6 ↓	Calculate the kinetic energy store of an object.	1, End of chapter 1, 6	Main 1, Plenary 2
	Calculate the elastic potential energy store of a stretched spring.	4	Main 2
	Investigate the relationship between the energy stored in a spring and the kinetic energy store of an object launched from it.	2	Main 2
Aiming for GRADE 8 ↓	Perform calculations involving the rearrangement of the kinetic energy equation.		Main 1
	Perform calculations involving the rearrangement of the elastic potential energy equation.	4	Main 2
	Perform a wide range of calculations involving transfer of energy.	2, End of chapter 5	Main 1, Main 2

Maths
Student will perform a wide range of calculations, including those for gravitational potential energy stores, kinetic energy stores, and elastic energy stores (3b, 3c).

Literacy
Students need to clearly describe the factors affecting changes in kinetic energy stores, including the interpretation of data or graphs.

Key words
elastic potential energy

Practical

Title	Investigating kinetic energy stores
Equipment	ramp (or drainpipe), tennis ball, velocity or distance sensor, balance to measure mass of object
Overview of method	This experiment can be demonstrated with a ball and motion sensor or with a dynamics trolley and light gates.
Safety considerations	Ensure that balls do not fall off desks.

P1 Conservation and dissipation of energy

Practical

Title	Investigating a catapult
Equipment	flat surface, elastic bands (fishing-pole elastic works well), a dynamics trolley or wheeled toy
Overview of method	The trolley is pulled back through different distances and fired by the band. The speed (or time taken to cover a distance) is measured and then the changes in kinetic energy stores for the object.
Safety considerations	Ensure that trolleys do not fall off desks.

Starter	Support/Extend	Resources
Mass and velocity (5 min) Using mini-whiteboards, the students must give accurate definitions of mass and velocity and their units.		
Kinetic objects (10 min) Show students various moving objects with the mass and the velocity of the object. Students use the interactive to put them into order from which object has the smallest kinetic energy store to the largest.	**Support:** Identify the factors that affect kinetic energy store beforehand through discussion.	**Interactive:** Kinetic objects

Main	Support/Extend	Resources
Investigating kinetic energy stores (25 min) Students carry out the practical to investigate the factors that affect the amount of energy in a kinetic store by using the practical. They may need reminding beforehand about gravitational potential energy stores. The data provided in the student book may be used if the experiment does not provide suitable results. Introduce the kinetic energy equation. Demonstrate a set of calculations before expecting students to perform their own.	**Support:** Simple clues for velocity and mass should be used. **Extend:** Calculations involving SI prefixes are very demanding, so try some. **Extend:** Ensure students rearrange this equation.	**Practical:** Investigating kinetic energy stores
Investigating a catapult (15 min) This energy transfer needs careful explanation as there are two linked concepts with corresponding equations. The practical can be used as a demonstration to show how stretching the band further stores more energy.	**Support:** As before, just use simple values for the measurements.	

Plenary	Support/Extend	Resources
Higher/lower (5 min) Go through a series of objects with different masses and velocities and ask the students to say (or calculate) if the kinetic energy store is higher or lower than the previous one.		
Kinetic cards revisited (10 min) The students now have to calculate the energy of each of the cards used in the second starter to check their order. Use this task to make sure that the students are treating the calculations correctly.	**Support:** Calculation frames can be provided for some of the cards.	

Homework		
Challenge students to build their own elastic-powered vehicles and hold a competition on whose can go the furthest. The vehicles should all have identical elastic bands and could be cars, boats, or aeroplanes.		

kerboodle

A Kerboodle highlight for this lesson is **Calculation sheet: Energy transfers**. Refer to the **Content map** on Kerboodle for a full list of resources and assessment.

P1.6 Energy dissipation

AQA spec Link: 1.2.1 Energy can be transferred usefully, stored, or dissipated, but cannot be created or destroyed.

Students should be able to describe, with examples, how in all system changes energy is dissipated, so that it is stored in less useful ways. This energy is often described as being 'wasted'.

Students should be able to explain ways of reducing unwanted energy transfers, for example, through lubrication and the use of thermal insulation.

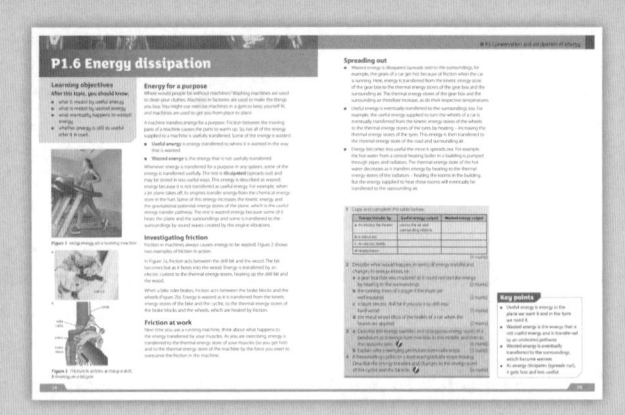

MS 3a

Aiming for	Outcome	Checkpoint	
		Question	Activity
Aiming for GRADE 4 ↓	Identify useful and wasted energy in simple scenarios.	1	Main
	Describe energy dissipation in terms of heating the surroundings.	2	Main
	Measure the frictional force acting on an object.		Main
Aiming for GRADE 6 ↓	Analyse energy transfers to identify useful and less useful energy transfers.	1	Main
	Describe energy dissipation and how this reduces the capacity of a system to do work.	2, 3	Main
	Investigate the factors that affect frictional forces.		Main
Aiming for GRADE 8 ↓	Use a wide range of energy stores and physical processes to decide on wasted and useful energy transfers.		Main
	Apply the concept of energy dissipation in a wide range of scenarios.	2, 3, 4	Main
	Evaluate in detail an experiment to measure the frictional forces acting on an object.		Main

Maths
Students can compare transfers of energy in quantitative terms (3a).

Literacy
Students should discuss different transfers of energy and collaborate to decide which transfers are the more useful ones.

Key words
useful energy, wasteful energy, dissipated

Practical

Title	Investigating friction
Equipment	string, pulley, clamp, selection of masses, 1 kg mass (with hoop), three different surfaces to test (desk surface, carpet tiles, sandpaper)
Overview of method	Students place the 1 kg mass on the surfaces and attach it to a mass holder hanging over the desk by the pulley. They then find out what mass is required to start the 1 kg sliding across the surface. To improve the accuracy of the measurements, encourage students to add smaller masses when they get near to the sliding point of the mass, so several runs will be required.
Safety considerations	Ensure that masses do not fall to the floor.

14

■ P1 Conservation and dissipation of energy

Starter	Support/Extend	Resources
Useful or useless? (5 min) Show energy transfer diagrams and ask students to use the interactive to identify the useful energy transfers and the useless ones in each case.	**Extend:** The specific 'useful pathways' and 'wasteful pathways' can be discussed.	**Interactive:** Useful or useless?
Overheating (10 min) Ask students to explain why humans become hot when they work hard. How is this excess energy transferred from the body? Why do people need to eat less in hot weather? Links can be made to biological processes. This can lead to a discussion about where the energy in food actually ends up.		

Main	Support/Extend	Resources
Investigating friction (40 min) Discuss some example energy transfers. Use as many examples as possible until the students are clear on the useful and wasteful transfers.	**Support:** A simple set of examples can be used with the key energy stores described.	**Practical:** Investigating friction
Students then observe or try the practicals, noting that heating of the surroundings is the ultimate effect of most energy transfers. The idea of a force being the pathway by which energy is transferred should be emphasised.	**Extend:** Some braking systems recharge batteries, and these can be described.	
Show a video clip of brakes in action – Formula One cars are ideal. Discuss whether the energy in the resulting thermal stores can be reused in any way. Link back to the earlier demonstrations when discussing dissipation. Ensure that the students know that there is still the same amount of energy but eventually it is too spread out to be useful. Ensure that the students can use the term dissipated correctly.		

Plenary	Support/Extend	Resources
Sticky problems (5 min) Ask students to draw a table of the ways friction can be reduced and give examples of exactly where this happens. A table of suggested places can be provided – ask students to complete it to explain how the friction could be reduced.	**Support:** Video clips of machines operating can be very helpful here.	
What's wrong? (10 min) Ask students to correct some sentences describing energy and friction. This can be used to challenge some misconceptions. Examples can include: 'When a car stops at traffic lights, the speed energy is destroyed by the brakes and is lost.'	**Support:** Ask the students for ideas about what confuses them in energy transfer.	

Homework		
Students complete the WebQuest activity where they use the Internet to help them answer a series of questions involving energy calculations and comparisons.		**WebQuest:** How many AA batteries?

P1.7 Energy and efficiency

AQA spec Link: 1.2.2 The energy efficiency for any energy transfer can be calculated using the equation:

$$\text{efficiency} = \frac{\text{useful output energy transfer}}{\text{total input energy transfer}}$$

(H) Students should be able to describe ways to increase the efficiency of an intended energy transfer.

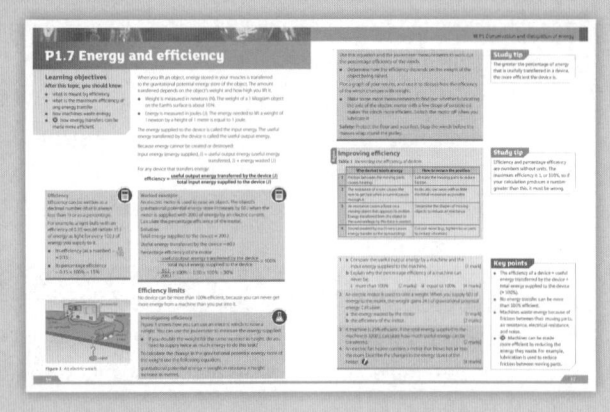

MS 1c, 3b, 3c

Aiming for	Outcome	Checkpoint	
		Question	Activity
Aiming for GRADE 4 ↓	Describe an efficient transfer as one that transfers more energy by a useful process.	4	Starter 1, Main
	State that the efficiency of an energy transfer is always less than 100%.	1	Main
	Calculate the efficiency of a simple energy transfer.	1	Main
Aiming for GRADE 6 ↓	Calculate the efficiency of a range of energy transfers.	2, End of chapter 7	Main
	Use the law of conservation of energy to explain why efficiency can never be greater than 100%.	1, 4	Main
	Investigate the efficiency of a motor.		Main
Aiming for GRADE 8 ↓	**(H)** Describe design features that can be used to improve the efficiency of an energy transfer.		Plenary 2
	Rearrange the efficiency equation to find input or total output energy.	2, 3	Main
	Evaluate in detail an efficiency investigation to justify conclusions.		Main

Maths
Students perform a range of efficiency calculations (1c, 3b, 3c).

Literacy
Students work in small groups to define efficiency, sharing their explanations.

Key words
efficiency

Practical

Title	Investigating efficiency
Equipment	joulemeter, variable low-voltage power supply, connecting leads, small electric winch (motor), five equal masses, metre rule, clamps to secure the winches to benches, cardboard box, or piece of carpet to protect the floor
Overview of method	Students lift a range of masses to a fixed height. A full metre is a good height – if the motor were 100% efficient it would require 0.1 J for a mass on 100 g.
Safety considerations	Protect the floor and keep feet clear from falling masses. Stop motor before masses reach the pulley.

P1 Conservation and dissipation of energy

Starter	Support/Extend	Resources
Staying on (5 min) Ask students to explain why some electrical devices of the same type (e.g., two different models of phone) last longer than others even though they use the same batteries. **Efficiency** (10 min) Ask students what is efficiency and why is it wanted? What are the advantages of an efficient device? Form students into groups and ask them to agree on a simple description of what efficiency is and why it is important.	**Extend:** Students link their explanations to the efficiency of the device. They should describe the subtle differences in what the devices do. For example, one phone may have many more applications running than another.	

Main	Support/Extend	Resources
Investigating efficiency (40 min) Recap the systems used for measuring quantities, particularly the joule and newton as these are required later. Discuss input and output energy in terms of how much energy is transferred from the starting stores into the stores we want it to be. This leads to calculations of efficiency based on these values. Students should try a few of the calculations to ensure that they can do them. Explain the limits to efficiency, linking this to the law of conservation of energy. Students try an efficiency measurement using the practical. Ensure that they are calculating work done correctly and finding the energy supplied to the motor.	**Extend:** Discuss the consequences if a machine was more than 100% efficient – energy could be created. Use Sankey diagrams to represent energy transfers and to find values for energy input and output.	**Practical:** Investigating efficiency

Plenary	Support/Extend	Resources
Car efficiency (5 min) Show students advertisements for car. Students use the interactive to arrange them in order of energy efficiency, using the fuel consumption figures in the small print. **Improving efficiency** (10 min) **H** Discuss the design features used to improve efficiency of a range of devices, supported by demonstration where possible.		**Interactive:** Car efficiency

Homework
Students research data on electrical devices, such as laptops or mobile phones, to determine which is most efficient. Students suggest the particular feature that improves the efficiency of the device.

kerboodle

A Kerboodle highlight for this lesson is **Extension sheet: Using energy conservation**. Refer to the **Content map** on Kerboodle for a full list of resources and assessment.

P1.8 Electrical appliances

AQA spec Link: 1.1.1 A system is an object or group of objects. There are changes in the way energy is stored when a system changes. Students should be able to describe all the changes involved in the way energy is stored when a system changes, for common situations. For example:
- bringing water to a boil in an electric kettle.

1.2.2 The energy efficiency for any energy transfer can be calculated using the equation:

$$\text{efficiency} = \frac{\text{useful output energy transfer}}{\text{total input energy transfer}}$$

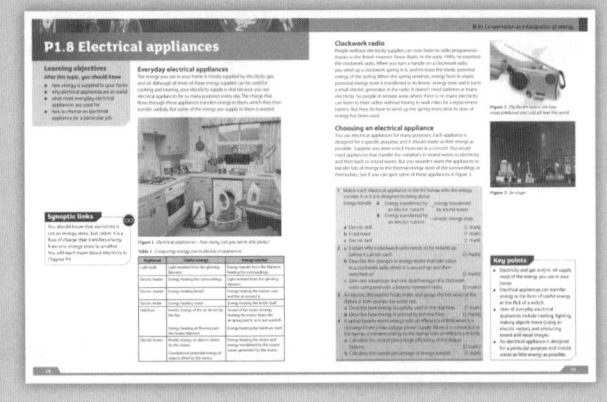

MS 1a, 1c, 3a, 3b, 3c

Aiming for	Outcome	Checkpoint Question	Checkpoint Activity
Aiming for GRADE 4 ↓	List some example electrical devices.		Starter 1, Main 1
	Survey a range of electrical devices and their operation.		Main 1
	Describe the energy transfers carried out by electrical devices.	1, End of chapter 1	Starter 1, Main 1
Aiming for GRADE 6 ↓	Rank electrical devices in terms of their power.		Main 2
	Compare mains-powered and battery-powered devices.	2	Starter 2, Main 2
	Describe the processes that waste energy in electrical devices.	3	Main 2
Aiming for GRADE 8 ↓	Compare electrical devices in terms of efficiency.		Main 2
	Calculate the efficiency of an electrical device.	4	Plenary 1
	Explain the operation of electrical devices in terms of forces and electric current.		Main 2

Maths
Students can rank appliances by their power ratings (3a).

Literacy
Descriptions of the operation of devices should be constructed by the students with links to energy transfer.

Practical

Title	Everyday electrical appliances
Equipment	Demo 1: low-voltage power supply (variable), connecting wires, resistance wire, heatproof mat
	Demo 2: low-voltage motor and power supply
	Demo 3: loudspeaker and signal generator
Overview of method	For the first demonstration, pass a current through the wire to observe it heating up and glowing.
	For the second demonstration, observe the motion of the motor.
	For the third demonstration, observe the motion of the loudspeaker.
Safety considerations	The wire in the first demonstration will be very hot. It should be allowed to cool.

■ P1 Conservation and dissipation of energy

Starter	Support/Extend	Resources
Electricity everywhere (5 min) Ask students to list all of the electrical appliances that they use during the day, including mains-powered and battery-powered. They then describe how their lives would be more difficult if these appliances did not exist.	**Support:** Provide some initial suggestions to get students going.	
Using energy (10 min) Challenge students to design an experiment to compare how much energy is stored in different batteries. Their ideas could include measuring how long a bulb could stay lit or even how long a toy operates.	**Extend:** Ask students to design appropriate results tables.	

Main	Support/Extend	Resources
Everyday electrical appliances (20 min) Discuss a range of electrical appliances with the students, ideally showing them some examples. The students can then list as many more as they can think of and explain their purpose. Carry out the practical demonstration to show the possible effects of an electric current.	**Support:** Limit the range of devices to simple ones. **Extend:** More complex devices can be used requiring a greater depth of understanding.	**Practical:** Everyday electrical appliances
Mains- or battery-powered (20 min) The students could compare mains- and battery-powered devices, noting that mains devices can transfer energy far more quickly. This can be linked to the voltage and size of the current. Students should also be made aware of clockwork devices and shown one if possible. Students then analyse the different devices mentioned in the student book, discussing how they operate and link this back to the effects of a current from earlier in the lesson.	**Extend:** The electrical power equation ($P = \frac{E}{t}$) can be covered. Look for explanations of the rate of energy transfer using the idea of larger and smaller electrical currents and/or voltages.	

Plenary	Support/Extend	Resources
Making connections (5 min) Interactive where students complete the paragraph 'Electrical current is a very convenient way of transferring energy because…' and include the words energy, transfer, and current. Students then calculate the efficiency of a series of electrical appliances.		**Interactive:** Making connections
Electrical appliances (10 min) Ask students to produce a table similar to the one in the student book with additional electrical appliances. You could use a mobile phone, projector, vacuum cleaner, and electric fan. For some students, you could add challenging appliances such as a computer.	**Support:** Physical cards can be used to assemble the table.	

Homework		
Students carry out a survey of electrical appliances found at school or at home. Record the useful and wasted energy transfers of each appliance.		

P1.9 Energy and power

AQA spec Link: 1.1.4 Power is defined as the rate at which energy is transferred or the rate at which work is done.

$$\text{power} = \frac{\text{energy transferred}}{\text{time}} \quad [P = \frac{E}{t}]$$

$$\text{power} = \frac{\text{work done}}{\text{time}} \quad [P = \frac{W}{t}]$$

power P in watts, W

energy transferred E in joules, J

time t in seconds, s

work done W in joules, J

An energy transfer of 1 joule per second is equal to a power of 1 watt.

Students should be able to give examples that illustrate the definition of power, for example, comparing two electric motors that both lift the same weight through the same height but one does it faster than the other.

1.2.2 The energy efficiency for any energy transfer can be calculated using the equation:

$$\text{efficiency} = \frac{\text{useful output energy transfer}}{\text{total input energy transfer}}$$

Efficiency may also be calculated using the equation:

$$\text{efficiency} = \frac{\text{useful power output}}{\text{total power input}}$$

(H) Students should be able to describe ways to increase the efficiency of an intended energy transfer.

MS 1a, 1b, 1c, 3b, 3c

Aiming for	Outcome	Checkpoint	
		Question	Activity
Aiming for GRADE 4 ↓	State the unit of power as the watt and kilowatt.	1	Starter 1, Main
	With support, rank electrical appliances in order of power.	1	Main
	Identify 'wasted' and 'useful' energy transfers in electrical devices.		Main
Aiming for GRADE 6 ↓	Calculate the energy transferred by an electrical device.	2	Main, Plenary 2
	Calculate the efficiency of a device from power ratings.	2, 3	Main
	Find the wasted power of a device.	3	Main
Aiming for GRADE 8 ↓	Compare the power ratings of devices using standard form.		Main
	Apply the efficiency equation in a range of situations, including rearrangement of the equation.	2, 3	Main, Plenary 2
	Combine the electrical power equation with other equations to solve complex problems.	4	Main, Plenary 2

Maths
There is a range of calculations involving power and efficiency that the students need to perform (1a, 1c, 3c). Higher-tier students are also required to rearrange the equations and can also use standard form (1b, 3b).

Literacy
Students discuss the power ratings of devices, linking this to the efficiency and function.

Key words
power

P1 Conservation and dissipation of energy

Practical

Title	Efficiency and power
Equipment	low-voltage power supply, low-voltage electrical appliances, joulemeter
Overview of method	Demonstrate the energy use of electrical appliances by connecting appliances to the low-voltage power supply and measuring the energy using the joulemeter. Demonstrate a range of bulbs so that students can link the energy use to the brightness. Then move on to motors, showing larger motors requiring more energy.

Starter	Support/Extend	Resources
Big numbers (5 min) Give students a set of units with SI prefixes and ask them to place the units in order of size. These could be mm, cm, m, km, and another set containing mg, g, and kg. Then add in larger units such as mega (M) and giga (G) that students may not have encountered. **Match up** (10 min) Ask students to sort a range of electrical appliances into order of energy transfer (power rating). You could do this with real objects or with cards to represent them. The objects could be set up on a long bench and students should add sticky notes for their ranking. Discuss these rankings after everybody has had a go.	**Support:** Provide examples of the use of each unit to assist students with their ideas of scale. **Extend:** Students guess the power ratings then add sticky notes indicating the useful energy transfers and wasted energy on each.	**Interactive:** Big numbers

Main	Support/Extend	Resources
Efficiency and power (40 min) Carry out the practical demonstration to show the difference in energy use between different devices. Discuss the transfer of energy at different rates leading to the power equation. The students need to try some calculations to ensure that they are performing them correctly and using the correct units. Describe some of the power ratings of typical devices using some of the examples from the student book so that the students understand the stages in the calculation. They should then try an example of their own. A maths skills interactive is available to support students with the calculations and provide some examples for them to carry out themselves. Students then identify the useful and wasted power output of a range of devices and then use this data to find the efficiency. Emphasise careful layout of calculations to avoid mistakes. A support sheet is available where students develop their knowledge of the units of energy and power and also practise using energy terms.	**Support:** Select appropriate questions for the students. **Extend:** Use numbers with SI prefixes and expect rearrangement of the base equation. **Support:** Assist students with identifying the useful and the wasted power transfers. **Extend:** Use kilowatts and watts for different examples.	**Practical:** Efficiency and power **Math skills:** Energy transfer by electricity **Support:** Power to the kitchen

Plenary	Support/Extend	Resources
Matching the power (5 min) Give students a set of pictures of household electrical appliances and a set of power ratings. Ask them to match the ratings with the appliances. For example, kettle 2 kW, washing machine 0.5 kW (average over washing cycle), desktop computer 200 W, dishwasher 1.5 kW, electric clock 1 W, iron 1 kW, CD player 30 W, blender 300 W. **Calculation loop** (10 min) Students match up calculation questions with their numerical answers. There should be a set of calculations and only one card with the correct answer. Students work out the correct answer and then ask the question on that card. Repeat until all of the questions are answered.	**Support:** Differentiate questions according to students' ability.	

Homework		
Students complete the WebQuest where they research how much energy their electronic devices (phone, ipad, mp3 player, laptop) use in a typical day/year, and how this compares with more obvious energy usage such as lighting and heating.		**WebQuest:** Your electronic devices

kerboodle

A Kerboodle highlight for this lesson is **Working scientifically: Working with units**. Refer to the **Content map** on Kerboodle for a full list of resources and assessment.

P1 Conservation and dissipation of energy

Overview of P1 Conservation and dissipation of energy

In this chapter, students developed their understanding of energy and energy transfer, begun in KS3. This included development of an energy stores model and the processes (pathways), such as forces and electrical currents, through which energy can be transferred.

Students have learnt how to measure the work done by a force acting over a distance and how this concept can be used to analyse energy transfers in gravitational stores, through lifting and falling, and elastic potential stores during stretching using the relevant mathematical relationships. The conservation of energy through changes in the gravitational, kinetic and elastic stores was also discussed.

They have considered the dissipation of energy during transfers, such as those caused by friction or electrical heating, leading to the idea of efficiency during different energy transfers and the calculation of efficiency calculation. The concept of efficiency has then been applied to the selection of electrical devices.

Finally, the students have learnt about the rate of energy transfer in different systems through the concept of power and how this power rating can be used to determine the total energy transfer over time.

MyMaths

You can find additional support for the maths skills covered in this chapter on **MyMaths**, including recognising and using expressions in standard form, using an appropriate number of significant figures, using of bar charts, and rearranging of equations.

kerboodle

For this chapter, the following assessments are available on Kerboodle:

P1 Checkpoint quiz: Conservation and dissipation of energy
P1 Progress quiz: Conservation and dissipation of energy 1
P1 Progress quiz: Conservation and dissipation of energy 2
P1 On your marks: Conservation and dissipation of energy
P1 Exam-style questions and mark scheme: Conservation and dissipation of energy

Checkpoint follow up lesson

A student's route through this lesson can be determined using the Checkpoint assessment. Percentage pass marks are supplied in the Checkpoint teacher notes.

For each successive route through it is assumed that the student can perform to their current route as well as previous routes. For example, students working at Aiming for 6 are assumed to be secure in Aiming for 4 knowledge and understanding and working towards achieving all the learning outcomes for Aiming for 6.

	Aiming for 4	**Aiming for 6**	**Aiming for 8**
Learning outcomes	Name different types of energy store.	Describe processes in terms of energy stores, and transfers.	Explain processes in terms of energy stores.
	Do calculations involving gravitational potential energy, kinetic energy, elastic potential energy, work done, power and efficiency.	Do calculations involving gravitational potential energy, kinetic energy, elastic potential energy, work done, power and efficiency, and change the subject of equations.	Do more complex calculations involving gravitational potential energy, kinetic energy, elastic potential energy, work done, power and efficiency, and change the subject of equations.
	Describe the difference between efficient and inefficient devices in terms of dissipation.		Apply what you know about power and efficiency.
Starter	**Spot the store! (5 min)** Give out cards with pictures of everyday situations, e.g. a camping stove, ball rolling down a hill, and ask students to identify the store or stores where the energy is increasing, and the store or stores where the energy is decreasing.		
	Guess the question (10 min) Make packs of cards with the keywords from the energy topic. In groups students take turns to select a card and everyone in the groups writes as many questions as they can think of where the word is the answer. Groups feedback their questions to the class, with a prize for the group with the most questions.		
Differentiated checkpoint activity	Aiming for 4 students use the Checkpoint follow-up sheet to model the transfer of energy between stores, and with help do calculations involving a bouncing ball and electrical appliances. The follow-up sheet is highly-structured to support students with the tasks, and they should work in pairs with input from the teacher.	Aiming for 6 students use the Checkpoint follow-up sheet to design an investigation into bouncing balls, model energy transfers with liquid and coins, and consider the efficiency of different types of light bulb. The follow-up sheet is fairly structured and students should be aiming to work independently.	Aiming for 8 students use the Checkpoint follow-up sheet to design an investigation into craters, model energy transfers with liquid and coins, and calculate the efficiency of different types of light bulb. The follow-up sheet provides minimal support for students and they should be working independently.
	Kerboodle resource P1 Checkpoint follow up: Aiming for 4, P1 Checkpoint follow up: Aiming for 6, P1 Checkpoint follow up: Aiming for 8		
Plenary	**Find the biggest (10 min)** Give out a set of cards with information on each relating to efficiency, work, and power. Students work in teams of three to work out the card in each category that shows the biggest efficiency, work done, or power. Pair the groups up to check the answers. The information on the cards can be differentiated with Aiming at 4 students also being given the equations.		
	Energy conservation...or not? (5 min) Show students one of more of three situations that appear to defy the law of conservation of energy: the Gaussian gun, the 'thunder popper' (a rubber hemisphere you turn inside out and drop, which goes higher than you dropped it from), dropping a tennis ball on a football. Ask them to account to the apparent appearance of more energy at the end than at the start. Groups feedback explanations and the class votes for the best one in each case.		
Progression	Students should be able to identify the energy stores involved in a range of energy transfers, and to do calculations involving stores, work, power and efficiency. Encourage students to think about the difference between the energy description of a process and what is physically happening by identifying the stores involved. Putting units in calculations will help them to get more answers correct.	Students should be able to describe a range of processes in terms of the energy stores involved, and to do calculations involving stores, work, power and efficiency, and convert between a variety of units. Encourage students to think about the difference between the energy description of a process and what is physically happening by identifying the stores involved. They should devise a system for remembering the relevant equations for the energy associated with different stores.	Students should be able to use ideas about stores to identify changes in energy in a range of processes, to do more complex calculations involving stores, work, power and efficiency, and convert between a variety of units, and apply what they know about efficiency to a range of situations. Encourage students to differentiate the energy description of a process and what is physically happening by identifying the stores involved, and to think critically about ways of modelling energy transfers.

P 2 Energy transfer by heating

2.1 Energy transfer by conduction

AQA spec Link: 1.2.1 Unwanted energy transfers can be reduced in a number of ways, for example through lubrication and the use of thermal insulation. Students should be able to explain ways of reducing unwanted energy transfers, for example, through lubrication and the use of thermal insulation.

The higher the thermal conductivity of a material the higher the rate of energy transfer by conduction across the material.

Students should be able to describe how the rate of cooling of a building is affected by the thickness and thermal conductivity of its walls.

Students do not need to know the definition of thermal conductivity.

3.2.1 Energy is stored inside a system by the particles (atoms and molecules) that make up the system. This is called internal energy.

Internal energy is the total kinetic energy and potential energy of all the particles (atoms and molecules) that make up a system.

Heating changes the energy stored within the system by increasing the energy of the particles that make up the system. This either raises the temperature of the system or produces a change of state.

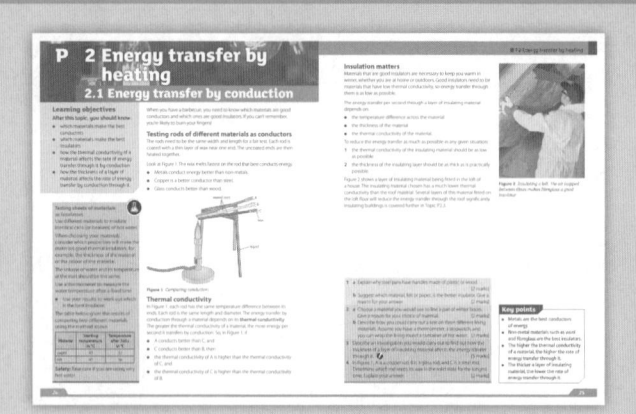

MS 2c, 4a

Aiming for	Outcome	Checkpoint	
		Question	Activity
Aiming for GRADE 4 ↓	Describe materials as good or poor thermal conductors.	1	Starter 1, Starter 2
	Compare the thermal conductivities of materials in simple terms.	1	Starter 1, Starter 2, Main
	Relate the thermal conductivities of a material to the uses of that material in familiar contexts.	1	Main
Aiming for GRADE 6 ↓	Analyse temperature change data to compare the thermal conductivity of materials.		Main
	Describe the changes in the behaviour of the particles in a material as the temperature of the material increases.	3	Main
	Apply understanding of thermal conductivity in reducing energy dissipation through the choice of appropriate insulating materials.	2, 4, End of chapter 4	Homework
Aiming for GRADE 8 ↓	Explain the different thermal conductivities of materials using the free electron and lattice vibration explanations of conduction.	3	Main, Plenary 2
	Evaluate the results of an experiment into thermal conductivity in terms of repeatability and reproducibility of data, and the validity of conclusions drawn from the data.		Main
	Justify the choices of a material involved in insulation or conduction using the concept of thermal conductivity and other data.	4	Homework

Maths
Students draw tables and plot graphs of their results from the practical (2c, 4a).

Literacy
Focus on the precise application of the scientific key terms in descriptions of conduction processes.

Key words
thermal conductivity

24

P2 Energy transfer by heating

Practical

Title	Testing sheets of materials as insulators
Equipment	containers for water (metals cans, beakers, or boiling tubes), access to hot water (kettle), thermometer (0–100 °C with 0.5 °C divisions), stopwatch, elastic bands or tape, aluminium foil (for lids), range of materials to test (wool, cotton wool, fur, corrugated card, etc.)
Overview of method	Insulate containers using different materials. Pour hot water into the containers and place a lid onto them. Allow the containers to cool for a fixed length of time and compare the temperature drop.
Safety considerations	Kettles can cause burns; a hot water tap may be sufficient as an alternative.

Starter	Support/Extend	Resources
Frying tonight? (10 min) Crack an egg onto a frying pan and a heat-resistant mat and use Bunsen burners to heat them. (Alternatively, show a video of an egg frying.) Students describe the processes that allow energy to reach the eggs and compare the rate of energy transfer. **Spoons** (5 min) Ask students to explain, if a metal spoon and a wooden spoon are put into boiling water, why only the end of one spoon will get hot.	**Extend:** Students should directly link the behaviour of the particles in a material to the material's temperature. **Extend:** Look for descriptions about energy transfer *within* the materials.	**Interactive:** Frying tonight?

Main	Support/Extend	Resources
Testing sheets of materials as insulators (40 min) Students complete the practical, focusing on producing results that are as accurate as possible from this experiment by refining the control of variables and eliminating sources of random error. Links should be made to the idea of trapped air in foams or fluffy materials used for insulation and reduction of energy dissipation.	**Extend:** Ask students to develop a quantitative test comparing the number of layers of insulation with the temperature change.	**Practical:** Testing sheets of materials as insulators

Plenary	Support/Extend	Resources
Chilling effect (5 min) Explain to students what a defrosting plate is. (You could show students a photo or video of one.) Ask students to explain why an ice cube will melt a lot quicker on a defrosting plate than on a plastic surface, in terms of conduction. (Defrosting trays are made of materials that have a high thermal conductivity and will transfer thermal energy more efficiently than a plastic surface.) **Conduction modelling** (10 min) Ask students to describe a large-scale model of conduction through lattice vibration to provide a visual idea of the process.	**Extend:** Students should incorporate the idea of free electrons into their physical model in some way and evaluate the model.	

Homework		
Students complete a survey of the materials used in their home for insulation or to allow efficient energy transfer. This can include the building materials and the furnishings.	**Extend:** Provide students with some numerical values for the thermal conductivity that they use to justify the choices of materials.	

P2.2 Specific heat capacity

AQA spec Link: 3.2.1 Heating changes the energy stored within the system by increasing the energy of the particles that make up the system. This either raises the temperature of the system or produces a change of state.

3.2.2 If the temperature of the system increases, the increase in temperature depends on the mass of the substance heated, the type of material, and the energy input to the system.
The following equation applies:
change in thermal energy = mass × specific heat capacity × temperature change

$$[\Delta E = m\, c\, \Delta \theta]$$

change in thermal energy ΔE in joules, J
mass m in kilograms, kg
specific heat capacity c in joules per kilogram per degree Celsius, J/kg °C
temperature change $\Delta \theta$ in degrees Celsius, °C.
The specific heat capacity of a substance is the amount of energy required to raise the temperature of one kilogram of the substance by one degree Celsius.

1.1.3 The amount of energy stored in or released from a system as its temperature changes can be calculated using the equation:

change in thermal energy = mass × specific heat capacity × temperature change

$$[\Delta E = m\, c\, \Delta \theta]$$

change in thermal energy ΔE in joules, J
mass m in kilograms, kg
specific heat capacity c in joules per kilogram per degree Celsius, J/kg °C
temperature change $\Delta \theta$ in degrees Celsius, °C
The specific heat capacity of a substance is the amount of energy required to raise the temperature of one kilogram of the substance by one degree Celsius.

Required practical: investigation to determine the specific heat capacity of one or more materials. The investigation will involve linking the decrease of one energy store (or work done) to the increase in temperature and subsequent increase in thermal energy stored.

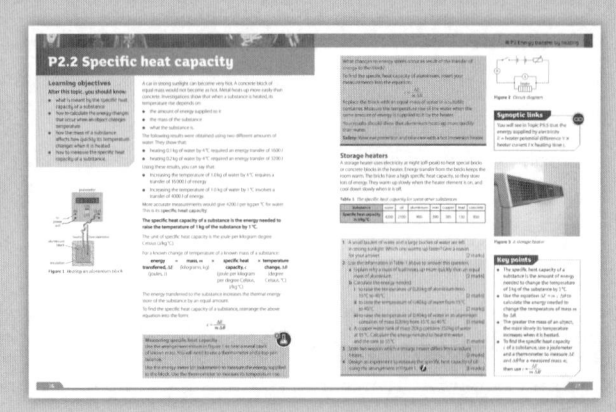

MS 1a, 3b, 3c, 3d

Aiming for	Outcome	Checkpoint	
		Question	Activity
Aiming for GRADE 4	Describe materials in terms of being difficult or easy to heat up (increase the temperature of).	2, 3	Starter 1, Starter 2, Main
↓	List the factors that affect the amount of energy required to increase the temperature of an object.	1	Main
	With some support, measure the specific heat capacity of a material.		Main
Aiming for GRADE 6	Describe the effects of changing the factors involved in the equation.		Starter 1, Main
↓	Calculate the energy required to change the temperature of an object.	2	Main
	Measure the specific heat capacity of a material and find a mean value.		Main
Aiming for GRADE 8	Evaluate materials used for transferring energy in terms of their specific heat capacity.		Main
↓	Use the specific heat capacity equation to perform a wide range of calculations in unfamiliar contexts.	2	Main
	Evaluate in detail the results of an experiment to measure specific heat capacity.	4	Main

Maths
The students perform calculations involving specific heat capacity using an equation with variables (1a, 3b, 3c).

Literacy
Students work in small groups to discuss results of experiments and describe them accurately.

Key words
specific heat capacity

P2 Energy transfer by heating

Required practical

Title	Measuring specific heat capacity
Equipment	low-voltage power supply, aluminium heating block, heating element, thermometer, joulemeter, connecting leads, stopwatch, beaker (size depends on the mass of the metal block), water
Overview of method	Students heat the aluminium block for five minutes recording the temperature rise and energy supplied. They use this data and the mass of the block to calculate the specific heat capacity. They then repeat the process with a beaker of water of the same mass and compare the two temperature rises and notice that the aluminium's temperature rise is greater. An ammeter, a voltmeter, and a stopwatch can be used instead of the joulemeter to measure the energy supplied to the block. The ammeter is used to measure the heater current, and the voltmeter is used to measure the heater voltage. If this method is used, the heating time also needs to be measured.
Safety considerations	The block should not be heated to high temperatures – a maximum of 40 °C is sufficient.

Starter	Support/Extend	Resources
Hot metal (10 min) Heat a relatively small block of metal until it is clearly very hot using a Bunsen burner, gauze, and tripod. Use tongs to drop it into a bucket of water. Students explain the small change in temperature for the water. Safety: Take care with the hot metal. Put the hot metal carefully into the bucket of water. Make sure the bucket or container of water is made of an appropriate material for the experiment. **Boiling up** (5 min) Explain to students that of two kettles, one full and one half full, the half full kettle will boil first. Ask students to come up with their own explanation as to why the half full kettle boils first.	**Extend:** Ask for discussion of the temperature change of both the metal block and the water.	

Main	Support/Extend	Resources
Measuring specific heat capacity (40 min) Discuss the factors that may affect the temperature change of a material when it is heated, using ideas from the starters. Lead the students through the calculation for specific heat capacity step by step, ensuring they understand each of the terms of the equation. Students then carry out the practical to attempt to find a value for the specific heat capacity of a metal. It is likely that their value will not match an accepted value and so they should discuss the reasons that their values are different. This is mainly due to energy transferred to the environment. Students can use the Maths skills interactive to rearrange the equation for specific heat capacity.	**Support:** A calculation frame showing each of the steps will help a great deal. **Extension:** The Extension sheet provides opportunity for students to rearrange the equation and apply it in a wider range of contexts.	**Required practical:** Measuring specific heat capacity **Extension:** Specific heat capacity **Maths skills:** Specific heat capacity

Plenary	Support/Extend	Resources
Hot water (5 min) Why is water used in central heating systems? Students could come up with a range of reasons why it is chosen. **Crossword** (10 min) Students use the interactive to complete a crossword on the content from this and the previous lessons. This should form a summary of their learning about energy transfer.	**Extend:** Suggest alternative materials such as mercury. **Support:** Provide differentiated clues to different groups of students.	**Interactive:** Crossword

Homework		
Students complete the Calculation sheet for further practice in using the equation for specific heat capacity.		**Calculation sheet:** Specific heat capacity

kerboodle

A Kerboodle highlight for this lesson is **Bump up your grades: Specific heat capacity**. Refer to the **Content map** on Kerboodle for a full list of resources and assessment.

P2.3 Heating and insulating buildings

AQA spec Link: 1.2.1 Students should be able to describe, with examples, how in all system changes energy is dissipated, so that it is stored in less useful ways. This energy is often described as being 'wasted'.

Students should be able to describe how the rate of cooling of a building is affected by the thickness and thermal conductivity of its walls.

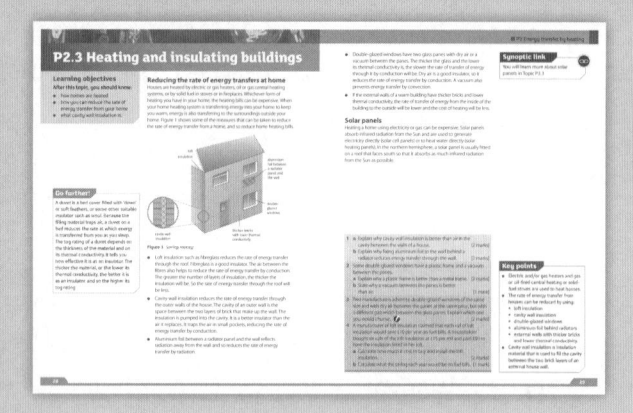

MS 2h, 3c

Aiming for	Outcome	Checkpoint	
		Question	Activity
Aiming for GRADE 4 ↓	Describe some design features used to prevent energy transfer to the surroundings in the home.	1, 2, 3	Starter 1, Main 1
	Calculate the payback time of a simple home improvement feature.	4	Main 2
Aiming for GRADE 6 ↓	Describe how some design features are used to reduce energy transfers from a home.	1, 2, 3	Starter 1, Main 1
	Compare home improvement features in terms of payback time.	4	Main 2
Aiming for GRADE 8 ↓	Evaluate in detail design features used to reduce the rate of energy transferred from the home.	1, 2, 3	Main 1, Main 2
	Decide on home improvement features using payback time and savings beyond the payback time.	4	Main 2, Plenary 1

Maths
Students calculate the payback time for a home improvement feature (2h). Some may also use specific heat capacity calculations (3c).

Literacy
Students work in small groups to discuss energy saving features and their operation.

P2 Energy transfer by heating

Starter	Support/Extend	Resources
Worth it? (10 min) Swapping over your mobile phone to a new one will cost you £200 but you will be able to enter a new contract for £10 less each month on a two-year contract. Should you swap your phone? What other factors would you have to consider? **Hot house** (5 min) Show students a large diagram of a house showing the various locations where energy can be transferred to its surroundings. Students suggest ways to save energy. Students could copy the diagram, or the diagram could be provided to students for them to annotate.	**Extend:** Provide additional information about data tariffs.	

Main	Support/Extend	Resources
Reducing energy transfers in the home (25 min) Discuss the features used to prevent energy transferred in a house one by one. Use example materials (e.g., bricks, insulation foam) if any are available. Provide students with some examples of costs, as these will be useful later. **Payback time** (15 min) The students compare the payback time of some of the design features, using real data.	**Support:** Students work in groups to produce a large, annotated poster describing the features. **Extension:** Students complete the Extension sheet to consider some of the energy transfers from a house and think about some of the best ways to save money. **Extend:** Provide more detailed data such as lifetime of improvements.	**Activity:** Reducing energy transfers in the home **Extension:** Energy and buildings

Plenary	Support/Extend	Resources
Energy neutral house (10 min) Students can use their knowledge of energy transfer to design an energy neutral house. They can use all of the design features here and may include some of the developing ideas in electricity generation. **House analysis** (5 min) Provide a set of home improvements costs and savings. Students use the interactive to sequence them in the order in which the improvements should be done.	**Support:** Provide a simple table for the students to complete.	**Interactive:** House analysis

Homework		
Students complete the WebQuest where they research different methods that can be used to improve the insulation of a house.		**WebQuest:** House insulation

kerboodle

A Kerboodle highlight for this lesson is **Bump up your grade: Thermal conductivity**. Refer to the **Content map** on Kerboodle for a full list of resources and assessment.

P2 Energy transfer by heating

Overview of P2 Energy transfer by heating

In this chapter the students have developed their understanding of the heating and cooling processes, which transfer energy within a material or from one object to another. They have investigated thermal conductivity and the differences in the processes of thermal conduction in metals and non-metals.

All students have analysed the changes in temperature when a material is heated, leading to the experimental determination of specific heat capacity along with corresponding calculations. The concept of specific heat capacity was then used to explain the choice of materials used in heating systems.

Finally, the reduction of energy transfers to the surroundings by insulation has been studied and applied to the context of reducing the rate of energy transfer from buildings to reduce heating costs including the idea prioritising home improvements in line with payback time.

MyMaths

You can find additional support for the maths skills covered in this chapter on **MyMaths**, including recognising and using expressions in decimal form, solving simple algebraic equations, plotting graphs, using equations and standard form.

Required practical

All students are expected to have carried out the required practical:

Practical	Topic
An investigation to determine the specific heat capacity of one or more materials. The investigation will involve linking the decrease of one energy store (or work done) to the increase in temperature and subsequent increase in thermal energy stored.	P2.2

kerboodle

For this chapter, the following assessments are available on Kerboodle:

P2 Checkpoint quiz Energy transfer by heating
P2 Progress quiz: Energy transfer by heating 1
P2 Progress quiz: Energy transfer by heating 2
P2 On your marks: Energy transfer by heating
P2 Exam-style questions and mark scheme: Energy transfer by heating

Checkpoint follow up lesson

A student's route through this lesson can be determined using the Checkpoint assessment. Percentage pass marks are supplied in the Checkpoint teacher notes.

For each successive route through it is assumed that the student can perform to their current route as well as previous routes. For example, students working at Aiming for 6 are assumed to be secure in Aiming for 4 knowledge and understanding and working towards achieving all the learning outcomes for Aiming for 6.

	Aiming for 4	**Aiming for 6**	**Aiming for 8**
Learning outcomes	Calculate change in thermal energy.	Describe what thermal conductivity depends on.	Calculate specific heat capacity and apply knowledge of specific heat capacity to make predictions.
	Describe what thermal conductivity means.	Describe a variety of ways to keep your house warm.	Apply what you know about thermal conductivity to buildings and other situations.
	Describe how to keep your house warm.	Calculate change in thermal energy and convert between units.	Analyse data in terms of specific heat capacity.
Starter	**Keeping warm (10 min)** Give students two minutes to come up with as many different ways to keep a house warm as they can think of. Then ask them to join with a partner to collate their ideas, and finally join with another pair. Bring the ideas together, and discuss the reasons why these methods would keep a house warm.		
Differentiated checkpoint activity	Students use the checkpoint follow-up sheets to investigate into how the volume of water affects the time it takes to heat water.		
	The Aiming for 4 follow-up sheet provides a structured method for students to follow and students should work in pairs with teacher input.		
	The Aiming for 6 follow-up sheet provides limited support for students plan their own investigation. They should be aiming to work independently. Any plans should be checked by the teacher before students carry out any practical work.		
	The Aiming for 8 follow-up sheet provides minimal support and students should plan their own investigation. They should work independently and any plans should be checked by the teacher before students carry out any practical work.		
	All students should also plot given data on different materials' thermal conductivity, and analyse their graph. Students will need graph paper.		
	Kerboodle resource P2 Checkpoint follow up: Aiming for 4, P2 Checkpoint follow up: Aiming for 6, P2 Checkpoint follow up: Aiming for 8		
Plenary	**Baked Alaska (10 min)** Give students A4 dry wipe boards, pens, and an eraser. Ask them to do a calculation of the thermal energy required to melt 1 kg of ice cream. Tell them roughly how long it would take a normal oven to transfer this energy. Show a video of a Baked Alaska coming out of the oven and in groups get them to write the best explanation as to why the ice cream does not melt. Display a mark scheme and get them to peer mark the work.		
Progression	Encourage students to think about specific heat capacity in terms of rise in temperature, and thermal conductivity in terms of time for energy transfer and to apply what they know to keeping a house warm.	Encourage students to think of the link between specific heat capacity and thermal conductivity when choosing building materials.	Encourage students to think of the link between specific heat capacity and thermal conductivity when choosing building materials.

P 3 Energy resources
3.1 Energy demands

AQA spec Link: 1.3 The main energy resources available for use on Earth include: fossil fuels (coal, oil and gas), nuclear fuel, biofuel, wind, hydro-electricity, geothermal, the tides, the Sun, and water waves.

A renewable energy resource is one that is being (or can be) replenished as it is used.

The uses of energy resources include transport, electricity generation, and heating.

Students should be able to:
- describe the main energy sources available
- compare ways that different energy resources are used, the uses to include transport, electricity generation, and heating
- understand why some energy resources are more reliable than others.

Descriptions of how energy resources are used to generate electricity are **not** required.

WS 4.4
MS 1b

Aiming for	Outcome	Checkpoint	
		Question	Activity
Aiming for GRADE 4 ↓	Identify which fuels are renewable and which are non-renewable.	1	Starter 1, Starter 2, Main 1
	Identify activities that require large energy transfers.	4	Main 1
	Describe biofuels as carbon neutral whereas fossil fuels are not.	1	Starter 2
Aiming for GRADE 6 ↓	Outline the operation of a fossil fuel burning power station.		Main 1
	Outline the operation of a nuclear power station.		Main 2
	Explain why biofuels are considered carbon neutral.	3	Main 1
Aiming for GRADE 8 ↓	Compare energy use from different sources and different societies from available data.	2	Main 1
	Compare fossil fuels and nuclear fuels in terms of energy provided, waste, and pollution.	1	Main 2
	Discuss some of the problems associated with biofuel use and production.	3	Main 1

Maths
Students handle large numbers when discussing energy; some using SI prefixes and standard form (1b).

Literacy
Students describe complex processes in power stations and work together to discuss the advantages and disadvantages of different fuels.

Key words
biofuel, renewable, carbon-neutral, nuclear fuel, nucleus

Practical

Title	Burning fuels for energy
Equipment	heat-resistant mat, small sample of ethanol, spirit burner
Overview of method	Put a small sample of ethanol into the spirit burner, and light the wick.
Safety considerations	Burn the sample on top of the heat-resistant mat and allow the container to cool before handling.

P3 Energy resources

Starter	Support/Extend	Resources
Fossil fuels (5 min) Students use the interactive to put in order statements that describe how coal, oil, and natural gas are formed. **The burning question** (10 min) Students draw a spider diagram or visual summary covering what they know about combustion of fuels. They can do this whilst watching a birthday candle burn, stopping when the candle is finished. Choose a candle that will last for a few minutes.	**Support:** Provide the key stages for the students to put in order. **Support:** Provide example fuels for the students and expect simple word equations. **Extend:** Students should produce some balanced symbol equations for combustion reactions.	**Interactive:** Fossil fuels

Main	Support/Extend	Resources
Burning fuels for energy (25 min) Begin with an explanation of the very high energy demands of developed countries and ask the students about what they already understand about how these needs are met. Discuss which activities may be responsible for the very large energy demands, such as transport and heating of homes. Show students the structure of a conventional (fossil fuel) power station, supported with animations or video clips where possible. Demonstrate the combustion of a biofuel (e.g., ethanol) whilst discussing how it is produced. Place emphasis on the carbon-neutral nature, identifying photosynthesis and combustion and the key processes. Explain how the process of burning a fuel is used to produce electricity. **Nuclear power** (15 min) Outline the operation of a nuclear power plant, noting the different heating processes taking place in the core with much of the rest of the plant similar to fossil fuel power plants. A quick comparison of nuclear and fossil fuels should be made.	**Extend:** Discuss the additional costs of producing biofuels in terms of land and food shortage, and energy costs and emissions in processing. Ask students to use standard form to represent large numbers.	**Practical:** Burning fuels for energy

Plenary	Support/Extend	Resources
Anagrams (5 min) Ask students to decipher anagrams of important key words from this lesson. Add a few more about energy resources to see if the students can figure them out. Students then define each key term. **Lightning storm** (10 min) Some people propose harnessing the electricity from lightning strikes for power. Students could discuss the advantages and disadvantages of this idea.	**Support:** Differentiate according to students' abilities by using single words or more complex phrases.	

Homework		
Students complete the WebQuest where they research the differences, of biofuels and fossil fuels, the advantages and disadvantages of biofuels, and the effect biofuels have on the environment. They use their research to prepare a presentation or debate.		**WebQuest:** Biofuels

P3.2 Energy from wind and water

AQA spec Link: 1.3 The main energy resources available for use on Earth include: fossil fuels (coal, oil and gas), nuclear fuel, biofuel, wind, hydro-electricity, geothermal, the tides, the Sun, and water waves.

A renewable energy resource is one that is being (or can be) replenished as it is used.

The uses of energy resources include transport, electricity generation, and heating.

Students should be able to:
- describe the main energy sources available
- distinguish between energy resources that are renewable and energy resources that are non-renewable
- compare ways that different energy resources are used, the uses to include transport, electricity generation, and heating
- understand why some energy resources are more reliable than others
- describe the environmental impact arising from the use of different energy resources.

Students should be able to:
- consider the environmental issues that may arise from the use of different energy resources
- show that science has the ability to identify environmental issues arising from the use of energy resources but not always the power to deal with the issues because of political, social, ethical, or economic considerations.

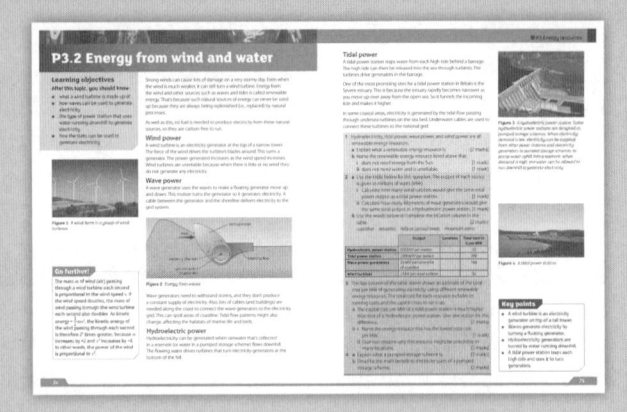

WS 1.3, 4, 4.4
MS 1c, 2c, 4a

Aiming for	Outcome	Checkpoint	
		Question	Activity
Aiming for GRADE 4	State that wind turbines, wave generators, hydroelectric systems, and tidal systems are renewable energy resources.	1	Main
	Describe some simple advantages or disadvantages of renewable energy systems.	End of chapter 4	Main
	Outline the operation of a renewable energy source.	1, End of chapter 3, 4	
Aiming for GRADE 6	Describe the operation of a wind farm.	2	Main
	Describe the operation of a hydroelectric system.	End of chapter 2	Main
	Suggest the most appropriate energy resource to use in a range of scenarios.	2	Plenary 1
Aiming for GRADE 8	Compare the operation of hydroelectric, wave, and tidal systems in terms of reliability, potential power output, and costs.	2, 3, End of chapter 2	Main
	Explain in detail the purpose, operation, and advantages of a pumped storage system.	4	Main
	Justify the choice of an energy resource by using numerical and other appropriate data.	End of chapter 5, 6	Plenary

Maths
Students can use numerical values such as power output to compare different schemes of electricity generation (2c).

Literacy
There are several opportunities for students to discuss in small groups the advantages and disadvantages of energy resources.

34

P3 Energy resources

Practical

Title	Wind and wave power
Equipment	model wind turbine, desk fan, voltmeter, metre rule, clamp stand, clamp, boss
Overview of method	Attach the voltmeter to the model wind turbine, and use the clamp to hold the turbine at the height of the desk fan. Use the metre rule to measure how far the desk fan is from the turbine. Demonstrate how the number of turbine blades affects voltage output.
Safety considerations	Switch off the desk fan and ensure all parts stop moving before making any changes to the equipment.

Starter	Support/Extend	Resources
Wind and convection currents (5 min) Ask students to suggest the cause of wind in the atmosphere.	**Extend:** Ask students to explain for themselves the causes of the flow of air in terms of expansion, density changes, and pressure.	
Water cycle recap (10 min) Students use the interactive to label a diagram of the water cycle with the key words evaporation, condensation, and precipitation. They then choose the correct words to complete sentences that explain how the water cycle is linked to hydroelectricity.	**Support:** Provide a basic diagram showing an ocean, land, mountains, and a river for the students to annotate.	**Interactive:** Water cycle recap

Main	Support/Extend	Resources
Wind and water power (40 min) Show a video clip of a wind farm and ask students to explain what is happening. Link back to the idea of a turbine generating electricity. Carry out the simple practical to investigate wind turbines. Discuss the advantages and disadvantages of wind power including its renewable nature.	**Support:** Students can complete a simple advantages/disadvantages table for this and other resources discussed this lesson.	**Practical:** Wind and water power
Discuss the operation of a simple system ensuring the students are clear on some of the advantages and disadvantages.		
Then explain how a water turbine works and discuss the energy transfers involved, linking back to the idea of gravitational potential energy stores.	**Extend:** Students can discuss the efficiency of pumped storage systems, linking this to a graph of base load. Students can also discuss smaller-scale tidal pools, which do not 'block off' whole rivers.	
Include a discussion of a pumped storage system, ensuring that the students know that, although these systems are not efficient, they allow some of the excess power produced at night by the base load of the network to be used usefully. Renewability should be addressed.		
Tidal power can be linked to the hydroelectric systems but with a different supply of water – the tides.		

Plenary	Support/Extend	Resources
Local solutions (10 min) Give students some example towns and their local environments. Students should decide which of the systems covered today would best suit each town, and determine if the systems are a better solution to local needs than a fossil fuel power station.	**Extend:** Students analyse their local environment and suggest the best way to generate electricity.	
Wind farm controversy (5 min) Ask students to suggest why local communities may campaign against wind farms.		

Homework		
Ask students to design a poster to persuade a local community to allow a wind farm in the vicinity. Other students could design an 'anti' poster. The poster could include information about new jobs, noise, reliability, cheaper or more expensive electricity. Students can then evaluate each other's work.		

kerboodle

A Kerboodle highlight for this lesson is **Working scientifically: Wind turbines**. Refer to the **Content map** on Kerboodle for a full list of resources and assessment.

P3.3 Power from the Sun and the Earth

AQA spec Link: 1.3 The main energy resources available for use on Earth include: fossil fuels (coal, oil and gas), nuclear fuel, biofuel, wind, hydro-electricity, geothermal, the tides, the Sun, and water waves.

The uses of energy resources include transport, electricity generation, and heating.

Students should be able to:
- describe the main energy sources available
- distinguish between energy resources that are renewable and energy resources that are non-renewable
- compare ways that different energy resources are used, the uses to include transport, electricity generation, and heating
- understand why some energy resources are more reliable than others
- describe the environmental impact arising from the use of different energy resources.

Students should be able to:
- consider the environmental issues that may arise from the use of different energy resources.

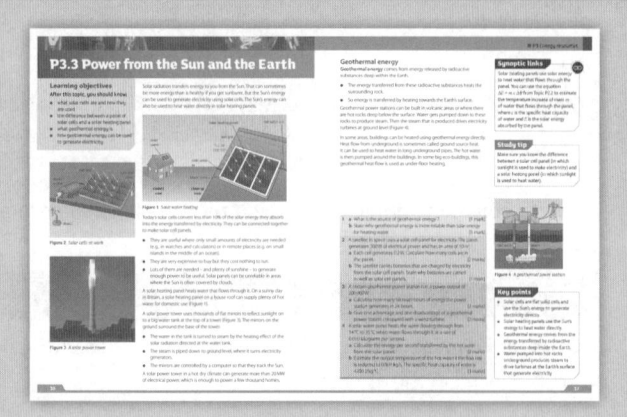

WS 4.4
MS 1c, 2c, 4a

Aiming for	Outcome	Checkpoint	
		Question	Activity
Aiming for GRADE 4	Explore the operation of a solar cell.		Main 1, Plenary 1
	Describe one difference between solar cells and solar heating systems.		Main 2
	State that radioactive decay is the source of heating in geothermal systems.	1	Main 2
Aiming for GRADE 6	Compare and contrast the operation of solar cells (photovoltaic cells) with solar heating panels.		Main 2
	Describe the operation of a solar power tower.		Main 2
	Describe the operation of a geothermal power plant.	3, End of chapter 3	Main 2
Aiming for GRADE 8	Analyse the power output of a variety of energy resources.	2, 3	Main 2
	Calculate the energy provided by a solar heating system by using the increase in water temperature.	4	Main 2
	Plan in detail an investigation into the factors that affect the power output of a solar cell.		Homework

Maths
Students compare and evaluate systems in terms of power output (2c). They may use graphical information to assess the effectiveness of a system (4a).

Literacy
There are plenty of opportunities for students to discuss the functions of energy resources and their advantages and disadvantages.

Key words
geothermal energy

Practical

Title	Using solar cells
Equipment	solar cell, motor, bulb, voltmeter
Overview of method	A low-power motor will be required; complete kits containing a matched solar cell and motor are available. Students should be able to investigate how the voltage output of the motor changes with the distance of the bulb from the solar cell. They may like to compare the speed of the motor in bright sunlight to that produced by a bulb. Covering part of the solar cell will reduce the energy output too.

P3 Energy resources

Starter	Support/Extend	Resources
Old Faithful (10 min) Show a video clip of 'Old Faithful' and ask students if they have ever seen a geyser and if they know what causes geysers. Ask them to explain why the water is so hot.	**Support:** Show a video clip of Old Faithful Geyser located in the Yellowstone National Park.	
To the centre of the Earth (5 min) Interactive where students label a simple diagram showing the layers of the Earth (crust, mantle, and core). They then match each layer with its properties. They should be aware that the outer core is a molten layer and that the centre of the Earth is very hot.	**Extend:** Ask for a more detailed description of the properties of the layers, such as the density.	**Interactive:** To the centre of the Earth

Main	Support/Extend	Resources
Using solar cells (20 min) Students use the practical to investigate the operation of a solar cell. They can measure the effect of reducing the area exposed to light on the current and voltage output, and the effect of increasing the light level by moving a lamp closer or further away.	**Extend:** Students can use some cost data to support discussions of larger-scale solar power schemes.	**Practical:** Using solar cells
Solar and geothermal heating systems (20 min) Remind students about the ideas around heating and the temperature rise caused by absorbing infrared radiation. Discuss the renewable nature of geothermal systems. Students can struggle to remember the heating source in geothermal systems, so emphasise the radioactive decay. Students should compare systems that use high pressure steam with ones that simply provide hot water for direct heating.	**Support:** Place cool water in a black container and a silver container near a lamp at the start of the lesson. Measure the temperature now to remind students of the principles involved. **Extend:** Students should try a calculation such as Summary Question 4. Models of radioactive decay can be used, linking to Chapter P7 Radioactivity later in the course.	

Plenary	Support/Extend	Resources
Solar car (5 min) Ask students to list the advantages and disadvantages of the design of solar cars.	**Support:** Show students a video clip of a solar car in action, or use a toy one.	
Keep cool (10 min) Ask students to produce a design for a device that keeps them cooler, the brighter the Sun is. A solar-powered fan is a typical design but colour-changing clothing is a possibility with smart materials (white on the side that faces the Sun but black on the opposite side).	**Support:** Show your own design and ask students to evaluate it.	

Homework		
Students can plan an investigation into the power output from solar cells. This could focus on the area of the cells (parts can be covered by black card) or the distance from the light source (moving a lamp closer or further away).	**Extend:** This can form a full investigation over the course of a pair of lessons, allowing students to choose their own independent variable(s) to investigate.	**Working scientifically:** Solar cells

kerboodle

A Kerboodle highlight for this lesson is **WebQuest: Solar panels**. Refer to the **Content map** on Kerboodle for a full list of resources and assessment.

P3.4 Energy and the environment

AQA spec Link: 1.3

A renewable energy resource is one that is being (or can be) replenished as it is used.

Students should be able to:
- describe the main energy sources available
- distinguish between energy resources that are renewable and energy resources that are non-renewable
- compare ways that different energy resources are used, the uses to include transport, electricity generation, and heating
- understand why some energy resources are more reliable than others
- describe the environmental impact arising from the use of different energy resources.

Students should be able to:
- consider the environmental issues that may arise from the use of different energy resources
- show that science has the ability to identify environmental issues arising from the use of energy resources but not always the power to deal with the issues because of political, social, ethical, or economic considerations.

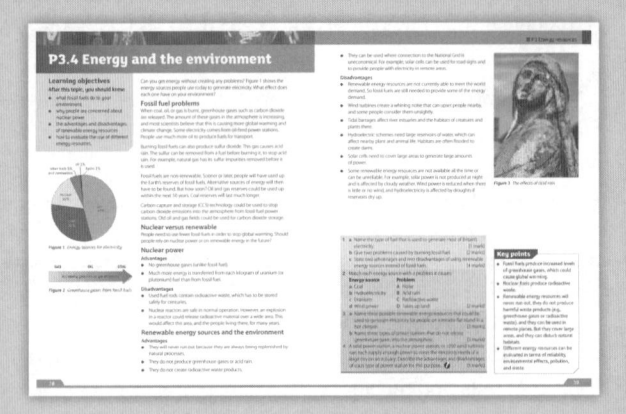

WS 4.4
MS 1c, 2c, 4a

Aiming for	Outcome	Checkpoint	
		Question	Activity
Aiming for GRADE 4	List some environmental problems associated with burning fossil fuels.	2	Main 1
	Identify the waste products of fossil fuels and nuclear fuel.	1	Main 1, Main 2
	Describe simple advantages and disadvantages of a variety of renewable energy resources.	3, End of chapter 1	Starter 1, Main 1
Aiming for GRADE 6	Describe the effects of acid rain and climate change.		Main 1
	Describe techniques to reduce the harmful products of burning fossil fuels.		Main 1
	Compare a wide range of energy resources in terms of advantages and disadvantages.	3, 4	Plenary 1
Aiming for GRADE 8	Evaluate methods of reducing damage caused by waste products of fossil fuels and nuclear fuels.		Main 1, Main 2
	Discuss in detail the problems associated with nuclear accidents and the public perception of nuclear safety.		Main 2
	Evaluate the suitability of an energy resource for a range of scenarios, taking into account a wide range of factors.	3, 4	Main 1, Main 2, Plenary 2

Maths
Numerical data can be introduced during comparisons of resources (2c, 4a), and a timeline of nuclear accidents can be produced by the students.

Literacy
There is considerable scope for small groups of students to discuss the issues with each energy resource.

P3 Energy resources

Practical

Title	Acid rain
Equipment	test tubes, universal indicator solution (range pH 4–7), a variety of samples of 'rainwater' (see method) with pH range 4–6, distilled water
Overview of method	Students use the indicator solution to test the pH of the samples. Include real, local rainwater in the samples, but also include a few samples that have been 'doctored' to produce a variety of results to show students that acid rain can have a pH as low as 4.0. Students should note that 'natural' rain has a pH of 5.6.
Safety considerations	Ensure that eye protection is worn.

Starter	Support/Extend	Resources
Renewable or not? (5 min) Give students a list of energy resources and ask them to sort the resources into either renewable or non-renewable. Use coal, oil, natural gas, and uranium for non-renewable resources and tidal, solar, geothermal, wind, wave, and biofuel for renewable resources. **Acid rain** (10 min) Demonstrate the acidity of rainwater with universal indicator and ask students to explain what causes this acidity.	**Extend:** Students should justify their decisions by giving clear definitions of the differences.	

Main	Support/Extend	Resources
The problems with fossil fuels (20 min) Cover the range of problems with fossil fuels, making sure that the students do not confuse the problems of acid rain and climate change. There is scope here to discuss some of the problems associated with climate change, or this can form a larger part of the debate in Topic P3.5. A simple discussion of the advantages or disadvantages of renewable systems should take place. Students can compile this information in preparation for the debate in Topic P3.5. **Nuclear power** (20 min) Recap on the differences between nuclear fuel and other fuels – no combustion and so no carbon dioxide or sulfur dioxide. This leads to discussion of the alternative problems with the waste. Discuss the Chernobyl disaster and its effects but also link to more recent accidents such as Fukushima Daiichi. Emphasise the fact that accidents are rare but very significant.	**Support:** Students can match problems with explanations by using a simple table. **Extend:** Discuss whether carbon-capture technology is a permanent solution to global warming. **Support:** A timeline of serious incidents can be produced. **Extend:** Ask students to evaluate a few possible solutions for the storage or disposal of nuclear waste. Ask students why nuclear power stations are often built on coastlines.	**Activity:** Energy and the environment

Plenary	Support/Extend	Resources
What's the problem? (5 min) Students use the interactive to match environmental problems with their likely causes. **Energy resource crossword** (10 min) Students create a crossword that includes all of the key words covered so far in this chapter. They then swap and complete a partner's.	**Support:** Illustrate with photographs of damage and the possible causes. **Support:** Provide a list of the key words. **Extend:** Include more challenging clues, including cryptic ones.	**Interactive:** What's the problem?

Homework		
In Topic P3.5 students will debate energy resources. They can be given preparatory materials for this or asked to research relevant information for the discussion.		

kerboodle

A Kerboodle highlight for this lesson is **Maths skills: Energy resources**. Refer to the **Content map** on Kerboodle for a full list of resources and assessment.

P3.5 Big energy issues

AQA spec Link: 1.3

A renewable energy resource is one that is being (or can be) replenished as it is used.

The uses of energy resources include transport, electricity generation, and heating.

Students should be able to:
- describe the main energy sources available
- distinguish between energy resources that are renewable and energy resources that are non-renewable
- compare ways that different energy resources are used, the uses to include transport, electricity generation, and heating
- understand why some energy resources are more reliable than others
- describe the environmental impact arising from the use of different energy resources
- explain patterns and trends in the use of energy resources.

Descriptions of how energy resources are used to generate electricity are **not** required.

Students should be able to:
- consider the environmental issues that may arise from the use of different energy resources
- show that science has the ability to identify environmental issues arising from the use of energy resources but not always the power to deal with the issues because of political, social, ethical, or economic considerations.

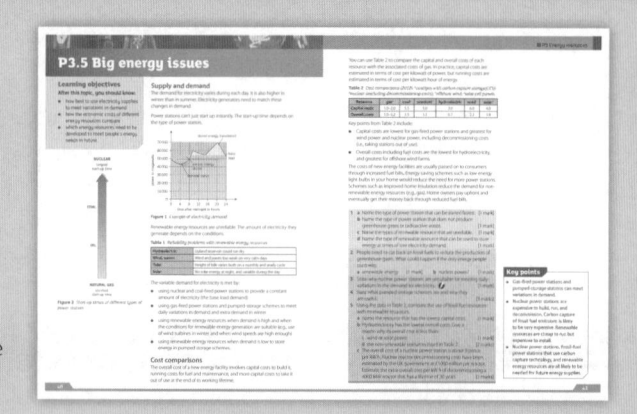

WS 1.3, 4, 4.4
MS 1a, 1c, 2c, 4a

Aiming for	Outcome	Checkpoint	
		Question	Activity
Aiming for GRADE 4	Rank the start-up times of various power stations.	1, 2	Main 1
	Compare some of the advantages and disadvantages of various energy resources.	2	Main 2
	Discuss the construction of a power plant in the local area in simple terms by using information provided.		Main 2
Aiming for GRADE 6	Use base load and start-up time data to explain why some power stations are in constant operation whereas others may be switched on and off.	1, 3	Main 1
	Compare energy resources in terms of capital and operational costs.	4	Main 2
	Debate the construction of a power plant in the local area by using a wide range of information, much of which is provided.		Starter 1, Main 2
Aiming for GRADE 8	Use the capital and operational costs of energy resources to evaluate their usefulness.	4	Main 1
	Form persuasive arguments for and against a variety of energy resources.		Main 2, Homework
	Debate the construction of a power plant in the local area by using a wide range of information, much of which is independently researched.		Starter 1, Main 2

Maths
Students calculate the effective costs of a variety of energy resources (1a, 1c).

Literacy
Students debate significant issues in small and large teams. They write persuasive arguments for and against specific energy resources.

■ P3 Energy resources

Starter	Support/Extend	Resources
Energy recap (5 min) In preparation for the debate, use the interactive to complete a series of paragraphs to summarise the basic principles of each energy resource studied in this chapter.		**Interactive:** Energy recap
Energy resources (10 min) Students complete the calculation sheet to interpret data about different energy sources, evaluate the data to make conclusions, and calculate cost of energy.	**Support:** Provide tables for students to complete. **Extend:** Ask students to design their own fact sheets.	**Calculation sheet:** Energy resources

Main	Support/Extend	Resources
Supply and demand (10 min) Discuss the advantages of various resources in terms of reliability and start-up times. Make sure the students are clear on the concept of base load. Students must be able to make comparisons of not only running costs but initial (start-up) and final (decommissioning) costs to judge the cost effectiveness of the different resources.	**Support:** Remind students of the base load graph and the power stations that are in constant operation to provide this power. **Extend:** Students can also consider the decommissioning costs of power stations.	
The big energy debate (30 min) The remainder of the lesson can be centred on a debate about how to meet future energy needs. The debate is relevant because the students will probably not have access to 'unlimited' fossil fuel supplies as the last few generations have. This could be as a result of shortages or commitments to reduce carbon emissions by the government. The result of this is an energy gap that needs to be filled by new resources. Explain the purpose of the debate and the outcomes that are needed (a set of proposals) so that the students know that they have to reach conclusions. Give timings and establish roles within the groups if they are needed. To avoid a chaotic argument, discuss the ground rules for a successful discussion. Rules need to include who can speak and when, who is recording discussions or decisions, and whether roles will be assigned or students will be free to take on any position they want to.	**Support:** Roles can be assigned and partial scripts provided for the students to complete. **Extend:** Students should prepare their own discussions after carrying out research into their chosen areas.	**Activity:** The big energy debate

Plenary	Support/Extend	Resources
Democracy in action (5 min) Students vote on a range of proposals for energy production. Make this an anonymous vote with ballot papers giving various options. The results can be declared immediately or during the next lesson.		
Cut it out (10 min) Demand for electricity is increasing as more electrical devices are produced. One way to preserve resources is to cut back on waste and to stop using some devices altogether. What are the students willing to cut back on?	**Support:** Provide a list of options for the students to prioritise.	

Homework		
Students write a letter to their MP outlining the decision they have reached in the big debate. They need to explain what they have decided and ask their MP to act on the decision. This should be a formal letter if possible.	**Support:** Provide the basic structure of the letter. **Extend:** Provide clear success criteria about the content of the letter, including how many facts and figures are required.	

> kerboodle
> A Kerboodle highlight for this lesson is **Literacy sheet: Renewable and non-renewable resources**. Refer to the **Content map** on Kerboodle for a full list of resources and assessment.

P3 Energy resources

Overview of P3 Energy resources

In this chapter the students have examined the different sources of energy that are used to generate electricity or provide heating for homes. They have considered the effect of the production and use of biofuels on the environment along with the concept of carbon-neutrality before outlining the use of nuclear power in comparison to fossil fuels.

Students have described and evaluated renewable resources such as wave power, wind power, hydroelectricity and tidal technology and how these can be used to generate electricity in specific locations. In addition, students have described the operation of geothermal power stations and their links to radioactive decay. The principles of solar cells and both small-scale and large-scale solar heating systems have been outlined.

The students have compared all of the energy resources in terms of local environmental impacts, such as pollution, and global environment impacts, such as acid rain, and their contribution to global warming. Finally, the students have described how the different resources could be applied in combination to meet the base load and changing energy demands throughout a single day before finally considering the capital costs and operating costs over the operational lifetime of the resource.

MyMaths

You can find additional support for the maths skills covered in this chapter on **MyMaths**, including constructing and interpreting frequency tables and diagrams, bar charts and histograms and changing the subject of an equation.

kerboodle

For this chapter, the following assessments are available on Kerboodle:

P3 Checkpoint quiz Energy resources
P3 Progress quiz: Energy resources 1
P3 Progress quiz: Energy resources 2
P3 On your marks: Energy resources
P3 Exam-style questions and mark scheme: Energy resources

Checkpoint follow up lesson

A student's route through this lesson can be determined using the Checkpoint assessment. Percentage pass marks are supplied in the Checkpoint teacher notes.

For each successive route through it is assumed that the student can perform to their current route as well as previous routes. For example, students working at Aiming for 6 are assumed to be secure in Aiming for 4 knowledge and understanding and working towards achieving all the learning outcomes for Aiming for 6.

	Aiming for 4	**Aiming for 6**	**Aiming for 8**
Learning outcomes	Describe how current energy demands are met.	Describe how current energy demands are met, including how electricity is generated.	Describe how current energy demands are met, including how electricity is generated and variable demand is met.
	Describe the difference between renewable and non-renewable sources of energy.	Describe how to generate electricity with renewable sources.	Suggest and explain how demand for energy can be met in the future.
	Describe how to generate electricity with renewable sources.	Suggest how demand for energy can be met in the future.	Discuss the issues relating to future energy supply.
Starter	**Sort the resource (10 min)** Give out cards for a pairs matching game that contains the names of renewable and non-renewable energy resources on blue card, with the same number of each card in yellow that has 'renewable' or 'non-renewable' on it. Student put the cards face down, and pick up pairs of different colours, keeping any pairs that match. When they have completed the game they use the names of the resources to make a pyramid with the most important source for electricity production at the top.		
Differentiated checkpoint activity	Students use the Checkpoint follow-up sheet to complete one of two activities: • create a leaflet to describe how our energy demands are met • prepare a presentation about how an island community can meet its energy demands using renewable resources. The Aiming for 4 follow-up sheet is highly structured and students could work in pairs for support. Students should then analyse data to make predictions about future use of resources. Students will need access to graph paper.	Students use the Checkpoint follow-up sheet to complete one of two activities: • create a leaflet to describe how our energy demands are met • prepare a presentation about how an island community can meet its energy demands using renewable resources. The Aiming for 6 follow-up sheet provides some support and students should be aiming to work independently. Students should then analyse data to make predictions about future use of resources. Students will need access to graph paper.	Students use the Checkpoint follow-up sheet to complete one of two activities: • create a leaflet on nuclear power and other ways of generating electricity • devise a method to investigate solar cells and wind turbines. The Aiming for 8 follow-up sheet provides minimal support. Students could work in pairs for support, but should attempt to work independently. Students then analyse data to make predictions about future use of resources. Students will need access to graph paper.
	Kerboodle resource P3 Checkpoint follow up: Aiming for 4, P3 Checkpoint follow up: Aiming for 6, P3 Checkpoint follow up: Aiming for 8		
Plenary	**Mini balloon debate (10 min)** In groups each student selects a resource at random from the cards used in the starter. They prepare a series of 5 points in favour of their resource being included in future plans to meet energy demand. They each share those points, and the others in the group.		
Progression	Encourage students to think about the pros and cons of different energy sources.	Encourage students to think about the pros and cons of different energy sources, including the economic as well as environmental issues.	Encourage students to think about the need to balance the use of energy from a range of sources in the future both to meet baseline requirements and to meet fluctuations in demand.

2 Particles at work

Specification links

AQA specification section	Assessment paper
2.1 Current, potential difference, and resistance	Paper 1
2.2 Series and parallel circuits	Paper 1
2.3 Domestic uses and safety	Paper 1
2.4 Energy transfers	Paper 1
3.1 Changes of state and the particle model	Paper 1
3.2 Internal energy and energy transfers	Paper 1
3.3 Particle model and pressure	Paper 1
4.1 Atoms and isotopes	Paper 1
4.2 Atoms and nuclear radiation	Paper 1

Required practicals

AQA required practicals	Practical skills	Topic
Use circuit diagrams to set up and check appropriate circuits to investigate the factors affecting the resistance of electrical circuits. This should include: • the length of a wire at constant temperature • combinations of resistors in series and parallel.	AT 1 – use appropriate apparatus to measure and record length accurately. AT 6 – use appropriate apparatus to measure current, potential difference, and resistance. AT 7 – use circuit diagrams to construct and check series and parallel circuits.	P4.2, P4.5
Use circuit diagrams to construct appropriate circuits to investigate the I–V characteristics of a variety of circuit elements including a filament lamp, a diode, and a resistor at constant temperature.	AT 6 – use appropriate apparatus to measure current and potential difference, and to explore the characteristics of a variety of circuit elements. AT 7 – use circuit diagrams to construct and check series and parallel circuits including a variety of common circuit elements.	P4.3
Use appropriate apparatus to make and record the measurements needed to determine the densities of regular and irregular solid objects and liquids. Volume should be determined from the dimensions of a regularly shaped object and by a displacement technique for irregularly shaped objects. Dimensions to be measured using appropriate apparatus such as a ruler, micrometre, or Vernier callipers.	AT 1 – use appropriate apparatus to make and record measurements of length, area, mass, and volume accurately. Use such measurements to determine the density of solid objects and liquids.	P6.1

Maths skills

AQA maths skills	Topic
1a Recognise and use expressions in decimal form.	P4.2, P4.3, P4.4, P4.5, P5.4, P5.5, P5.6, P6.4, P7.1
1b Recognise and use expressions in standard form.	P7.1, P7.2
1c Use ratios, fractions, and percentages.	P7.4, P7.5
2a Use an appropriate number of significant figures.	P4.2, P4.3, P4.4, P4.5, P5.4, P5.5, P5.6, P7.1
2g Use a scatter diagram to identify a correlation between two variables.	P6.3, P6.6
3a Understand and use the symbols: $=, <, \ll, \gg, >, \propto, \sim$.	P4.2, P4.3, P4.4, P4.5, P5.4, P5.5, P5.6, P6.1, P6.5, P7.5
3b Change the subject of an equation.	P4.2, P4.3, P4.4, P4.5, P5.4, P5.5, P5.6, P6.1, P6.4, P6.5
3c Substitute numerical values into algebraic equations using appropriate units for physical quantities.	P4.2, P4.3, P4.4, P4.5, P5.4, P5.5, P5.6, P6.1, P6.4, P6.5
3d Solve simple algebraic equations.	P4.2, P4.3, P4.4, P4.5, P5.4, P5.5, P5.6, P6.1, P6.4, P6.5

P2 Particles at work

AQA maths skills	Topic
4a Translate information between graphical and numeric form.	P4.3, P5.1, P6.6, P7.5
4b Understand that $y = mx + c$ represents a linear relationship.	P4.3, P6.6
4c Plot two variables from experimental or other data.	P4.3, P6.3, P6.6
5b Visualise and represent 2D and 3D forms including two dimensional representations of 3D objects.	P6.4, P7.2
5c Calculate areas of triangles and rectangles, surface areas and volumes of cubes.	P6.1

KS3 concept	GCSE topic	Checkpoint	Revision
A cell or a battery pushes electrons round a circuit.	P4.1 Current and charge	Ask the students to describe how a simple circuit using a cell, two leads, and a bulb operates.	The students describe the effect on the current in a simple circuit if additional cells are added and then if a resistor is added.
Potential difference (p.d.) is measured in volts and current is measured in amperes.	P4.2 Potential difference and resistance	Ask the students to draw a circuit diagram showing how current in and p.d. across a bulb can be measured.	Give the students a set of circuit diagrams and ask them identify the voltmeters and ammeters being used.
Power is how much energy is transferred per second.	P5.4 Electrical power and potential difference	Show the students two different light bulbs and ask them to explain why one is brighter than the other.	Students can rank devices in terms of power using data about their operating current and voltage using a card sort or similar.
Mass is the amount of matter in a substance and is measured in kilograms.	P6.1 Density	Ask the students why an object, such as a metal block, has a weight and whether this weight can change.	Students can use data about the weight of objects to sort them in order of mass.
Gas particles move about very fast and collide with the surface of the gas container.	P6.6 Gas pressure and temperature	Ask students to describe why a balloon will 'pop' if you continue to inflate it.	Inflate a balloon, describing the increase in pressure and its cause.
The nucleus of an atom is composed of protons and neutrons.	P7.1 Atoms and radiation	Ask students to draw a diagram showing the components of an atom.	The students can assemble model nuclei from descriptions (some in atomic notation) and small amounts of coloured modelling clay.
Understand that scientific methods and theories develop as earlier explanations are modified to take account of new evidence and ideas.	P7.2 The discovery of the nucleus	Ask students if our understanding of the nucleus has always been the same or if it has changed over time.	Students can sort a timeline of discoveries about atomic structure from ancient Greek ideas to the modern interpretation.

P 4 Electric circuits
4.1 Current and charge

AQA spec Link: 2.1.1 Circuit diagrams use standard symbols.

Students should be able to draw and interpret circuit diagrams.

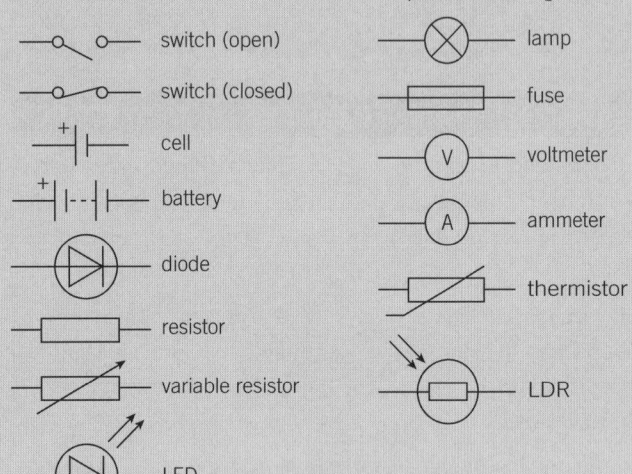

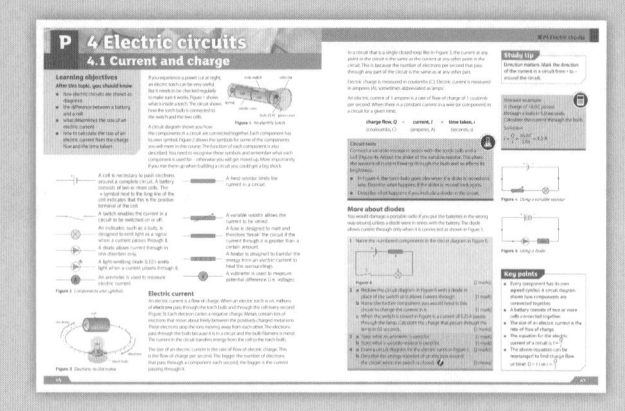

- switch (open)
- switch (closed)
- cell
- battery
- diode
- resistor
- variable resistor
- LED
- lamp
- fuse
- voltmeter
- ammeter
- thermistor
- LDR

WS 1.2

MS 3b, 3c

2.1.2 For electrical charge to flow through a closed circuit the circuit must include a source of potential difference.

Electric current is a flow of electrical charge. The size of the electric current is the rate of flow of electrical charge. Charge flow, current, and time are linked by the equation:

charge flow = current × time

$$[Q = I\,t]$$

charge flow Q in coulombs, C

current I in amperes, A (amp is acceptable for ampere)

time t in seconds, s

A current has the same value at any point in a single closed loop.

Aiming for	Outcome	Checkpoint	
		Question	Activity
Aiming for GRADE 4 ↓	Identify circuit components from their symbols.	1	Plenary 2
	Draw and interpret simple circuit diagrams.	4	Starter 2
	Construct a simple electrical circuit.		Main
Aiming for GRADE 6 ↓	Describe the operation of a variable resistor and a diode and their effects on current.	2, 3, End of chapter 2	Main
	Calculate the charge transferred by a steady current in a given time.	2	Main, Plenary 1
	Construct an electrical circuit and accurately measure the current.		Main
Aiming for GRADE 8 ↓	Explain the nature of an electric current in wires in terms of electron behaviour.		Main
	Perform a range of calculations, including rearrangement of the equation $Q = It$.		Main, Plenary 1
	Measure the current in a circuit accurately and use it to calculate the rate of flow of electrons.		Main

Maths
Students calculate charge and current with the appropriate equation (3b, 3c).

Literacy
Students need to describe the operation of a variety of electrical components and the nature of a current. They discuss the current model with each other.

Key words
electrons

P4 Electric circuits

Practical

Title	Circuit tests
Equipment	For each group: cells (1.5 V), torch bulb (1.5 V), leads, diode, variable resistor, ammeter.
Overview of method	The students set up a simple circuit with the variable resistor and the bulb and explore the effect of altering the resistor. The students then include a diode in the circuit in forward then reverse position. This will show that the diode allows the current in only one direction.

Starter	Support/Extend	Resources
It's symbolic (5 min) Show a set of slides/diagrams to the students containing common symbols and ask them to say what they mean. Use road signs, hazard symbols, washing symbols, and so on. **Describe the circuit** (10 min) Give the students diagrams of two circuits containing cells, switches, and bulbs, one series and one parallel. Ask them to describe both in one paragraph. The students can demonstrate their understanding of circuit symbols, establishing prior knowledge of concepts such as current, voltage, series, and parallel.	**Support:** Use simple circuits with a minimal number of components. **Extend:** Ask students to draw a circuit based on a written description of it.	

Main	Support/Extend	Resources
Circuit tests (40 min) Construct a 'torch' circuit, showing the students each component and discussing its operation. Demonstrate how circuits should be constructed methodically to avoid problems later. At the same time show some of the other components that will be introduced later. Discuss the nature of a current, with a focus on the rate of flow of charge, leading to the equation $Q = It$. A few example calculations are required to embed the units. Students then construct the circuit described in the practical and test it, with the focus on connecting the apparatus correctly. They can then add the ammeter to collect numerical information and practise using it. Students add a diode to their circuit, note the effect, and discuss its operation ensuring the students link the direction of the arrow on the symbol to the direction of the current.	**Extend:** Provide the charge of an electron and ask the students to find the number of electrons passing through the bulb per second.	**Practical:** Circuit tests

Plenary	Support/Extend	Resources
Current calculations (5 min) Give the students a few calculations based on the equation to perform. **Circuit symbols and resistance** (10 min) Students work through the interactive to match the circuit symbols and relevant units with their definitions.	**Support:** Use relatively simple quantities and calculations requiring no rearrangement.	**Interactive:** Circuit symbols and resistance

Homework
Students describe an important development in electronics, such as development of the battery or discovery of the electron.

kerboodle

A Kerboodle highlight for this lesson is **WebQuest: A short history of electricity**. Refer to the **Content map** on Kerboodle for a full list of resources and assessment.

P4.2 Potential difference and resistance

AQA spec Link: 2.1.3 The current I through a component depends on both the resistance R of the component and the potential difference V across the component. The greater the resistance of the component the smaller the current for a given potential difference (p.d.) across the component.

Questions will be set using the term potential difference. Students will gain credit for the correct use of either potential difference or voltage.

Current, potential difference, or resistance can be calculated using the equation:

potential difference = current × resistance [$V = I R$]

potential difference V in volts, V

current I in amperes, A (amp is acceptable for ampere)

resistance R in ohms, Ω

Students should be able to recall and/or apply this equation.

2.1.4 Students should be able to explain that, for some resistors, the value of R remains constant but that in others it can change as the current changes.

The current through an ohmic conductor (at a constant temperature) is directly proportional to the potential difference across the resistor. This means that the resistance remains constant as the current changes.

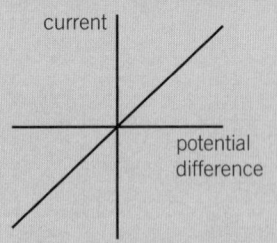

The resistance of components such as lamps, diodes, thermistors, and LDRs is not constant; it changes with the current through the component.

Required practical: use circuit diagrams to set up and check appropriate circuits to investigate the factors affecting the resistance of electrical circuits. This should include:

- the length of a wire at constant temperature.

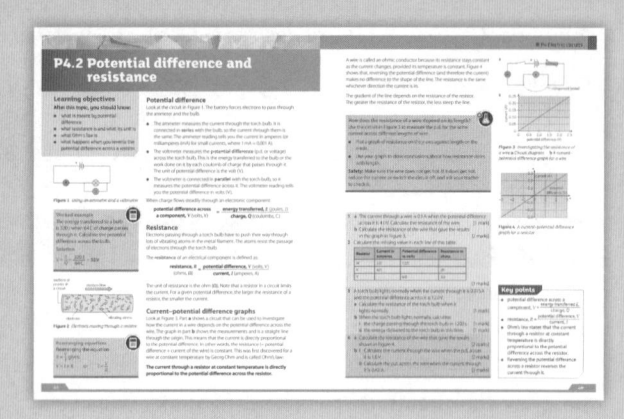

MS 3b, 3c

Aiming for	Outcome	Checkpoint	
		Question	Activity
Aiming for GRADE 4 ↓	State that resistance restricts the size of a current in a circuit.		Main
	State Ohm's law and describe its conditions.	End of chapter 1	Main
	Measure the current and potential difference in a circuit to determine the resistance.		Main
Aiming for GRADE 6 ↓	Calculate the potential difference.	3	Main
	Calculate the resistance of a component.	1, 3, 4	Homework
	Measure the effect of changing the length of a wire on its resistance in a controlled experiment.		Main
Aiming for GRADE 8 ↓	Describe potential difference in terms of work done per unit charge.		Main
	Rearrange equations for resistance and potential difference.	2, 3, 4	Main, Homework
	Investigate a variety of factors that may affect the resistance of a metal wire, such as the current through it, length, cross-sectional area, and metal used.		Main

48

■ P4 Electric circuits

Maths
The students will use a range of electrical equations and analyse components graphically. They will use the concept of inverse proportionality.

Literacy
Students discuss the factors that may affect the resistance of a metal wire and plan an investigation into these factors.

Key words
series, potential difference, parallel, resistance

Required practical

Title	How does the resistance of a wire depend on the length?
Equipment	power supply or battery pack, connecting leads, switch, crocodile clips, variable resistor, constantan wire (selection of different lengths), heat-resistant mat, ammeter, voltmeter.
Overview of method	Connect the circuit with the variable resistor and test wire in series. Using the variable resistor, control the current through the test wire and measure both the current and the potential difference. Reverse the power supply and repeat the measurements.
	Use a series circuit with the variable resistor to limit the current to below 0.5 A. Adjust the length of the wire being tested by using the crocodile clips. Constantan or nichrome wire has a high resistivity and gives results that are easier to interpret
Safety considerations	The wire can become very hot – students must not touch it, and the heat-resistant mat should be used to protect surfaces.

Starter	Support/Extend	Resources
Resistors (5 min) Show the students the circuit symbols for all of the different types of resistor and ask them to describe the similarities in the symbols.		
Rearranging equations (10 min) Students use the interactive to identify the three correct arrangements of the equation for charge flow. They then answer an example calculation for each arrangement.		**Interactive:** Rearranging equations
Main		**Resources**
How does the resistance of a wire depend on its length? (40 min) Discuss the nature of potential difference and demonstrate how it is measured in a circuit along with current. Use the Maths skills interactive to give students some practice using the equation.	**Extend:** Students can discuss interactions between electrons and metal ions and the cause of resistance.	**Maths skills:** Potential difference, current, and resistance
Students then investigate the effect of changing the length of a wire on the resistance.	**Support:** Provide blank results tables.	**Required practical:** How does the resistance of a wire depend on the length?
Different groups of students can be given wires of differ diameters or materials to show that the pattern is the same (resistance is proportional to length) and identify some other factors which affect resistance.	**Extend:** Students compare several wire characteristics to determine which has the greatest resistance.	
The second half of the required practical is covered in Topic P4.5.		
Plenary		**Resources**
An electron's tale (5 min) Students write a paragraph about the journey of an electron around a circuit containing a bulb and a resistor. They should write about the energy transfers that are going on in the circuit.		
Reinforced resistance (10 min) Additional calculations should be used to reinforce learning, differentiating by student ability as appropriate.	**Extend:** Students complete the Extension sheet on the mathematical relationships of charge, current, potential difference, and resistance.	**Extension:** Electrical quantities
Homework		
Provide students with further resistance and current calculations to complete. The calculations should involve rearranging the equations.		

kerboodle
A Kerboodle highlight for this lesson is **Working scientifically: What's the potential?** Refer to the **Content map** on Kerboodle for a full list of resources and assessment.

P4.3 Component characteristics

AQA spec Link: 2.1.4 Students should be able to explain that, for some resistors, the value of R remains constant but that in others it can change as the current changes.

The current through an ohmic conductor (at a constant temperature) is directly proportional to the potential difference across the resistor. This means that the resistance remains constant as the current changes.

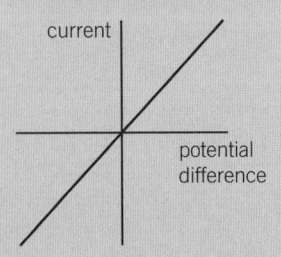

The resistance of components such as lamps, diodes, thermistors, and LDRs is not constant; it changes with the current through the component.

The resistance of a filament lamp increases as the temperature of the filament increases.

The current through a diode flows in one direction only. The diode has a very high resistance in the reverse direction.

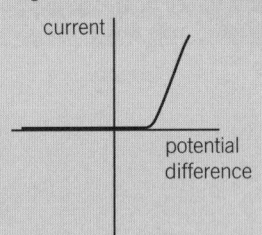

The resistance of a thermistor decreases as the temperature increases.

The applications of thermistors in circuits, for example, a thermostat is required.

The resistance of an LDR decreases as light intensity increases.

The application of LDRs in circuits, for example, switching lights on when it gets dark is required.

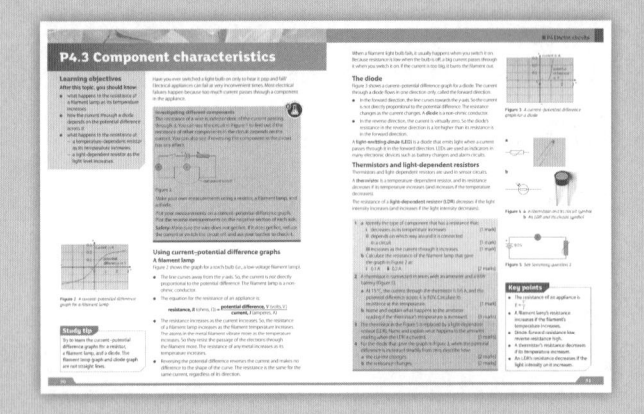

Students should be able to:

- explain the design and use of a circuit to measure the resistance of a component by measuring the current through, and potential difference across, the component
- draw an appropriate circuit diagram using correct circuit symbols.

Students should be able to use graphs to explore whether circuit elements are linear or non-linear and relate the curves produced to their function and properties.

Required practical: Use circuit diagrams to construct circuits to investigate the I–V characteristics of a variety of circuit elements, including a filament lamp, a diode, and a resistor at constant temperature.

WS 1.2, 1.4

MS 4c, 4d, 4e

Aiming for	Outcome	Checkpoint	
		Question	Activity
Aiming for GRADE 4 ↓	Identify the key characteristics of electrical devices.	1, End of chapter 1, 2	Plenary 1, Main
	Identify components from simple I–V graphs.		Main
	State the operation of a diode in simple terms.	1	Main
Aiming for GRADE 6 ↓	Describe the resistance characteristics of a filament lamp.		Main
	Describe the characteristics of a diode and light-emitting diode.	3	Main
	Investigate the resistance characteristics of a thermistor and a LDR.	2	Starter 2, Plenary 2
Aiming for GRADE 8 ↓	Explain the resistance characteristics of a filament lamp in terms of electrons and ion collisions.		Main
	Determine the resistance of a component based on information extracted from a I–V graph.	4	Main
	Compare the characteristics of a variety of electrical components, describing how the components can be used.	2	Main

Maths
Students will apply graphical skills in analysis of the behaviour of electrical devices (4c, 4d, 4e).

Literacy
Students translate graphical information into prose.

Key words
diode, light-emitting diode (LED), thermistor, light-dependent resistor (LDR)

P4 Electric circuits

Required practical

Title	Investigating different components
Equipment	power supply or battery pack, connecting leads, variable resistor, ammeter, voltmeter, filament lamp, fixed resistor, diode
Overview of method	Connect the circuit with the component being tested in series with the variable resistor and ammeter and a voltmeter in parallel with the component. Using the variable resistor, the students change the p.d. across the component and record the current and potential difference. From the results, the students produce a current–potential difference graph. They should try the circuit with the current in the opposite direction to show that this does not affect the bulb but is very important for the diode.
Safety considerations	Current in the circuits should be kept low.

Starter	Support/Extend	Resources
Comparing wires (5 min) Show the students a graph of the current–p.d. characteristics of three wires. They use the interactive to put the three wires in order of highest resistance to lowest resistance. They then complete a paragraph to describe what characteristics affect the resistance of a wire. **Thermistors and LDRs** (10 min) Introduce thermistors and LDRs briefly. Set up a circuit with a thermistor attached by crocodile clips and place the thermistor into a beaker of hot water. Measure the resistance of the thermistor, and ask students to predict what would happen to the resistance measurement as the water cools.	**Extend:** Students calculate the resistance of each wire by using the graph. **Support:** Provide a brief recap of the effect of high resistance. **Extend:** Students explain in terms of electrons and ions.	**Interactive:** Comparing wires

Main		Resources
Investigating different components (40 min) Discuss the results of the investigation into the characteristics of a wire from Topic P4.3. The students then investigate the behaviour of a filament lamp, a diode, and a resistor, as described. Ensure that the students can identify and describe the resulting I–V graphs clearly. Results should be shared so that all students are aware of the characteristics of the components.	**Support:** Students can investigate only one of the components and share their results with a group that has investigated the other component.	**Required practical:** Investigating different components

Plenary		Resources
What's in the box? (5 min) An electrical component has been placed inside a black box with only the two connections visible. The students should suggest an experiment to find out what it is. This should involve a detailed analysis of the V–I characteristics. **Thermistors and LDRs – revisited** (10 min) Revisit the circuit with the thermistor from the start of the lesson to see how the resistance of the thermistor has increased as the water cooled. Then ask students to predict what would happen to the resistance of an LDR if it was placed closer to a bright light. Set up the circuit to demonstrate.	**Support:** Suggest some equipment to the students.	

Homework		
Students plan an investigation into the behaviour of a thermistor or LDR.		

kerboodle

A Kerboodle highlight for this lesson is **Bump up your grade: IV graphs**. Refer to the **Content map** on Kerboodle for a full list of resources and assessment.

P4.4 Series circuits

AQA spec Link: 2.2 There are two ways of joining electrical components, in series and in parallel. Some circuits include both series and parallel parts.

For components connected in series:

- there is the same current through each component
- the total potential difference of the power supply is shared between the components
- the total resistance of two components is the sum of the resistance of each component.

$$R_{total} = R_1 + R_2$$

resistance R in ohms, Ω

Students should be able to:

- use circuit diagrams to construct and check series and parallel circuits that include a variety of common circuit components
- describe the difference between series and parallel circuits
- explain qualitatively why adding resistors in series increases the total resistance whilst adding resistors in parallel decreases the total resistance
- explain the design and use of d.c. series circuits for measurement and testing purposes
- calculate the currents, potential differences, and resistances in d.c. series circuits
- solve problems for circuits which include resistors in series using the concept of equivalent resistance.

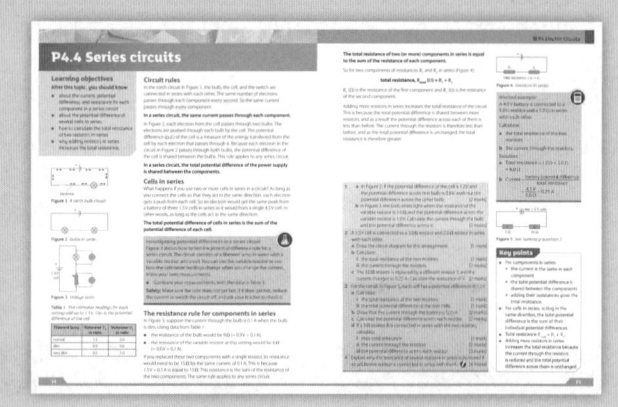

WS 1.4

MS 1c, 3b, 3c, 3d

Aiming for	Outcome	Checkpoint	
		Question	Activity
Aiming for GRADE 4 ↓	State that the current in any part of a series circuit is the same.		
	Calculate the potential difference provided by cell combinations.	3	Main 1
	Calculate the total resistance of two resistors placed in series.	3	Plenary 1
Aiming for GRADE 6 ↓	Find the potential difference across a component in a circuit by using the p.d. rule.	1	Main 1
	Calculate the current in a series circuit containing more than one resistor.	2	Main 2, Plenary 1
	Investigate the resistance of series circuits with several components.		Main 2
Aiming for GRADE 8 ↓	Explain in detail why the current in a series circuit is the same at all points by using the concept of conservation of charge (electrons).		Main 1
	Analyse a variety of series circuits to determine the current through, p.d. across, and resistance of combinations of components.	1, 3, End of chapter 3, 7	Main 1, Main 2, Plenary 1
	Evaluate in detail the investigation of series circuits and explain discrepancies.		Main 1

Maths
Students calculate the sum of resistances and current in series circuits (3b, 3c, 3d).

Literacy
Students describe the current in circuits and explain why it must be the same at all points.

Practical

Title	Investigating potential differences in a series circuit
Equipment	power supply or battery pack (1.5 V), connecting leads, variable resistor, 1.5 V bulb, three voltmeters
Overview of method	The students connect a bulb and variable resistor in series. Connect one voltmeter across the bulb V_1 and one across the variable resistor V_2. When the circuit is switched on, the students should find that $V_1 + V_2 = V_{total}$ when the variable resistor is set to any position.
Safety considerations	Use low potential differences to produce small currents.

■ P4 Electric circuits

Starter	Support/Extend	Resources
Adding wires (10 min) Show the students a circuit with a wire of resistance 2 Ω and ask them what would happen if a second length of identical wire was placed 'in series'. Would the resistance go up or down? What would happen if the wire was placed in parallel with the first?	**Extend:** Students should give numerical values and suggest scientific explanations.	
One way only (5 min) Ask students: In what situation are we allowed only one way through something? Suggest a tour or road system. Discuss the idea of conservation – the same number of people or cars go out and come in.	**Support:** Use an animation of flow to show that the same number of objects must leave as enter.	

Main		Resources
Investigating potential differences in a series circuit (25 min) Demonstrate the conservation of current and the addition of potential differences by using ammeters and voltmeters in a series circuit, accounting for any discrepancies. Students then investigate potential difference, discovering that the total p.d. around a branch (summing the p.d.s across the series components) is the same as the p.d. provided by the power supply. There will be some variation in measurements and a discussion of meter precision and error should take place. **Resistors in series** (15 min) Discuss resistance in series and allow students to confirm the information using fixed resistors in a circuit by constructing a circuit containing fixed value resistors.	**Support:** Use simulations of electron movement in the circuit to show that the electrons pass all the way around the circuit and are not 'used up'. **Extend:** Students should discuss why the meters can sometimes give different readings even though the current is the same at all points. **Extend:** The variation in resistance of particular resistors can be discussed.	**Practical:** Investigating potential differences in a series circuit

Plenary		Resources
Controlling current (5 min) Interactive where students are given combinations of cells and resistors and the current they would produce, some correct and some incorrect. Students identify which combinations are correct. **Circuit rules** (10 min) The students should start making a list of circuit rules to help them work out the currents, potential differences, and resistances in series and parallel circuits.	**Support:** Give only simple possibilities.	**Interactive:** Controlling current

Homework		
The students can research the developments in batteries, including the materials used to construct them and the hazards associated with these materials.		

P4.5 Parallel circuits

AQA spec Link: 2.2 There are two ways of joining electrical components, in series and in parallel. Some circuits include both series and parallel parts.

For components connected in parallel:
- the potential difference across each component is the same
- the total current through the whole circuit is the sum of the currents through the separate components
- the total resistance of two resistors is less than the resistance of the smallest individual resistor.

Students should be able to:
- use circuit diagrams to construct and check series and parallel circuits that include a variety of common circuit components
- describe the difference between series and parallel circuits
- explain qualitatively why adding resistors in series increases the total resistance whilst adding resistors in parallel decreases the total resistance.

Students are **not** required to calculate the total resistance of two resistors joined in parallel.

2.1.4 Required practical: use circuit diagrams to set up and check appropriate circuits to investigate the factors affecting the resistance of electrical circuits. This should include:
- combinations of resistors in series and parallel.

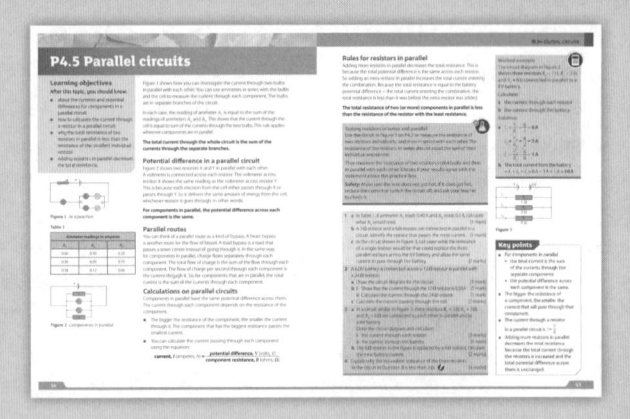

MS 1c, 3b, 3c, 3d

Aiming for	Outcome	Checkpoint	
		Question	Activity
Aiming for GRADE 4 ↓	Identify parallel sections in circuit diagrams.	1	Starter 1
	State the effect of adding resistors in parallel on the size of the current in a circuit.		Main 1
	State that the p.d. across parallel sections of a circuit is the same.		Main 1
Aiming for GRADE 6 ↓	Measure the p.d. across parallel circuits and explain any discrepancies.		Main 1
	Describe the effect on the resistance in a circuit of adding a resistor in parallel.	1, 4	Main 1, Main 2
	Investigate the effect of adding resistors in parallel on the size of the current in a circuit.		Main 2
Aiming for GRADE 8 ↓	Analyse parallel circuits in terms of current loops.		Main 2, Plenary 2
	Calculate the current at any point in a circuit.	2, 3, End of chapter 4	Main 1, Plenary 2
	Evaluate in detail an investigation into the effect of adding resistors in parallel on a circuit.		Main 2

Maths
Students calculate the current in parallel circuits (3b, 3c, 3d).

Literacy
Students discuss the changes in resistance in parallel circuits and how these changes affect the current in the circuits.

Required practical

Title	Testing resistors in series and parallel
Equipment	battery or power supply, connecting leads, two voltmeters, two ammeters, two fixed value resistors (10 ohms)
Overview of method	The students measure the resistance of the individual resistors and then the two resistors in series and finally the two resistors in parallel.
Safety considerations	Ensure the wires do not overheat.

■ P4 Electric circuits

Starter	Support/Extend	Resources
Circuit jumble (5 min) Show the students a diagram of a parallel circuit with three branches and several components on each branch. The wires and components are jumbled up, and the students must redraw the circuit properly. **The river** (10 min) Show the students a picture of a river branching and re-joining. Ask them to explain what happens to the current in the river (mass of water passing a point each second) before, during, and after the split. They should compare this to the current in circuits.	**Support:** Provide students with a partially completed circuit diagram. **Extend:** At the end of the lesson, students should be asked to identify the limitations of this model of current and p.d.	

Main		Resources
Investigating parallel circuits (30 min) Students construct a simple parallel circuit and measure the current in the two branches. Use a conservation model to explain this – electrons are not created or destroyed, so the current into a junction is the same as the current out of it. The students should perform some example calculations on parallel circuits. Students need to analyse a circuit with the worked example in the student book to consolidate the current and p.d. rules. **Resistors in parallel** (10 min) The students should test a pair of resistors in series and parallel using the practical task. Explain this by discussing the new current loop provided by the new branch whilst the old current loop still exists. The first half of this required practical is covered in topic P4.2.	**Extend:** Emphasise the formal definition of potential difference. Additional branches can be incorporated. **Support:** Lead the students through the stages methodically.	**Required practical:** Testing resistors in series and parallel

Plenary		Resources
Stair lights (5 min) Students design a simple circuit that can be used to turn the lights on and off from the top and bottom of a set of stairs. **Another circuit** (10 min) Interactive where students analyse a parallel circuit to determine the current from a battery.	**Support:** Demonstrate the circuit and show the diagram, asking the students to explain how it operates. **Extend:** Use more complex resistors such as 1.2 kΩ.	**Interactive:** Another circuit

Homework		
Students explain why thicker wires are used in applications where high currents are needed, using the idea of resistance and heating.		

kerboodle

A Kerboodle highlight for this lesson is **Extension sheet: Analysis circuits**. Refer to the **Content map** on Kerboodle for a full list of resources and assessment.

P4 Electric circuits

Overview of P4 Electric circuits

In this chapter students described electric circuits and the components used to construct them using the concept of current as the rate of charge flow through components due to a potential difference between points in the circuit. Resistance was introduced and the cause of a heating effect and corresponding energy transfer. Students then investigated the factors affecting the resistance of a wire and the corresponding current-potential difference graphs. Further investigations of the components and analysis of the current-potential difference graphs have shown ohmic and non-ohmic behaviours for wires, filaments, and diodes. The relationship between the resistance of a thermistor and its temperature along with the relationship between the resistance of a light-dependent resistor and light level have been investigated.

Finally, the students investigated and analysed a range of series and parallel circuits describing the path of current at junctions, the potential difference across branches and components, and the effect on resistance of series and parallel branches.

MyMaths

You can find additional support for the maths skills covered in this chapter on **MyMaths**, including recognising and using expressions in decimal form, using an appropriate number of significant figures, understanding and using the symbols: =, <, <<, >>, >, ∝, ~, and solving simple algebraic equations.

kerboodle

For this chapter, the following assessments are available on Kerboodle:

P4 Checkpoint quiz: Electric circuits
P4 Progress quiz: Electric circuits 1
P4 Progress quiz: Electric circuits 2
P4 On your marks: Electric circuits
P4 Exam-style questions and mark scheme: Electric circuits

Checkpoint follow up lesson

A student's route through this lesson can be determined using the Checkpoint assessment. Percentage pass marks are supplied in the Checkpoint teacher notes.

For each successive route through it is assumed that the student can perform to their current route as well as previous routes. For example, students working at Aiming for 6 are assumed to be secure in Aiming for 4 knowledge and understanding and working towards achieving all the learning outcomes for Aiming for 6.

	Aiming for 4	**Aiming for 6**	**Aiming for 8**
Learning outcomes	Describe and explain what happens in series and parallel circuits.	Apply knowledge of series and parallel circuits.	Apply what you know to a range of problems involving series and parallel circuits.
Starter	**Brightest/dimmest (10 min)** Give students A4 dry wipe boards, pens and an eraser. Ask them to draw a circuit diagram containing three bulbs and a battery, where the bulbs are: dimmest, brightest, two bulbs are dim and one is bright. Students compare their diagrams and hold up the best diagram in each category.		
Differentiated checkpoint activity	Aiming for 4 students use the Checkpoint follow-up sheet to solve problems involving series and parallel circuits and practise using the equations involving potential difference, current, resistance, energy, power, and time. The follow-up sheet provides structured tasks and questions to help students complete these activities and check their understanding of series and parallel circuits, and to do calculations involving current, charge, time, potential difference, and resistance.	Aiming for 6 students use the Checkpoint follow-up sheet to play a game involving series and parallel circuits and practise using the equations involving potential difference, current, resistance, energy, power, and time, and identify mystery components by plotting a characteristic curve for each. The follow-up sheet provides tasks and questions to help students complete these activities and check their understanding of series and parallel circuits, and to do calculations involving current, charge, time, potential difference, and resistance, and revise characteristic curves, and sensor circuits.	Aiming for 8 students use the Checkpoint follow-up sheet to play a game involving series and parallel circuits and practise using the equations involving potential difference, current, resistance, energy, power, and time, and identify mystery components by plotting a characteristic curve for each, and then produce a calibration graph. Finally, they will apply what they know about measurement circuits. The follow-up sheet provides tasks and questions to help them complete these activities and check their understanding of electrostatics, series and parallel circuits, do calculations involving current, charge, time, potential difference, and resistance, and revise characteristic curves, and the use of LDRs and thermistors in sensor circuits.
	Kerboodle resource P4 Checkpoint follow up: Aiming for 4, P4 Checkpoint follow up: Aiming for 6, P4 Checkpoint follow up: Aiming for 8		
Plenary	**How did you get that? (10 min)** Give students A4 dry wipe boards, pens and an eraser. Display a number and unit, for example, 10 Ω, and ask students to devise a calculation where that is the answer. You can put up different quantities to check the equations involving current, charge, time, and potential difference, current, resistance and steer students towards different calculations depending on the level at which they are aiming. Students swap boards and check their calculations.		
Progression	Encourage students to use the idea of net resistance in series and parallel circuits.	Encourage students to use the ideas about thermistors and light dependent resistors to make sensor circuits.	Encourage students to use the idea that potential dividers make sensor circuits. You could also introduce students to the sub-atomic particles and electrostatics.

P5 Electricity in the home

5.1 Alternating current

AQA spec Link: 2.3.1 Mains electricity is an a.c. supply. In the United Kingdom the domestic electricity supply has a frequency of 50 Hz and is about 230 V.

Students should be able to explain the difference between direct and alternating potential difference.

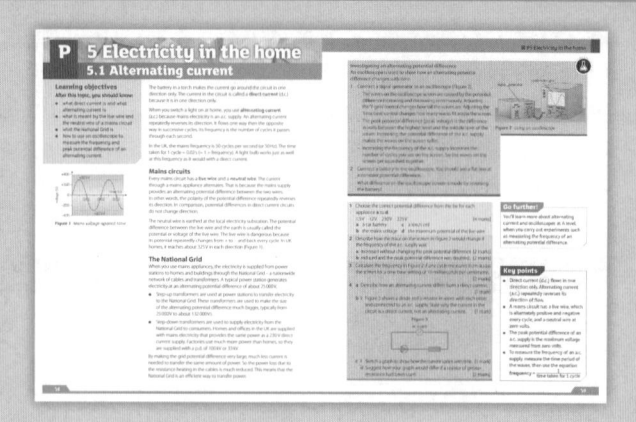

MS 4a

Aiming for	Outcome	Checkpoint	
		Question	Activity
Aiming for GRADE 4 ↓	State that the UK mains supply is a high-voltage alternating current supply.		Main 1
	State simple differences between a.c. and d.c. sources.	1	Main 1
	Describe how the trace on an oscilloscope changes when the frequency or amplitude of the signal is changed.	2	Main 2, Plenary 2
Aiming for GRADE 6 ↓	Describe the characteristics of the UK mains supply.	End of chapter 1	Main 1
	Compare a.c. traces in terms of period and amplitude (voltage).	3, End of chapter 1	Main 2
	Operate a cathode ray oscilloscope to display an a.c. trace.		Main 2
Aiming for GRADE 8 ↓	Explain the process of half-wave rectification of an a.c. source.		Main 2
	Analyse a.c. traces with an oscilloscope to determine the voltage and frequency.	3	Main 2, Plenary 2
	Compare and contrast the behaviour of electrons in a wire connected to d.c. and a.c. supplies.		Main 1

Maths
Students read graphical data from an oscilloscope and translate this into numerical data (4a). They also calculate the frequency of a waveform from its period.

Literacy
Students will need to collaborate to describe how an oscilloscope operates and to describe the observed waveforms.

Key words
direct current, alternating current, live wire, neutral wire

Practical

Title	Investigating an alternating potential difference
Equipment	cathode ray oscilloscope (CRO), low-voltage a.c. source (e.g., signal generator), battery, leads
Overview of method	The greatest problem the students will have with this experiment is setting the time base and volts per centimetre (Y-gain) dials on the CRO. If these are incorrectly set, then the students will not get a useful trace. To make things easier, put small blobs of paint on the scale around the dials showing the correct setting for displaying a 2 V, 50 Hz trace clearly. Digital oscilloscopes connected to a computer can be easier to use.
Safety considerations	Ensure that only low-voltage sources are used.

P5 Electricity in the home

Starter	Support/Extend	Resources
Waveforms (5 min) Show the students a wave diagram (e.g., picture from the student book) and ask them to discuss it. They should recognise the sine wave shape of the wavelength (or period) and the amplitude. **Mains facts** (10 min) Ask the students some true/false questions about mains electricity to see what they already know. These should include some basic questions that have already been covered on d.c. and some testing of their knowledge of mains electricity.	**Support:** Provide a wave diagram for students to annotate. **Support:** Differentiate by selecting appropriately challenging questions.	**Interactive:** Mains facts

Main	Support/Extend	Resources
Alternating and direct current (20 min) Discuss d.c. using a simple series circuit and ask students to describe electron movement. Introduce the idea that the electrons can be made to move back and forth rapidly (an a.c. supply), which still transfers energy to devices. Discuss the structure of a mains circuit, outlining the function of the live, neutral, and then earth wires. Emphasise the higher, rapidly varying voltages. The characteristics of the mains (50 Hz and around 230 V) should also be covered, noting that the peak voltage is significantly higher (325 V). Outline the basic features of the National Grid in terms of transformers and changes in voltage. **Investigating an alternating potential difference** (20 min) Demonstrate or allow students to use an oscilloscope. They should be able to form a steady trace and measure the key characteristics of a.c. and d.c. sources by using the scales. They should also interpret some additional traces when given the oscilloscope settings in questions. Show students the waveform produced by half-wave rectification by placing a diode in series with a resistor and a low-voltage a.c. source.	**Extend:** Introduce the concept that the energy is transferred by a varying electric field within the wire. Discuss electron behaviour in the a.c. wire. **Support:** Teaching assistants or technicians should support students with a CRO as CROs are difficult to access. **Extend:** Ask students to explain the waveform in terms of electron movement.	**Practical:** Investigating an alternating potential difference

Plenary	Support/Extend	Resources
a.c./d.c.? (5 min) Give the students a set of electrical appliances and ask them to stack them into one of two piles: a.c. operation and d.c. operation. **Traces** (10 min) Show the students a series of oscilloscope traces with settings data (time base) and ask them to extract data from them, such as the peak p.d. and period.	**Extend:** Include less obvious devices such as laptops and phones. **Support:** Use a single time-base setting for most of the diagrams. **Extend:** Students should calculate frequency from the period.	

Homework		
Students suggest the differences between the European and US mains electric systems. How and why were these choices made by each country?		

P5.2 Cables and plugs

AQA spec Link: 2.3.2 Most electrical appliances are connected to the mains using three-core cable.

The insulation covering each wire is colour coded for easy identification: live wire – brown; neutral wire – blue; earth wire – green and yellow stripes.

The live wire carries the alternating potential difference from the supply. The neutral wire completes the circuit. The earth wire is a safety wire to stop the appliance becoming live.

The potential difference between the live wire and earth (0 V) is about 230 V. The neutral wire is at, or close to, earth potential (0 V). The earth wire is at 0 V, it only carries a current if there is a fault.

Students should be able to explain:

- that a live wire may be dangerous even when a switch in the mains circuit is open
- the dangers of providing any connection between the live wire and earth.

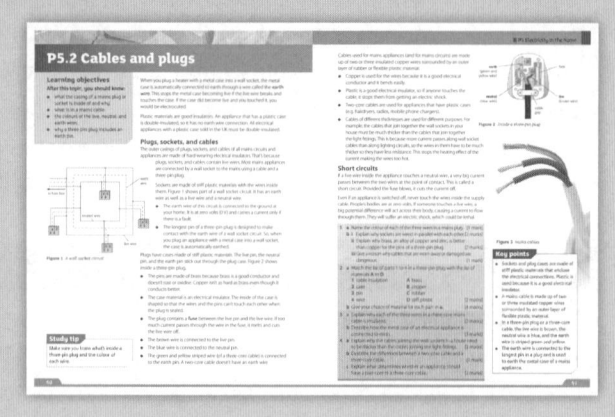

WS 1.5

Aiming for	Outcome	Checkpoint	
		Question	Activity
Aiming for GRADE 4 ↓	Identify the live, neutral, and earth wires in a three-pin plug.	End of chapter 2	Main
	Identify the key components of a typical three-pin plug and socket.	2	Main
	Identify simple and obvious hazards in electrical wiring.	1	Main, Plenary 2
Aiming for GRADE 6 ↓	Discuss the choices of materials used in cables and plugs in terms of their physical and electrical properties.	1, 2	Starter 2, Main, Plenary 1
	Describe why a short circuit inside a device presents a hazard.	3	Main
	Identify a variety of electrical hazards associated with plugs and sockets.	1	Plenary 2
Aiming for GRADE 8 ↓	Explain when there will be a current in the live, neutral, and earth wires of an appliance.	4	Main
	Discuss in detail the hazards associated with poor electrical wiring.	3	Main

Literacy
Students discuss electrical hazards associated with electrical wiring and their potential consequences.

Key words
earth wire, fuse

Practical

Title	Short circuit
Equipment	6 V battery pack or power supply, 6 V bulb and holder, connecting leads, crocodile clips, heat-resistant mat, very thin nichrome or constantan wire
Overview of method	Connect the bulb and battery, showing it illuminated. Use the crocodile clips to carefully connect the wire in parallel with the bulb. The wire will become very hot and could melt.
Safety considerations	Place the apparatus on the heat-resistant mat, and do not touch the wire.

P5 Electricity in the home

Starter	Support/Extend	Resources
Mystery object (5 min) Place a mains plug in a bag and ask one student to describe it to the rest of the class but only using shape and texture. This can be made more difficult by using a continental plug.		
Material sorting (10 min) Give each group of students a bag containing a range of materials and ask them to sort the materials in any way they wish. They must explain how they sorted them to other student groups in terms of the properties. Ensure that sorting criteria include conductors, insulators, hard, and flexible.	**Support:** Provide a list of properties to use during the sorting process.	

Main	Support/Extend	Resources
Plugs, cables, and short circuits (40 min) Show the students appliances with three-pin plugs (do not use loose plugs without devices connected). The students discuss the choices of materials and physical design of the pins and socket. Recap the purpose of each of the three wires. Show partially stripped three-core and two-core cables and discuss the materials and design. Compare these to the leads used in low-voltage experiments. Students need to understand that thick cables are less likely to overheat than thin ones. Demonstrate the practical and discuss what would happen if the wire was in contact with flammable materials.	**Extend:** Emphasise the heating effect and the higher resistance of thin wires in this discussion, and ask students to suggest an explanation.	**Activity:** Plugs, cables, and short circuits

Plenary	Support/Extend	Resources
Materials summary (5 min) Students make a table listing the parts of a plug and cable, the materials used, and the reasons for those choices. This should be centred on ideas about good conductors and insulators along with flexibility or rigidity.		
Wonky wiring (10 min) Students use the interactive to match the colour of a wire's insulation with what pin of a plug it is attached to. They then complete a paragraph to describe the hazards associated with plugs and sockets.	**Support:** Ask students to match known problems with particular pictures of plugs.	**Interactive:** Wonky wiring

Homework		
Students complete the WebQuest where they research plug designs from around the world, discussing which they think is the safest and/or best design.	**Extend:** Expect justification of shapes and materials.	**WebQuest:** Plugs

kerboodle

A Kerboodle highlight for this lesson is **Bump up your grade: Mains electricity**. Refer to the **Content map** on Kerboodle for a full list of resources and assessment.

P5.3 Electrical power and potential difference

AQA spec Link: 2.4.1 Students should be able to explain how the power transfer in any circuit device is related to the potential difference across it and the current through it, and to the energy changes over time:

$$\text{power} = \text{potential difference} \times \text{current} \quad [P = V I]$$

$$\text{power} = (\text{current})^2 \times \text{resistance} \quad [P = I^2 R]$$

power P in watts, W; potential difference V in volts, V; current I in amperes, A (amp is acceptable for ampere); resistance R in ohms, Ω

2.4.2 Everyday electrical appliances are designed to bring about energy transfers.

The amount of energy an appliance transfers depends on how long the appliance is switched on for and the power of the appliance.

Work is done when charge flows in a circuit.

The amount of energy transferred by electrical work can be calculated using the equation:

$$\text{energy transferred} = \text{power} \times \text{time} \quad [E = P t]$$

$$\text{energy transferred} = \text{charge flow} \times \text{potential difference} \quad [E = Q V]$$

energy transferred E in joules, J; power P in watts, W; time t in seconds, s; charge flow Q in coulombs, C; potential difference V in volts, V

Students should be able to explain how the power of a circuit device is related to:

- the potential difference across it and the current through it
- the energy transferred over a given time.

Students should be able to describe, with examples, the relationship between the power ratings for domestic electrical appliances and the changes in stored energy when they are in use.

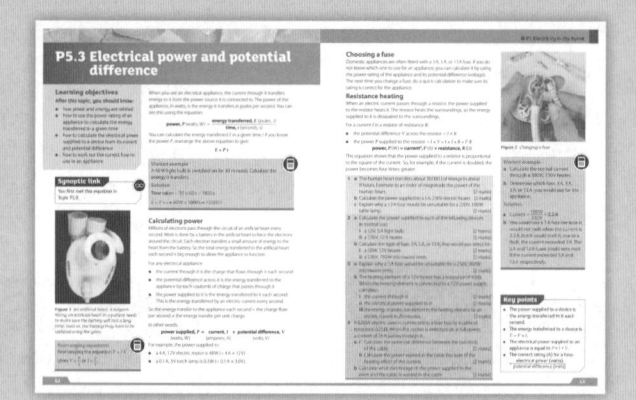

WS 1.2, 1.4
MS 3b, 3c

Aiming for	Outcome	Checkpoint	
		Question	Activity
Aiming for GRADE 4	State that the power of a device is the amount of energy transferred by it each second.		Starter 1, Main 1
	Describe the factors that affect the rate of energy transfer by a current in a circuit.		Main 1
	Explain why different fuses are required for different electrical devices in simple terms.	1, 3	Main 2, Plenary 1
Aiming for GRADE 6	Calculate the power of systems.	1, End of chapter 6	Main 1
	Calculate the power of electrical devices.	1, 2	Main 1
	Select an appropriate fuse for a device.	2, End of chapter 4	Main 2, Plenary 2
Aiming for GRADE 8	Measure and compare the power of electrical devices and explain variations in readings.		Main 1
	Calculate the electrical heating caused by resistance.	4, End of chapter 5	Main 2
	Combine a variety of calculations to analyse electrical systems.	4	Main 2

Maths
Students use a range of electrical equations in their analysis of electrical power (3b, 3c).

Literacy
Students describe energy transfer in terms of work done on or by electrons in a current.

■ P5 Electricity in the home

Practical

Title	Energy and power
Equipment	power supply (12 V), joulemeter (or ammeter and voltmeter combination), leads and a few appliances that operate at 12 V. The appliances could be a lamp, clocks, a small heater
Overview of method	The students connect the power supply to the appliance along with the joulemeter and determine the electrical power by measuring the energy transfer over one minute. Alternatively, they can connect the ammeter in series and voltmeter in parallel and determine the power rating using the electrical equation power = current × potential difference.
Safety considerations	Ensure that devices do not become hot.

Starter	Support/Extend	Resources
Power (5 min) Can the students give a scientific definition (and an equation) for power? Once a formal definition has been made, ask how this could be connected to electrical current where no force is apparently causing anything to move.	**Support:** Provide a definition and ask students to find an equation that matches the definition.	
Electrical units (10 min) Students use the interactive to match up electrical quantities with their definitions, abbreviations, and units. Include current I (amperes), voltage V (volts), resistance Ω (ohms), power P (watts), and energy (E, joules). Can the students provide any definitions for these units?	**Support:** Frame the activity as a jigsaw puzzle that can be assembled to produce a table of the information.	**Interactive:** Electrical units

Main	Support/Extend	Resources
Energy and power (25 min) Recap the concept of energy and the power equation that was met when studying mechanical power. The students should try some simple calculations to refresh their understanding. Ask students what factors will affect the rate of energy transfer by a current and then introduce the equation $P = IV$. The practical can be used to support this section. As usual, several example calculations will be required to embed this.	**Extend:** Calculations should include units such as kW, mA, and so on.	**Practical:** Energy and power
Fuses, resistance and heating (15 min) The students should apply the power calculation to select fuses for a variety of devices using the mains p.d. of 230 V. Show how the equations $V = IR$ and $P = IV$ can be combined algebraically, and ask the students to perform some heating calculations based on $P = I^2R$.	**Extend:** Combinations of devices can be used (e.g., through an extension lead) Do not exceed the rating of the extension cable. Link the equation back to all of the heating effects mentioned during fuses and electrical safety in earlier lessons.	**Maths skills:** Electrical power and charge

Plenary	Support/Extend	Resources
Electrical error (5 min) 'I'm sick of all my stuff fusing; I'm going to put a 13 A fuse in all of my things, so that they'll all keep working.' Ask students to discuss the hazards associated with doing this.		
Match the fuse (10 min) The students need to find the correct fuse for an electrical appliance after being told the power rating. This involves calculating the current and then choosing the fuse that is slightly higher. Use 3 A, 5 A, 13 A, and 30 A fuses.	**Extend:** Ask the students to select fuses for circuits where there are several appliances connected (e.g., a four-socket extension).	

Homework		
The students should perform additional calculations using the equations covered in this lesson.	**Support:** Differentiate the questions by students' ability.	

kerboodle

A Kerboodle highlight for this lesson is **Working scientifically: Are you energy smart?** Refer to the **Content map** on Kerboodle for a full list of resources and assessment.

P5.4 Electrical currents and energy transfer

AQA spec Link: 2.4.1 Students should be able to explain how the power transfer in any circuit device is related to the potential difference across it and the current through it, and to the energy changes over time:

$$\text{power} = \text{potential difference} \times \text{current} \quad [P = V I]$$

$$\text{power} = (\text{current})^2 \times \text{resistance} \quad [P = I^2 R]$$

power P in watts, W; potential difference V in volts, V; current I in amperes, A (amp is acceptable for ampere); resistance R in ohms, Ω

2.4.2 Everyday electrical appliances are designed to bring about energy transfers.

The amount of energy an appliance transfers depends on how long the appliance is switched on for and the power of the appliance.

Students should be able to describe how different domestic appliances transfer energy from batteries or a.c. mains to the kinetic energy of electric motors or the energy of heating devices.

Work is done when charge flows in a circuit.

The amount of energy transferred by electrical work can be calculated using the equation:

$$\text{energy transferred} = \text{power} \times \text{time} \quad [E = P t]$$

$$\text{energy transferred} = \text{charge flow} \times \text{potential difference} \quad [E = Q V]$$

energy transferred E in joules, J; power P in watts, W; time t in seconds, s; charge flow Q in coulombs, C; potential difference V in volts, V

Students should be able to explain how the power of a circuit device is related to:

- the potential difference across it and the current through it
- the energy transferred over a given time.

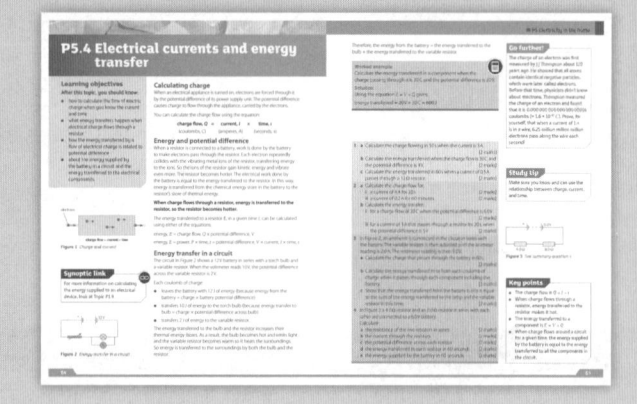

WS 1.2, 1.4
MS 3b, 3c

Aiming for	Outcome	Checkpoint	
		Question	Activity
Aiming for GRADE 4	Describe how an electric current consists of a flow of charge (electrons in a wire).		Main 1
	Identify the factors that affect the energy transfer in a circuit.		Main 2
	State that a battery or power supply provides energy to a current whereas a resistor causes a transfer of energy to the surroundings.		Main 2
Aiming for GRADE 6	Calculate the charge transferred by a current in a given time.	1, 2	Main 1, Homework
	Calculate the energy transferred by a charge passing through a potential difference.	1, 2, 3	Main 2
	Apply the law of conservation of energy in a circuit.	3	Main 2
Aiming for GRADE 8	Perform calculations involving rearrangement of the equations $Q = It$ and $E = VQ$.	2, 4, End of chapter 5	Main 1, Main 2, Homework
	Explain how energy is conserved in terms of current and p.d. during energy transfers by an electric current.	3	Main 2
	Use algebra to combine the equations $Q = It$ and $E = VQ$ to form the relationships $E = VIt$ and $P = IV$.	End of chapter 5	Main 2

Maths
The students will apply the relationships $Q = It$, $E = VQ$, $E = IVt$, and $P = IV$ for a variety of calculations (3b, 3c).

Literacy
Students describe energy transfer by using the various concepts about current in circuits.

P5 Electricity in the home

Practical

Title	The power of lamps
Equipment	12 V or 6 V lamp, power supply variable resistor, ammeter, voltmeter
Overview of method	The students use the variable resistor to gradually increase the current in the lamp whilst measuring the current in it and p.d. across it. They compare changes in these values to the brightness of the lamp.
Safety considerations	The lamp may become hot – allow time for cooling.

Starter	Support/Extend	Resources
Current and p.d. rules (5 min) Ask the students to describe the rules for current and potential difference in series and parallel circuits. **Energy transfer** (10 min) How many electrical appliances can the students describe energy transfers for? The students can also estimate the electrical efficiency of the appliances after they are clear about which of the energy pathways are useful.	**Extend:** Students should also describe the idea of conservation of energy. **Support:** Provide simple appliances and possible starting points for the diagrams.	

Main	Support/Extend	Resources
Charge and current (15 min) Show a simulation or model of an electric current and discuss the movement of electrons around the circuit. Ensure that students understand that the charge is conserved throughout the circuit. Introduce the equation $Q = It$ and ask the students to perform a few calculations with it.		
The power of lamps (25 min) Use the idea of a potential difference to describe energy transfer when charges pass through a resistor. Support this with measurement of the current and p.d. for a lamp with increasing brightness, as described in the practical, so that the students can relate the two factors to energy transfer.	**Extend:** Discuss the similar equation about energy provided *to* the charges (charge field) by a power supply such as a battery.	**Practical:** The power of lamps

Plenary	Support/Extend	Resources
Electrical spelling (5 min) Hold a spelling competition about electrical words using mini-whiteboards. **Electric crossword** (10 min) Interactive where students complete a crossword with answers based on the key words of the topics covered so far.	**Extend:** Give the students the completed crossword and ask them to write clues.	**Interactive:** Electric crossword

Homework		
Students should complete a range of electrical calculations based on the equations from the chapter so far.	**Support:** Differentiate the level of the questions according to students' ability.	

kerboodle

A Kerboodle highlight for this lesson is **Extension sheet: Electrical power.** Refer to the **Content map** on Kerboodle for a full list of resources and assessment.

P5.5 Appliances and efficiency

AQA spec Link: 2.4.2 Everyday electrical appliances are designed to bring about energy transfers.

The amount of energy an appliance transfers depends on how long the appliance is switched on for and the power of the appliance.

Students should be able to describe how different domestic appliances transfer energy from batteries or a.c. mains to the kinetic energy of electric motors or the energy of heating devices.

Work is done when charge flows in a circuit.

The amount of energy transferred by electrical work can be calculated using the equation:

energy transferred = power × time $[E = P\,t]$
energy transferred = charge flow × potential difference $[E = Q\,V]$

energy transferred E in joules, J; power P in watts, W; time t in seconds, s; charge flow Q in coulombs, C; potential difference V in volts, V

Students should be able to explain how the power of a circuit device is related to:
- the potential difference across it and the current through it
- the energy transferred over a given time.

Students should be able to describe, with examples, the relationship between the power ratings for domestic electrical appliances and the changes in stored energy when they are in use.

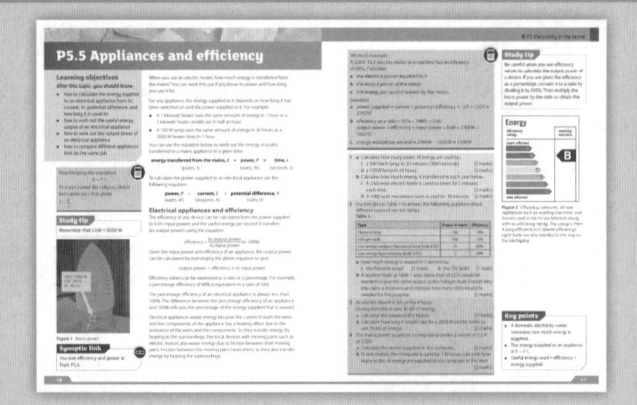

WS 1.4, 1.2
MS 3b, 3c

Aiming for	Outcome	Checkpoint	
		Question	Activity
Aiming for GRADE 4 ↓	Describe the factors that affect the cost of using various electrical devices.		Main 2
	Calculate energy transfer in joules.	1	Main 1
	State that energy transfer can be measured in kilowatt-hours.		Main 1
Aiming for GRADE 6 ↓	Calculate energy transfer in kilowatt-hours.	1, 2, End of chapter 4	Main 1
	Convert between efficiencies stated in percentages and those stated in decimal forms.		Main 2
	Calculate the power rating of a device from the energy transferred and the time of operation.	3	Main 1, Main 2
Aiming for GRADE 8 ↓	Convert between relevant units during calculations of energy transfer.		Starter 2, Main 1
	Analyse the use of a variety of electrical devices to determine their costs of operation.	4, End of chapter 4	Main 2
	Compare a range of electrical devices in terms of efficiency using calculations to support any conclusions.	2	Main 2, Plenary 1

Maths
Students calculate the energy transferred by a device and the cost of operation by using data from meter readings and electricity bills. Some students may convert between the units joule and kilowatt-hour (3b, 3c).

Literacy
Students discuss the nature of the units joule and kilowatt-hour and their use in a variety of situations. Students also discuss the idea of cost.

P5 Electricity in the home

Starter	Support/Extend	Resources
Multiple purchase (5 min) Ask the students to work out the unit cost of an everyday object from a bill (e.g., how much a chocolate bar costs when it is bought in a pack of five for £1.20). **Conversion factors** (10 min) Ask students to convert between some factors such as converting four days into hours then seconds, three miles into kilometres, and so on. Discuss why people use different units for the same quantity.	**Extend:** Include special offers such as buy two get one free. **Support:** Focus on the conversion of seconds into hours and vice versa.	

Main	Support/Extend	Resources
Electrical energy transfer (25 min) Replace earlier units with kilowatts as the base for power and hours for time to show that the values can be simpler for everyday devices. Ensure the students understand that the kilowatt-hour is just a different unit for energy, and show them how many joules the kWh represents. The students should try some simple calculations using the kWh to reinforce learning. Recap the energy and power equation ($E = Pt$), finding the energy transferred in joules but use larger values such as 200 W and 40 minutes. Show that using this system can produce large numbers that are difficult to understand. Discuss the idea that using kilowatts and hours as units may be better in some circumstances. **Electrical efficiency** (15 min) Recap on the concept of efficiency and the ideas of useful and less useful energy transfers. Describe the power version of the efficiency equation and ask the students to apply this equation to a range of calculations. Students should also discuss the reasons for inefficiency – heating by the current and frictional forces.	**Support:** Provide a simple calculation frame to develop students' skills. **Extend:** Students should try calculations that involve conversion between units. **Support:** Show the students some efficiency band labels. **Extend:** Students should also carry out calculations involving rearrangement of the equation.	**Activity:** Electrical energy transfer

Plenary	Support/Extend	Resources
Comparing kettles (10 min) Provide the students with data about UK and USA kettles including voltage, current, and operating time. Students identify which kettle is the most efficient. They then complete a paragraph to describe what makes electrical appliances efficient. **Big bill** (5 min) Ask the students to verify their school's electricity bill or a simplified version of it.	**Extend:** Include the volume of water each model of kettle can boil to add extra demand to the question. **Extend:** Include data on any standing charge.	**Interactive:** Comparing kettles

Homework		
The students should produce a summary or visual map of the information about current electricity, mains electricity, and electrical energy calculations. This has been quite a lot of information, so encourage the use of small diagrams on the map to enhance the readability.	**Support:** Provide a partially completed map for students to finish.	

kerboodle

A Kerboodle highlight for this lesson is **Literacy sheet: Electricity**. Refer to the **Content map** on Kerboodle for a full list of resources and assessment.

P5 Electricity in the home

Overview of P5 Electricity in the home

In this chapter the students have compared direct and alternating currents in terms of current direction. An oscilloscope has been used to analyse changes in the potential difference that causes the current and to measure the peak voltage, period and frequency of a low voltage sinusoidal a.c. signal.

The students have described the UK mains supply and the wires used within it, outlining the National Grid and the high voltages associated with it. Understanding of mains circuits, including the function of the neutral and earth wires, has been applied to three pin plugs and a simple ring-main. The choice of materials used for construction of mains circuits such as wires, cables, and plugs was discussed along with the need for a fuse to prevent overheating and insulation for protection from short circuits.

Students have mathematically analysed circuits to determine the power supplied by a current and the relationship between power and the resistance of components. This was linked back to the charge transfer in a circuit and the concept of electrical heating as charges move within or through components.

Finally, students have considered the importance of efficiency within mains powered electrical devices, linking this concept back to energy transfer by a current and to the simplified system of energy efficiency ratings used when considering the purchase of an appliance.

MyMaths

You can find additional support for the maths skills covered in this chapter on **MyMaths**, including recognising and using expressions in decimal form, using an appropriate number of significant figures, changing the subject of an equation, translating information between graphical and numeric form.

kerboodle

For this chapter, the following assessments are available on Kerboodle:

P5 Checkpoint quiz: Electricity in the home
P5 Progress quiz: Electricity in the home 1
P5 Progress quiz: Electricity in the home 2
P5 On your marks: Electricity in the home
P5 Exam-style questions and mark scheme: Electricity in the home

Checkpoint follow up lesson

A student's route through this lesson can be determined using the Checkpoint assessment. Percentage pass marks are supplied in the Checkpoint teacher notes.

For each successive route through it is assumed that the student can perform to their current route as well as previous routes. For example, students working at Aiming for 6 are assumed to be secure in Aiming for 4 knowledge and understanding and working towards achieving all the learning outcomes for Aiming for 6.

	Aiming for 4	**Aiming for 6**	**Aiming for 8**
Learning outcomes	Describe the purpose of fuses, earthing, circuit breakers, and plastic casings in electrical safety.	Explain the purpose of fuses, earthing, circuit breakers, and plastic casings in electrical safety.	Explain the purpose of fuses, earthing, circuit breakers, and plastic casings in electrical safety, and how a circuit breaker works.
	Calculate power, charge flow, energy transferred from the mains, and efficiency.	Describe the link between charge, potential difference, current, time, energy and power and do calculations involving those quantities.	Explain the link between charge, potential difference, current, time, energy and power, and do more complex calculations involving those quantities.
		Calculate peak potential difference and frequency from measurements of a trace on an oscilloscope screen.	Take measurements of peak potential difference and frequency from a trace on an oscilloscope screen.
Starter	**Mains danger (5 min)** Show an image of a kitchen with a range of appliances in it. Discuss what mains electricity is, and how large currents can be fatal. Ask students to 'snowball' ideas for preventing that happening when you are in the kitchen. Make a list of the words/phrases on the board (to use in the bingo later).		
	Efficient or not? (5 min) Give groups a large piece of paper and ask them to draw a line down the middle. On the left they should write down three situations in real life where we use the word efficient. Then ask them to write three sentences using the word 'efficient' as we use it in science.		
Differentiated checkpoint activity	Aiming for 4 students use the Checkpoint follow-up sheet to produce a safety leaflet for primary school students that explains the purpose of fuses, earthing, plastic casing, circuit breakers, and what is inside a plug. They then practise using equations for power, energy, charge, current, and efficiency. The follow-up sheet is highly structured and students should work in pairs with teacher support.	Aiming for 6 students use the Checkpoint follow-up sheet to produce a safety leaflet for primary school students. They do an experiment with lamps that work on the same potential difference but have different powers. They then practise using equations for power, energy, charge, current, and efficiency. The follow-up sheet is fairly structured and students should be aiming to work independently.	Aiming for 8 students use the Checkpoint follow-up sheet to produce a safety leaflet for primary school students. They do an experiment with lamps that work on the same potential difference but have different powers. They practise using equations for power, energy, charge, current, and efficiency, and make estimates of the use of appliances in a year. The follow-up sheet provided minimal support and students should be working independently.
	Kerboodle resource P5 Checkpoint follow up: Aiming for 4, P5 Checkpoint follow up: Aiming for 6, P5 Checkpoint follow up: Aiming for 8		
Plenary	**Safety bingo (10 min)** Give out grids and ask students to make a bingo card with words related to plugs, wiring, and safety from the starter. You may want to add to the list before you start with the colours of the wires, the potential difference of the wires, and so on. Play bingo.		
	What's the question? (5 min) Display the rubric for an exam question that asks for a calculation, and ask students to write down the information from the question that they need, as well as the equation. If time allows, students can select a question and answer it. You can select different questions depending on the level at which the students are aiming, or make a set of cards based on the questions and give them to different groups.		
Progression	Students should be able to identify the wires in a plug, explain what they are for, and how fuses work. They should be able to do calculations involving power, potential difference, and kWh, and describe the impact of using more efficient devices. Encourage students to think about explaining the impact of efficient devices on energy bills.	Students should be able to explain the structure of plugs in terms of safety and to identify other ways of protecting appliances and people. They should be able to do a range of calculations involving power, current, potential difference, energy, time, cost and efficiency, and describe the impact of using more efficient devices. Encourage students to think about explaining the impact of efficient devices on energy bills.	Students should be able to describe and explain in detail features that protect appliances and people in terms of mains electricity. They should be able to apply equations involving electrical quantities in a range of situations, and to explain the impact of efficient devices on energy bills. Encourage students to think critically about issues involving efficiency.

P 6 Molecules and matter
6.1 Density

AQA spec Link: 3.1.1 The density of a material is defined by the equation:

$$\text{density} = \frac{\text{mass}}{\text{volume}} \quad [\rho = \frac{m}{v}]$$

density, ρ, in kilograms per metre cubed, kg/m^3

mass, m, in kilograms, kg

volume, V, in metres cubed, m^3

Required practical: Use appropriate apparatus to make and record the measurements needed to determine the densities of regular and irregular solid objects and liquids. Volume should be determined from the dimensions of regularly shaped objects, and by a displacement technique for irregularly shaped objects. Dimensions to be measured using appropriate apparatus such as a ruler, micrometer, or Vernier callipers.

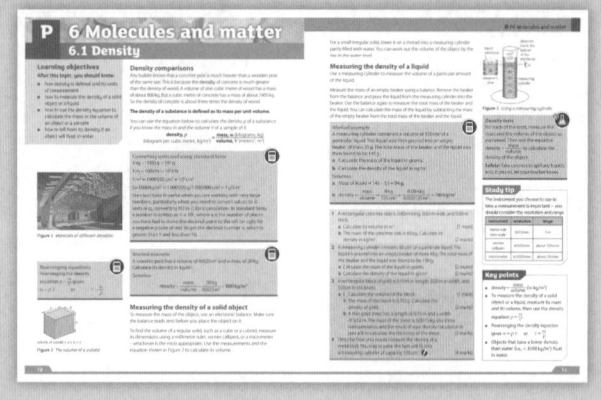

MS 1a, 1b, 1c, 3b, 3c, 5c

Aiming for	Outcome	Checkpoint	
		Question	Activity
Aiming for GRADE 4 ↓	Describe density as a property of a material and not a particular object.		Starter 1, Main
	State that the density of a material is the mass per unit volume.		Main
	Calculate the volume of some regular shapes and the density of materials, with support.	1, 3	Main
Aiming for GRADE 6 ↓	Explain why some materials will float on water.		Starter 2
	Calculate the density of materials.	1, 3	Main
	Measure the density of a solid and a liquid.	2	Main
Aiming for GRADE 8 ↓	Use the density equation in a wide variety of calculations.	3, End of chapter 1, 2	Main, Plenary 1
	Use appropriate significant figures in final answers when measuring density.		Main
	Evaluate in detail the experimental measurement of density, accounting for errors in measurements.		Main

Maths
Students calculate the volume and density of a range of objects (5c).

Literacy
Students use clear scientific language to compare the properties of a variety of materials in a fair way.

Key words
density

P6 Molecules and matter

Required practical

Title	Density tests – solids
Equipment	variety of regularly shaped objects (cubes, cylinders, etc.), ruler, top-pan balance
Overview of method	The students measure the dimensions of the object and calculate the volume. They then measure the mass and calculate the density.
Safety considerations	Do not use massive objects.

Title	Density tests – liquids
Equipment	measuring cylinders, beakers, top-pan balance, variety of liquids (water, oils, etc.)
Overview of method	Students measure the mass of the cylinder or beaker, add a measured volume of the liquid, and find the increase in mass. These values are used to find the density.
Safety considerations	Clear up spillages immediately.

Starter	Support/Extend	Resources
Material properties (10 min) Interactive where students match a list of material properties with its description (e.g., conductivity: How good a material is it at conducting electricity). Students then identify how the properties are measured.	**Extend:** Ask students to describe how some of the properties could be measured.	**Interactive:** Material properties
Cocktail (5 min) Pour some vegetable oil into a beaker partly full of water. Ask why the oil floats.	**Extend:** Add several immiscible liquids.	

Main	Support/Extend	Resources
Density tests (40 min) Students should analyse some materials and describe their properties, particularly how heavy they feel. They rank the materials in terms of heaviness. Discuss whether this ranking is fair (some objects are larger than others) and introduce the idea of density. Use the Maths skills interactive to provide students with some mass and volume data to calculate the density of a few sample materials using the equation. Discuss units of kg/m^3 and g/cm^3. Students then carry out the practical to measure the density of some samples. They should focus on the resolution of the instruments and the appropriate use of significant figures in their answers.	**Extend:** Students should use rearranged versions of the equation. **Support:** Provide the equations for volumes and some example calculations. **Extend:** Students should use the resolution of the instruments to estimate the uncertainty in their overall density answers.	**Required practical:** Density tests **Maths skills:** Density

Plenary	Support/Extend	Resources
Irregular solids (10 min) Students explain a way of finding the density of a rock or other irregular object.	**Support:** Provide a picture showing how this may be done and ask the students to explain it.	
Smoke signals (5 min) Light a candle and blow it out after a few seconds. The students should explain why the smoke rises. Link this to the idea of gasses floating on top of each other due to density differences.		

Homework		
The students should explain how a ship, constructed of a dense metal, can float on water. They can include data on real ship masses and volumes.		

kerboodle

A Kerboodle highlight for this lesson is **Extension sheet: Solving density puzzles**. Refer to the **Content map** on Kerboodle for a full list of resources and assessment.

P6.2 States of matter

AQA spec Link: 3.1.1 The particle model can be used to explain:
- the different states of matter
- differences in density.

Students should be able to recognise/draw simple diagrams to model the difference between solids, liquids, and gases.

Students should be able to explain the differences in density between the different states of matter in terms of the arrangement of atoms or molecules.

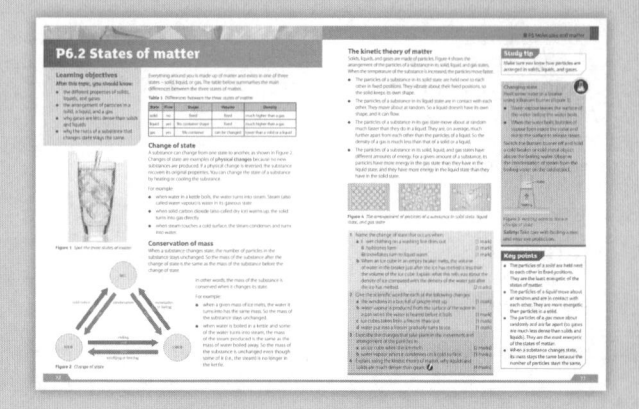

Aiming for	Outcome	Checkpoint Question	Checkpoint Activity
Aiming for GRADE 4	Describe the simple properties of solids, liquids, and gases.		Starter 1, Main 1
	Name the changes of state.	1, 2	Main 1
	State that there are changes in stores of energy associated with a material when its temperature is increased.	3	Main 1
Aiming for GRADE 6	Describe the arrangement of the particles in a solid, liquid, and gas.	3	Main 1, Main 2, Plenary 2
	Explain the behaviour of a material in terms of the arrangement of particles within it.	3, End of chapter 3	Main 1, Main 2
	Describe the changes in behaviour of the particles in a material during changes of state.	3	Main 1, Main 2
Aiming for GRADE 8	Describe the forces acting between particles in a solid, liquid, and gas.	3	Main 2, Plenary 1, Plenary 2
	Describe the changes in the energy of individual particles during changes of state.	4, End of chapter 3	Main 2
	Explain in detail why the density of a material changes during a change of state, using a particle model.	4, End of chapter 3	Main 2

Literacy
Students use a particle model to describe the changes of state and properties of a material.

Key words
physical changes

Practical

Title	Changing state
Equipment	Bunsen burner, tripod, heat-resistant mat, gauze, beaker (250 cm^3), icy cold spoon or something similar, ice (optional)
Overview of method	Students heat the water in a beaker using a Bunsen burner. They observe the changes of state and think about the idea of changes in energy and particle behaviour. Alternatively, half fill a beaker with ice and heat with a Bunsen burner to demonstrate melting then boiling.
Safety considerations	Clear up spillages immediately. The apparatus and water will become very hot.

P6 Molecules and matter

Title	Kinetic theory
Equipment	plastic tray, marbles, ping-pong balls or other small balls
Overview of method	Place a few balls in the tray and allow them to roll around – this is similar to a gas – the particles can move freely and are generally far apart. Almost fill the bottom layer of the tray – the particles can still move a bit, but there are few gaps between them, similar to a liquid. Finally, fill the tray so that the particles cannot move – they are closely packed together in a manner similar to the particles in a solid.
Safety considerations	Ensure that no marbles, or similar, are left on the floor.

Starter	Support/Extend	Resources
State the facts (5 min) Ask students to name the different changes of state and say whether energy is gained or dissipated by substances during these changes and where this energy is transferred from or to.	**Support:** Provide a diagram to add the labels to.	
Property match (10 min) Interactive where students sort the properties according to whether they describe solids, liquids, and gases. They then match descriptions of other properties – such as density, fluidity, and compressibility – with solids, liquids, and gases.	**Extend:** Challenge students to give explanations of these properties in terms of particle arrangement and movement.	**Interactive:** Property match

Main	Support/Extend	Resources
Changing state (40 min) Revise Key Stage 3 work by describing the three states of matter, using water as a simple example, using simple demonstrations in your explanations if appropriate. Ensure that the key properties of the three states are understood and that the concept of conservation of mass is covered. Model the particles of the three states using small balls and a plastic tray. Place a few balls in the tray and allow them to roll around – this is similar to a gas – the particles can move freely and are generally far apart. Almost fill the bottom layer of the tray – the particles can still move a bit, but there are few gaps between them, similar to a liquid. Finally, fill the tray so that the particles cannot move – they are closely packed together in a manner similar to the particles in a solid. Describe the changes in the forces between the particles. The students should use the model to explain the behaviours of solids, liquids, and gases.	**Support:** Demonstrate the conservation of mass when ice melts.	**Activity:** Changing state

Plenary	Support/Extend	Resources
Particle behaviour (5 min) Students could act out the states of matter. Ask them to behave like particles in a solid, a liquid, and a gas.		
Particle diagrams (10 min) Ask students to make particle diagrams. Provide them with a lot of discs from a hole-punch and let them create a diagram representing the three states and the transitions between them.	**Extend:** Ask student to discuss the limitations of these simple visual representations.	

Homework		
Students can research the evidence for the particle model, including Brownian motion.	**Support:** Provide students with observations of Brownian motion (or from a smoke cell) and ask them to complete a cloze exercise explaining these observations.	

kerboodle

A Kerboodle highlight for this lesson is **Working scientifically: Does melting ice expand?** Refer to the **Content map** on Kerboodle for a full list of resources and assessment.

73

P6.3 Changes of state

AQA spec Link: 3.1.2 Students should be able to describe how, when substances change state (melt, freeze, boil, evaporate, condense, or sublimate), mass is conserved.

Changes of state are physical changes which differ from chemical changes because the material recovers it original properties if the change is reversed.

3.2.3 Students should be able to interpret heating and cooling graphs that include changes of state.

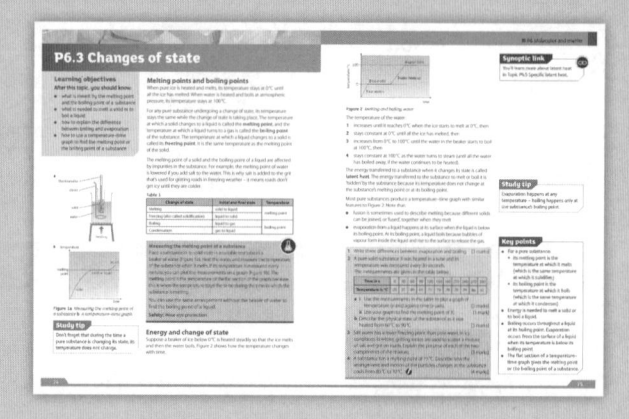

MS 4c

Aiming for	Outcome	Checkpoint	
		Question	Activity
Aiming for GRADE 4	State that the melting point of a substance is the temperature at which it changes from a solid to a liquid and vice versa.	1	Main
	State that the boiling point of a substance is the temperature at which it changes from a liquid to a gas and vice versa.	1	Main
	Describe the process of melting and boiling.	1, End of chapter 3	Main
Aiming for GRADE 6	State that the melting and boiling points of a pure substance are fixed.	3	Main
	Use the term 'latent heat' to describe the energy gained by a substance during heating for which there is no change in temperature.		Main
	Find the melting or boiling point of a substance by using a graphical technique.	2	Main, Plenary 1
Aiming for GRADE 8	Describe how the melting points and boiling points of a substance can be changed.	3	Main, Plenary 1
	Describe in detail the behaviour of the particles during changes of state.	4, End of chapter 3	Main
	Evaluate data produced by a heating experiment to discuss the reproducibility of the measurement of a melting point.		Main, Plenary 2

Maths
Students plot graphs of experimental data and identify their features (4c).

Literacy
Students describe the behaviour of materials and the features of a graph.

Key words
melting point, boiling point, freezing point, latent heat

Practical

Title	Measuring the melting point of a substance
Equipment	heating apparatus, stopwatch, 250 cm^3 beaker, stirrer, water, boiling tube containing a thermometer in solid wax or salicylic acid
Overview of method	The students set up the apparatus as shown in the student book and heat the water. They stir the water and measure the temperature of the solid every 30 seconds until it has completely melted.
Safety considerations	Wear eye protection, and clear up spillages immediately.

P6 Molecules and matter

Starter	Support/Extend	Resources
Water properties (5 min) Ask the students for the melting and boiling points for water. How can these be altered? **How hot?** (10 min) Provide the students with some important temperatures and ask them to match them to objects or changes (e.g., boiling point of water, temperature of the surface of the Sun).	**Extend:** Select more obscure temperatures to discuss.	

Main	Support/Extend	Resources
Measuring the melting point of a substance (40 min) Recap the changes in the behaviour of the particles as a material melts and then as it boils. Ask the students to suggest why, when the melting point is reached, all of the substance does not melt at once. The students carry out the practical and produce a temperature–time graph. The region in which the state changes (no increase in temperature) should be clearly identified. Discuss the identified region, emphasising that energy is still being transferred to the substance. This increase in the energy store is not obvious, hence the term latent heat. The terms fusion, boiling, and evaporation should be introduced.	**Support:** A simpler experiment measuring the boiling point of water can be used. Students use the equipment and method from Topic P6.2, measuring the temperature every 30 seconds until it boils, and for 3 minutes after (noting that there is no further increase in temperature). **Extend:** Discuss changes in melting and boiling points when the substances are not pure (e.g., salted water). Students should compare results to help evaluate the reproducibility of the measurements.	**Practical:** Measuring the melting point of a substance

Plenary	Support/Extend	Resources
Boiling at altitude (10 min) Show the students a graph of the boiling point of water compared with altitude. Students use the interactive to complete a description of this relationship and an explanation of why the boiling point changes. **Melting point** (5 min) Provide the students with a variety of measurements of the melting point for a substance and ask them to find the mean and range.	**Extend:** Students should use the data to discuss the reproducibility of the experiment and the precision and accuracy of their answer.	**Interactive:** Boiling at altitude

Homework		
Students complete the WebQuest where they research unusual materials. These include materials with extreme density values, melting points, and boiling points, and materials that cannot be easily categorised as solid or liquid.		**WebQuest:** Unusual materials

kerboodle

A Kerboodle highlight for this lesson is **Literacy skills: Changes of state**. Refer to the **Content map** on Kerboodle for a full list of resources and assessment.

P6.4 Internal energy

AQA spec Link: 3.2.1 Energy is stored inside a system by the particles (atoms and molecules) that make up the system. This is called internal energy.
Internal energy is the total kinetic energy and potential energy of all the particles (atoms and molecules) that make up a system.

Heating changes the energy stored within the system by increasing the energy of the particles that make up the system. This either raises the temperature of the system or produces a change of state.

3.2.2 If the temperature of the system increases, the increase in temperature depends on the mass of the substance heated, the type of material, and the energy input to the system.

The following equation applies:

change in thermal energy = mass × specific heat capacity × temperature change

$[\Delta E = m\, c\, \Delta \theta]$

change in thermal energy ΔE in joules, J

mass m in kilograms, kg

specific heat capacity c in joules per kilogram per degree Celsius, J/kg °C

temperature change $\Delta \theta$ in degrees Celsius, °C.

The specific heat capacity of a substance is the amount of energy required to raise the temperature of one kilogram of the substance by one degree Celsius.

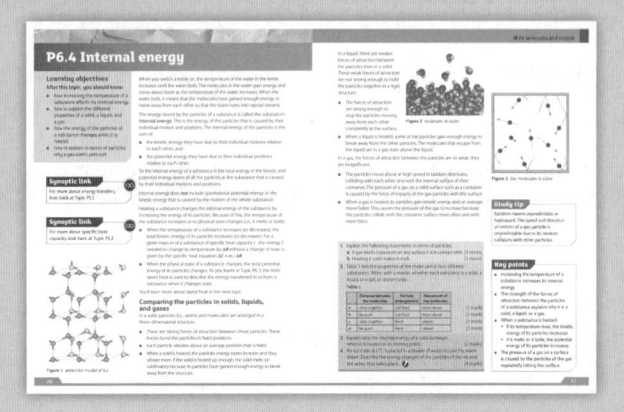

MS 1a, 3b, 3c, 3d

Aiming for	Outcome	Checkpoint	
		Question	Activity
Aiming for GRADE 4	State that the internal energy of a system increases as it is heated.		Starter 1, Main 1
	Identify which changes of state are related to increases in internal energy and which are related to decreases.		Main 1
↓	Outline the behaviour of particles in solids, liquids, and gases.	2, End of chapter 7	Main 2
Aiming for GRADE 6	Describe how the internal energy of an object can be increased by heating.		Main 1
	Describe how the behaviour of particles changes as the energy of a system increases.	1, 2, End of chapter 7	Main 2
↓	Describe the energy changes by heating between objects within the same system.	4	Main 2, Plenary 2
Aiming for GRADE 8	Use the concepts of kinetic and potential energy to explain changes in internal energy.		Main 1
↓	Describe the changes in the size of intermolecular forces during changes of state.	3, End of chapter 7	Main 2

Maths
Students calculate the energy changes associated with heating a material (3b, 3c, 3d).

Literacy
Students apply the particle model to describe changes in the internal energy of an object as it is heated.

Key words
internal energy

P6 Molecules and matter

Practical

Title	Internal energy
Equipment	heating apparatus, 500 cm³ beaker, water and crushed ice, thermometer
Overview of method	Place the iced water in the beaker and gradually heat it whilst discussing changes in the internal energy.
Safety considerations	Wear eye protection, and clear up spillages immediately. The apparatus will become very hot.

Starter	Support/Extend	Resources
Specific heat capacity (5 min) Introduce the equation $\Delta E = m\,c\,\Delta\theta$, then students complete the interactive where they work through some example calculations. **Convection** (10 min) Pour some hot water into a beaker and add ice cubes that have food colouring in them. Ask the students to describe the processes taking place.	**Extend:** Use non-base units such as grams. **Support:** Students can card sort the stages of a convection current.	**Interactive:** Specific heat capacity

Main	Support/Extend	Resources
Internal energy (20 min) Begin heating the beaker of iced water and discuss the energy transfers involved. Initially there will be no temperature increase, allowing discussion of the latent heat and the repositioning of the bonds of the particles. As the ice melts and the temperature starts to increase, begin to describe the changes in motion for the particles. By the time the water is boiling, the students should have a good understanding of internal energy. **Particle behaviour** (20 min) Describe the behaviour of the particles in a solid, liquid, and gas with a focus on the forces between the particles. Describe the attraction between individual particles and how the motion changes. Additional details about the behaviour of gasses will be covered in the next few lessons.	**Extend:** Discuss the processes causing temperature change throughout the liquid – convection and any dissipation to the surroundings. **Support:** Provide a table for students to summarise the forces and particle separation.	**Activity:** Internal energy

Plenary	Support/Extend	Resources
Convection revisited (10 min) Repeat the second starter, but ask the students to describe the changes in particle behaviour for the ice. **What forces?** (5 min) Can the students describe which forces are responsible for attraction and repulsion between molecules and atoms?	**Support:** Students can match up key terms describing the behaviour of atoms and molecules.	

Homework		
The students can describe energy changes in a variety of systems to revise their understanding of energy changes.	**Support:** Provide examples such as making a cup of tea or watching television.	

kerboodle

A Kerboodle highlight for this lesson is **Working scientifically: Assumptions in models**. Refer to the **Content map** on Kerboodle for a full list of resources and assessment.

P6.5 Specific latent heat

AQA spec Link: 3.2.3 If a change of state happens:

The energy needed for a substance to change state is called latent heat. When a change of state occurs, the energy supplied changes the energy stored (internal energy) but not the temperature.

The specific latent heat of a substance is the amount of energy required to change the state of one kilogram of the substance with no change in temperature.

energy for a change of state = mass × specific latent heat

$[E = m L]$

energy E in joules, J

mass m in kilograms, kg

specific latent heat L in joules per kilogram, J/kg

Specific latent heat of fusion – change of state from solid to liquid

Specific latent heat of vaporisation – change of state from liquid to vapour

Students should be able to distinguish between specific heat capacity and specific latent heat.

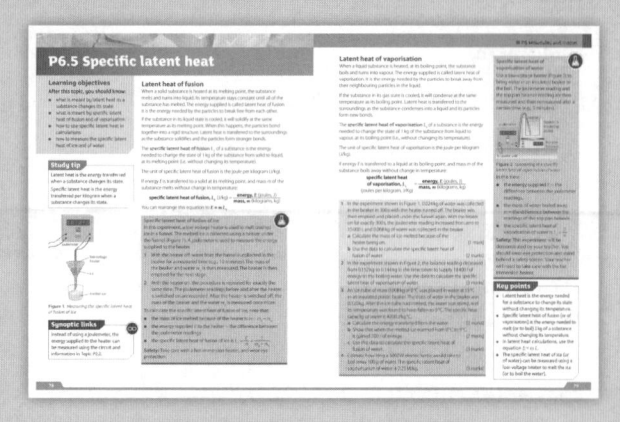

MS 1a, 3b, 3c, 3d, 4a

Aiming for	Outcome	Checkpoint	
		Question	Activity
Aiming for GRADE 4	State that heating a material will increase its internal energy.		Main
	Describe energy changes during melting and vaporisation.		Main
	Measure the latent heat of vaporisation for water.		Main
Aiming for GRADE 6	Describe the changes in particle bonding during changes of state.		Main
	Calculate the latent heat of fusion and latent heat of vaporisation for a substance.	2, End of chapter 4, 5	Main, Plenary 2
	Measure the latent heat of fusion for water.		Main
Aiming for GRADE 8	Perform a variety of calculations based on the latent heat equation.	4, End of chapter 4, 5	Main
	Combine a variety of equations to solve problems involving heating.	1, 2, 3	Main, Plenary 2
	Evaluate the reproducibility of a measurement of latent heat based on collated data.		Main

Maths
Students use the latent heat equation to solve a variety of problems (1a, 3b, 3c, 3d).

Literacy
Students use the particle model to discuss changes in internal energy.

Key words
specific latent heat of fusion, specific latent heat of vaporisation

Practical

Title	Specific latent heat of fusion of ice
Equipment	joulemeter, low-voltage electrical heating element and power supply, beaker, ice, funnel
Overview of method	Put a known mass of crushed ice into a funnel and secure over a beaker. Put the heating element of a low-voltage heater into the crushed ice but do not turn it on. Leave the experiment for a set period of time (e.g., 10 minutes) then measure the mass of water collected in the beaker. Repeat the procedure, this time with the heater on and the joulemeter measuring the energy supplied to the heater.
Safety considerations	Wear eye protection, and clear up spillages immediately.

P6 Molecules and matter

Title	Measuring the specific latent heat of vaporisation of water
Equipment	joulemeter, low-voltage electrical heating element and power supply, beaker, water, a top-pan balance
Overview of method	Wrap a beaker with some insulating material. Attach a low-voltage heater to a joulemeter and place the heater into the beaker of water. Place on a top-pan balance. Take a reading from the joulemeter and top-pan balance. Switch on the heater. After five minutes, take another reading from the joulemeter and top-pan balance.
Safety considerations	Wear eye protection, and clear up spillages immediately.

Starter	Support/Extend	Resources
Thermal conduction (10 min) Students should describe the process of thermal conduction in solids (metals and non-metals). **Puddle puzzle** (5 min) Interactive where students complete an explanation to explain why a puddle of water disappears over time.	**Support:** Provide a diagram for the students to annotate. **Extend:** Ask which factors affect the rate and why.	**Interactive:** Puddle puzzle

Main	Support/Extend	Resources
Specific latent heat (40 min) Recap the energy changes during the heating of a solid substance, with an emphasis on the breaking of bonds during melting. Define the latent heat as the energy change required for 1 kg of a substance to melt (with no change in temperature), pointing out that this is different for different substances. Students complete the Maths skills interactive to practice using the equation. Follow a similar method with vaporisation and energy change checking with a simple calculation before moving to the practical. Form students into groups and ask them to complete one of the two practicals. They should share data with another group that completed the same experiment to find a mean value for the latent heat. After this they share conclusions with the groups that completed the other practical.	**Support:** Show several example calculations before asking the students to perform one. **Support:** The vaporisation experiment is the simpler of the two. **Extend:** Students use the range of results to discuss the reproducibility of the experiment and the uncertainty in the answer.	**Maths skills:** Latent heat **Practical:** Specific latent heat

Plenary	Support/Extend	Resources
Overall heating (10 min) Ask the students to solve a problem involving the latent heat and specific heat capacity by finding the energy change when 2 kg of ice at −4 °C is melted. **A watched kettle** (5 min) Ask the students how long a 3.0 kW kettle would take to cause 1.5 kg of water to evaporate.	**Extend:** A similar task involving heating until the water boils can be used.	

Homework		
The students should write an explanation of why evaporation causes cooling of surfaces, for example, sweating.		

kerboodle

A Kerboodle highlight for this lesson is **Bump up your grade: Specific latent heat**. Refer to the **Content map** on Kerboodle for a full list of resources and assessment.

P6.6 Gas pressure and temperature

AQA spec Link: 3.3.1 The molecules of a gas are in constant random motion. The temperature of the gas is related to the average kinetic energy of the molecules.

Changing the temperature of a gas, held at constant volume, changes the pressure exerted by the gas.

Students should be able to:

- explain how the motion of the molecules in a gas is related to both its temperature and its pressure
- explain qualitatively the relation between the temperature of a gas and its pressure at constant volume.

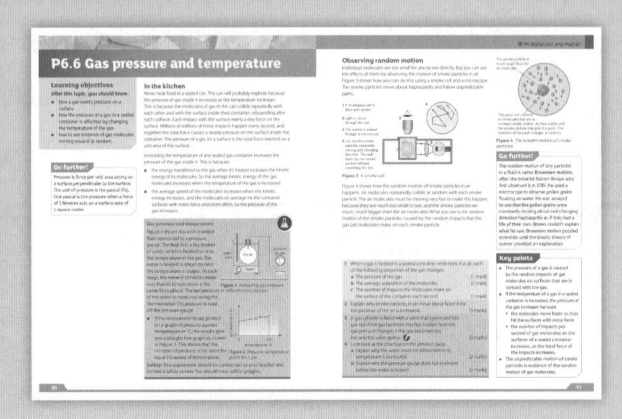

WS 1.2
MS 4b

Aiming for	Outcome	Checkpoint	
		Question	Activity
Aiming for GRADE 4 ↓	State that as the temperature of a gas in a sealed container increases, the pressure of the gas increases.	1	Main 1
	Describe a gas as consisting of a large number of rapidly moving particles.		Main 1, Main 2
	Describe pressure as being caused by collisions of gas particles with the walls of its container.	1	Main 1
Aiming for GRADE 6 ↓	Describe the behaviour of particles in a gas as the gas is heated.	1	Main 1
	Outline Brownian motion and how this provides evidence for the particle nature of matter.	2	Main 2, Plenary 1
	Describe the relationship between an increase in the temperature of a fixed volume of a gas and the increase in pressure of the gas.	3	Main 1, Plenary 2
Aiming for GRADE 8 ↓	Describe the linear relationship between changes in temperature and pressure for a gas.		Main 1
	Explain Brownian motion in terms of particle behaviour and collisions, relating the speeds of smoke particles and air molecules.	2	Main 2
	Describe in detail how the relationship between the pressure of a gas and its temperature can be investigated.	4	Main 1

Maths
Students describe linear relationships between quantities (4b).

Literacy
Students describe the motion of gas particles in detail as part of an explanation of gas pressure.

Practical

Title	Gas pressure and temperature
Equipment	water bath (large beaker of water), round flask, thermometer, heater, pressure gauge
Overview of method	Connect the apparatus as shown in the student book, making sure that the flask is completely submerged. Heat the water gradually, and record the temperature and pressure.
Safety considerations	Do not heat the water above 60 °C. Ensure glass vessels are in good condition and do not have any scratches or chips.

P6 Molecules and matter

Title	Theory of Brownian motion
Equipment	Brownian smoke cell with integrated light source, low-power microscope with large aperture, power supply, smoke source, pipette
Overview of method	Suck up some smoke from a source with the pipette and blow it into the chamber. Observe the behaviour of the smoke with the microscope. A single smoke cell can be connected to a visualiser so that the whole class can see it at once.
Safety considerations	Take care with the smoke source, and ensure that direct sunlight does not pass through the microscope.

Starter	Support/Extend	Resources
Pressure recap (10 min) Students use the interactive to recap their knowledge of pressure. They carry out some calculations, then complete a paragraph to describe what causes pressure when two surfaces are in contact with one another.	**Extend:** Introduce the idea of forces acting between the individual atoms of the two surfaces.	**Interactive:** Pressure recap
That's a bit random (5 min) Ask the students what the term random means, and discuss how random events can happen.	**Extend:** Ask whether random events are compatible with physical laws.	

Main	Support/Extend	Resources
Gas pressure and temperature (25 min) Discuss the behaviour of gases and what happens to their particles as they increase in energy through heating. Remind the students of the cause of gas pressure – particle collisions with container walls – and ask what will happen to pressure when temperature increases. Demonstrate the heating of a gas and find the relationship between gas temperature and pressure as outlined in the practical.	**Extend:** Sample data could be provided for students to plot a graph and to determine a pattern.	**Practical:** Gas pressure and temperature
Theory of Brownian motion (15 min) Show Brownian motion with a real smoke cell and discuss the conclusions that can be made using the Working scientifically sheet. Diffusion can also be demonstrated to show the random motion of particles and the gradual spreading effect.	**Support:** Back up any explanation with a simulation of the process. **Extend:** Discuss the relative speeds and masses of the smoke and air particles.	**Working scientifically:** Theory of Brownian motion

Plenary	Support/Extend	Resources
A random walk (5 min) Students place a counter in the central square of some graph paper. They roll a die (eight-sided ideally) to determine which direction to move the counter. Do this 10 times and compare the final position of the counter with other 'players'.		
Absolute zero (10 min) Show students two pressure–temperature graphs – one with the temperature in kelvin and the other in degrees Celsius. Students discuss why the two graphs are different and under what circumstances temperature is directly proportional to pressure. They then use the data to find the temperature when the pressure reaches zero.	**Extend:** Discuss this state as the lowest possible temperature.	

Homework		
The gas laws were important discoveries – students should find out who discovered them and how these were achieved. Students should also describe the properties of an 'ideal gas' in terms of the particles within it.	**Extend:** Students can describe the ideal gas law, which brings the gas laws together.	

P6 Molecules and matter

Overview of P6 Molecules and matter

In this chapter the students have increased their understanding of the concept of density as a property of a material or object by measuring and calculating the density of solids and liquids. This led to a discussion of the states of matter, the properties of matter in these states, and the changes that occur as a material changes from one state to another. The changes in the properties of matter were used to introduce the kinetic theory and to analyse the changes in temperature occurring during heating and the concept of latent heat.

The students moved on to discuss the concept of internal energy in more detail; analysing the behaviour of particles in a solid, liquid or gas as the temperature changed. Students described latent heat of fusion and vaporisation mathematically, calculating energy changes during the appropriate phase changes and attempted to measure the latent heat of fusion for ice using electrical heating.

The students analysed the relationships between the pressure and temperature of a fixed mass of gas, determining that the pressure is proportional to the absolute temperature. They described the cause of pressure in terms of random particle behaviour and impact between the particles and its container, explaining the changes in pressure in terms of changes in the motion of the gas particles as the temperature decreases.

MyMaths

You can find additional support for the maths skills covered in this chapter on **MyMaths**, including recognising and using expressions in decimal form, understanding and using the symbols: =, <, <<, >>, >, ∝, ~, and solving simple algebraic equations.

kerboodle

For this chapter, the following assessments are available on Kerboodle:

P6 Checkpoint quiz: Molecules and matter
P6 Progress quiz: Molecules and matter 1
P6 Progress quiz: Molecules and matter 2
P6 On your marks: Molecules and matter
P6 Exam-style questions and mark scheme: Molecules and matter

Checkpoint follow up lesson

A student's route through this lesson can be determined using the Checkpoint assessment. Percentage pass marks are supplied in the Checkpoint teacher notes.

For each successive route through it is assumed that the student can perform to their current route as well as previous routes. For example, students working at Aiming for 6 are assumed to be secure in Aiming for 4 knowledge and understanding and working towards achieving all the learning outcomes for Aiming for 6.

	Aiming for 4	**Aiming for 6**	**Aiming for 8**
Learning outcomes	Define density.	Calculate density and describe factors that affect it.	Calculate density, including converting between units, and describe factors that affect it.
	Describe the densities of different states.	Analyse data in terms of specific latent heat.	Analyse data in terms of specific latent heat in a range of situations
	Describe the effect of specific latent heat on the change of state of liquid.	Calculate energy transfer to produce a change in state.	Do calculations involving the equation for specific latent heat
	Describe and explain what happens when you increase the temperature or decrease the volume of a gas.	Explain why a gas exerts a pressure.	Use explanations of why a gas exerts a pressure to further explain the relationship between pressure and volume, and volume and temperature
Starter	**Melting and boiling (5 min)** Give students A4 dry wipe boards, pens and an eraser. Display or read a description of a material that melts then boils, giving details such as the temperatures and the times, and ask students to sketch the graph and label it with melting, boiling, solid, liquid, and gas, and with temperatures and times on the axes. Ask them to make the line where the density is highest into a zigzag line, and the line where it is lowest into a dotted line.		
Differentiated checkpoint activity	Aiming for 4 students use the Checkpoint follow-up sheet to complete one of two activities: • model density and states of matter using marbles • analyse data from an investigating into evaporation of liquids. The Checkpoint follow-up sheet is highly-structured and provides students with simple questions to consolidate their understanding from the tasks. Students will need access to graph paper.	Aiming for 6 students use the Checkpoint follow-up sheet to complete one of two activities: • create a of model density and states of matter using marbles • analyse data from an investigating into evaporation of liquids. The Checkpoint follow-up sheet provides limited support for students and includes more open-ended questions for students to consolidate their understanding of the tasks. Students will need access to graph paper.	Aiming for 8 students use the Checkpoint follow-up sheet to complete one of two activities: • design a of model density and states of matter using marbles, including qualitative analysis of their model • analyse data from an investigating into evaporation of liquids. The Checkpoint follow-up sheet provides limited support for students and includes open-ended questions for students to consolidate their understanding of the tasks. Students will need access to graph paper.
	Kerboodle resource P6 Checkpoint follow up: Aiming for 4, P6 Checkpoint follow up: Aiming for 6, P6 Checkpoint follow up: Aiming for 8		
Plenary	**What's wrong? (10 min)** Give students A4 dry wipe boards, pens, and an eraser. Show a calculation of density and specific latent heat that is incorrect and ask students to write the correct calculation. You can have the wrong numbers, equation, or units. Aiming for 4 students could be given the equations. **SHC vs SLH (10 min)** On the whiteboards ask students to make a Venn diagram for specific heat capacity (from chapter P2) and specific latent heat and to compare with the others in their group. Aiming for 8 students discuss how or if thermal conductivity can be added as a third circle.		
Progression	Encourage students to think about both the arrangement of the particles and the bonds between them when explaining latent heat.	Encourage students to think about the effect on the collisions of particles with a container when talking about the factors affecting gas pressure.	Encourage students to think about the assumptions of the particle model when using it to explain phenomena.

P 7 Radioactivity
7.1 Atoms and radiation

AQA spec Link: 4.1.1 Atoms are very small, having a radius of about 1×10^{-10} metres.

The basic structure of an atom is a positively charged nucleus composed of both protons and neutrons surrounded by negatively charged electrons.

The radius of a nucleus is less than $\frac{1}{10\,000}$ of the radius of an atom. Most of the mass of an atom is concentrated in the nucleus.

The electrons are arranged at different distances from the nucleus (different energy levels). The electron arrangements may change with the absorption of electromagnetic radiation (move further from the nucleus; a higher energy level) or by the emission of electromagnetic radiation (move closer to the nucleus; a lower energy level).

4.2.1 Some atomic nuclei are unstable. The nucleus gives out radiation as it changes to become more stable. This is a random process called radioactive decay.

Required knowledge of the properties of alpha particles, beta particles, and gamma rays is limited to their penetration through materials, their range in air, and ionising power.

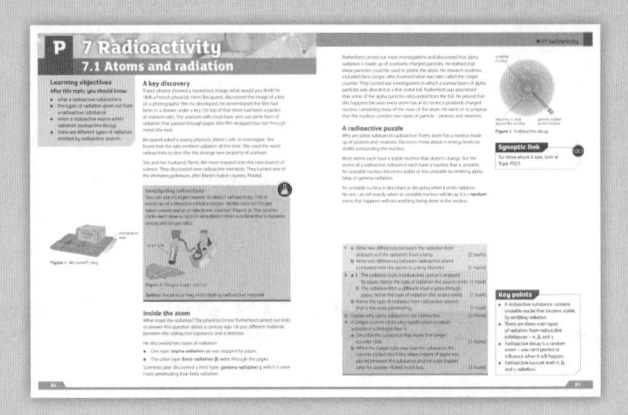

MS 1a, 1b, 2a

Aiming for	Outcome	Checkpoint	
		Question	Activity
Aiming for GRADE 4	Name the three types of nuclear radiation.		Main
	Name the three sub-atomic particles found in an atom (proton, neutron, and electron).		Starter 1, Starter 2, Main
	Identify some sources of background radiation.	3, 4, End of chapter 5	Main
Aiming for GRADE 6	Describe some safety precautions used when dealing with radioactive materials.		Main
	Describe how a Geiger counter can be used to detect radiation.	4	Main
	Identify natural and man-made sources of background radiation.	End of chapter 5	Main
Aiming for GRADE 8	Describe in detail the decay of an unstable nucleus.	3	Main
	Explain the similarities and differences between nuclear radiation and visible light.	2	Main, Plenary 2
	Describe the relative penetrating powers of the three types of nuclear radiation.	1	Main

Maths
Students compare count rates to describe the activity of a source or the level of background radiation.

Literacy
Students describe the operation of a Geiger counter and what the count rate says about the level of radiation present.

Key words
alpha radiation, beta radiation, gamma radiation, random

P7 Radioactivity

Practical

Title	Investigating radioactivity
Equipment	Geiger–Müller tube, ratemeter (and possibly high-voltage power supply), large plastic tray, tongs, radioactive sources, laboratory coat
Overview of method	Position the detector in the tray and switch it on. Bring the sources close to the tube window (and above the tray), and the ratemeter should count. If you can find a ratemeter that clicks, the demonstration is a lot more fun. A video camera connected to a data projector can be used to show the demonstrations more clearly.
Safety considerations	Follow local rules on the use of radioactive sources.

Starter	Support/Extend	Resources
Look alike (5 min) Ask students to draw and label an atom and discuss whether it is a realistic model. Show the students some caricatures of famous people to see whether these capture the essence of each person. **Atom models** (10 min) Ask students to draw some simple atomic models. Ask them to note any of the properties of the sub-atomic particles that they already know, for example, from studying electricity or from atomic structure in chemistry.	**Extend:** Discuss whether a model must look exactly like the object/situation it is meant to be describing. **Support:** Give students a set of cut-out protons, neutrons, and electrons to use. **Extend:** Ask for specific atoms to be constructed.	

Main	Support/Extend	Resources
Investigating radioactivity (40 min) Discuss the discovery of nuclear radiation, outlining the initial evidence and the efforts made to explain it. Show how the Geiger counter can be used to detect nuclear radiation, starting with a background count. Some sample rocks or salts can be used to show that natural substances are radioactive. Introduce the explanation of the source of the radiation – radioactive decay. Outline that there must be changes to the nucleus itself to produce these particles. Discuss some of the sources of background radiation, differentiating between natural sources and some man-made ones, particularly medical sources.	**Extend:** Discuss the operation of the counter, including the need for ionisation. **Support:** Introduce simple animations of the decay; these will be expanded on in future lessons. Provide a table of the sources of background radiation and relative importance.	**Activity:** Investigating radioactivity

Plenary	Support/Extend	Resources
Murder mystery (5 min) The body of a press photographer has been found in a sealed room, and all of the film in her camera has gone black even though it hasn't been used. Students explain what they think happened and how they know. **Comparing locations** (10 min) Interactive where students are provided with some data about the sources of background radiation in different locations in a pie chart. They use the pie chart to answer questions that compare the risks in each of the locations.	 **Extend:** Provide the data and ask students to draw their own pie chart. **Extend:** Provide extra information, including the actual values, and ask students to calculate percentages from the source information.	**Interactive:** Comparing locations

Homework		
Students should write a report on the work of one of the named scientists in this lesson. As an alternative, the students may research the occurrence of radioactive radon gas in the UK and find out whether there are any links to an increase in lung cancer.	**Support:** Provide some initial research links to websites.	

kerboodle

A Kerboodle highlight for this lesson is **Bump up your grade: Atoms and isotopes**. Refer to the **Content map** on Kerboodle for a full list of resources and assessment.

P7.2 The discovery of the nucleus

AQA spec Link: 4.1.3 New experimental evidence may lead to a scientific model being changed or replaced.

Before the discovery of the electron, atoms were thought to be tiny spheres that could not be divided.

The discovery of the electron led to the plum pudding model of the atom. The plum pudding model suggested that the atom is a ball of positive charge with negative electrons embedded in it.

The results from the alpha scattering experiment led to the conclusion that the mass of an atom was concentrated at the centre (nucleus) and that the nucleus was charged. This nuclear model replaced the plum pudding model.

Niels Bohr adapted the nuclear model by suggesting that electrons orbit the nucleus at specific distances. The theoretical calculations of Bohr agreed with experimental observation.

Later experiments led to the idea that the positive charge of any nucleus can be subdivided into a whole number of smaller particles, each particle having the same amount of positive charge. The name proton was given to these particles.

The experimental work of James Chadwick provided the evidence to show the existence of neutrons within the nucleus. This was about 20 years after the nucleus became an accepted scientific idea.

Students should be able to describe:

- why the new evidence from the scattering experiment led to a change in the atomic model
- the difference between the plum pudding model of the atom and the nuclear model of the atom.

Details of experimental work supporting the Bohr model are not required.

Details of Chadwick's experimental work are not required.

WS 1.1, 1.2, 4.1
MS 1b

Aiming for	Outcome	Checkpoint	
		Question	Activity
Aiming for GRADE 4 ↓	Identify the Rutherford (nuclear) model of an atom.	1	Main 1
	Identify the locations of protons, neutrons, and electrons in the nuclear model.	1	Main 1
	State that electrons can move between fixed energy levels within an atom.		Main 2, Plenary 1
Aiming for GRADE 6 ↓	Describe the plum pudding model of the atom.	3	Main 1
	Describe the evidence provided by the Rutherford scattering experiment.		Main 1
	Describe the properties of protons, neutrons, and electrons.	4	Main 1
Aiming for GRADE 8 ↓	Compare the plum pudding model, Rutherford model, and Bohr model of the atom in terms of the evidence for each model.	3	Main 2
	Explain how Rutherford and Marsden's experiment caused a rejection of the plum pudding model.	2	Main 1
	Describe how the initial evidence for the nuclear model was processed and how the model came to be accepted.	3	Main 1

Maths
Students discuss the size of an atom and that of a nucleus by using standard form (1b).

Literacy
Students discuss how a scientific model is accepted or becomes rejected as new evidence is discovered.

■ P7 Radioactivity

Starter	Support/Extend	Resources
What's in the tin? (5 min) Peel the label off a tin of sponge pudding. Show the unmarked tin to the students and ask them to describe ways they could find out what's inside without opening it. **Believe it or not?** (10 min) What does it take to change the students' minds about something? How much evidence would be needed to convince them that NASA has sent men to the Moon? Discuss how difficult it is to change people's strongly held beliefs, and point out that scientists also find it difficult to change ideas that they may have been working with for many years.	**Support:** Suggest some methods and discuss them (e.g., X-rays, ultrasound). **Support:** Provide a set of cards showing possible evidence and ask students to prioritise them (e.g., photographs, testimony, rock samples, and radio communications).	

Main	Support/Extend	Resources
The Rutherford model of the atom (25 min) Discuss the atomic model that students will have used in KS3 and ask them what evidence there is for it. Outline Rutherford's work and allow the students to discuss the idea of discovery by firing particles. Emphasise Rutherford's mathematical analysis of the Geiger and Marsden experiment that confirmed the model and how the model matched the behaviour observed during nuclear decay. Compare the Rutherford model briefly with the plum pudding model. **Further changes to the model of the atom** (15 min) Show the students the typical electron arrangement diagram used in Chemistry lessons, and discuss the nature of energy levels using the Bohr model. Ensure the students know that electrons can move between these levels when the electron's energy changes. Explain the need for a neutron as a component of most nuclei, and outline its discovery. The students should now know the key properties of all three sub-atomic particles.	**Support:** Animations and simulations can be very useful here. **Extend:** Students should discuss the relative size of an atom and a nucleus using standard form. They may also discuss the nature of the interaction – electric fields and forces. **Extend:** Discuss the need for specific amounts of energy for electrons to move between energy levels. The students should also explain why neutrons were initially difficult to detect.	**Activity:** The Rutherford model of the atom

Plenary	Support/Extend	Resources
Not like a solar system (5 min) The students should make a list of similarities and particularly differences between atomic models and solar systems. **I don't believe it** (10 min) Interactive where students choose the missing words to complete a paragraph summarising the evidence that led to the plum pudding model being replaced. Students then use this summary to write a letter to an unconvinced scientist who wants to hold on to the plum pudding model.		**Interactive:** I don't believe it

Homework		
Students finish writing their letter to an unconvinced scientist from Plenary 2 (or start their letter if Plenary 1 was chosen). They should also include the evidence provided by the work of Bohr and Chadwick in their letter.	**Support:** Differentiate by asking for different levels of detail for different students.	

kerboodle

A Kerboodle highlight for this lesson is **Working scientifically: Changing models of the atom.** Refer to the **Content map** on Kerboodle for a full list of resources and assessment.

P7.3 Changes in the nucleus

AQA spec Link: 4.1.2 In an atom the number of electrons is equal to the number of protons in the nucleus. Atoms have no overall electrical charge.

All atoms of a particular element have the same number of protons. The number of protons in an atom of an element is called its atomic number.

The total number of protons and neutrons in an atom is called its mass number.

Atoms can be represented as shown in this example:

$$^{23}_{11}\text{Na}$$
(Mass number) 23, (Atomic number) 11

Atoms of the same element can have different numbers of neutrons; these atoms are called isotopes of that element.

Atoms turn into positive ions if they lose one or more outer electron(s).

Students should be able to relate differences between isotopes to differences in conventional representations of their identities, charges, and masses.

4.2.2 Nuclear equations are used to represent radioactive decay.

In a nuclear equation an alpha particle may be represented by the symbol:

$$^{4}_{2}\text{He}$$

and a beta particle by the symbol:

$$^{0}_{-1}\text{e}$$

The emission of the different types of nuclear radiation may cause a change in the mass and/or the charge of the nucleus. For example:

$$^{219}_{86}\text{radon} \rightarrow ^{215}_{84}\text{polonium} + ^{4}_{2}\text{He}$$

So alpha decay causes both the mass and charge of the nucleus to decrease.

$$^{14}_{6}\text{carbon} \rightarrow ^{14}_{7}\text{nitrogen} + ^{0}_{-1}\text{e}$$

So beta decay does not cause the mass of the nucleus to change but does cause the charge of the nucleus to increase.

Students are not required to recall these two examples.

Students should be able to use the names and symbols of common nuclei and particles to write balanced equations that show single alpha (α) and beta (β) decay. This is limited to balancing the atomic numbers and mass numbers. The identification of daughter elements from such decays is not required.

The emission of a gamma ray does not cause the mass or the charge of the nucleus to change.

WS 1.2, 4.1
MS 3c

Aiming for	Outcome	Checkpoint Question	Activity
Aiming for GRADE 4 ↓	Identify the mass and atomic number by using nuclear notation.	1, 2, End of chapter 1	Main 1, Plenary 2
	Identify the type of decay taking place from a nuclear equation.		Main 2
	Describe how isotopes are atoms of the same element with different mass numbers.		Main 1
Aiming for GRADE 6 ↓	Calculate the number of neutrons in an isotope by using nuclear notation.	1, End of chapter 1	Main 1
	Describe the differences between isotopes.	1	Main 1
	Complete decay equations for alpha and beta decay.	2, 3	Main 2
Aiming for GRADE 8 ↓	Explain why particles are ejected from the nucleus during nuclear decay.		Main 2
	Describe the changes in the nucleus that occur during nuclear decay.		Main 2
	Write full decay equations, for example, nuclear decays.	4	Main 2

■ P7 Radioactivity

Maths
Students calculate changes in mass and atomic number in nuclear equations (3c).

Literacy
Students describe how a nucleus changes during decay.

Key words
atomic number, mass number, isotopes

Starter	Support/Extend	Resources
Fact or fiction (5 min) Give the students a set of 'facts' about radioactivity and atoms and let them use traffic light cards to indicate whether they agree (green), don't know (amber), or disagree (red).' **Chemical change** (10 min) Give the students a demonstration of a chemical reaction (magnesium + oxygen → magnesium oxide). Ask the students to describe what is happening in terms of particles and see if they understand basic conservation of particles in chemical reactions.	**Support:** Differentiate questions as appropriate. **Support:** Provide simple atom diagrams showing the process and ask students to describe the making or breaking of bonds. **Extend:** Require descriptions of energy changes.	

Main	Support/Extend	Resources
Nuclear notation (10 min) Show some examples of nuclear notation, ensuring the students can identify the atomic number (proton number) and mass number (nucleon number). Students should calculate the number of neutrons in some examples. Discuss isotopes, showing some in nuclear notation and noting the difference in mass numbers. **Alpha, beta, and gamma emission** (30 min) Describe an alpha decay and the changes it causes in a nucleus. The students should look at an example and then try to construct a few additional equations by using a periodic table. Move on to beta emission, focusing on the change of a neutron to a proton and how this affects the decay equation. Show a few examples and ask the students to complete a few more. Discuss gamma emission, pointing out that there is no change in the particle structure of the nucleus and so no decay equations are needed. Students then calculate changes in atomic number and mass number of an atom after it emits alpha and beta radiation.	**Support:** Students can construct atomic models from cut-out circles to match the notation. **Support:** A support sheet is available to help develop students understanding on alpha and beta radiation. **Extend:** An extension sheet is available where students write and interpret equations to represent nuclear reactions. **Extend:** The students can be made aware of the production of an anti-electron neutrino during beta emission.	**Activity:** Alpha, beta, and gamma emission **Support:** Nuclear decay equations **Extension:** Nuclear equations

Plenary	Support/Extend	Resources
Name that isotope (5 min) Students use the interactive to complete a table describing various isotopes. They need to fill in missing details such as element name, proton number, mass number, and number of electrons. **Definitions** (10 min) The students must give accurate definitions of the terms 'proton', 'neutron', 'electron', 'ion', 'mass number', 'atomic number', 'alpha particle', 'beta particle', and 'gamma ray'.	**Support:** Make this activity a simple phrase- or card-matching task.	**Interactive:** Name that isotope

Homework		
Students can each be given a particular isotope to research how it may be useful.		

kerboodle
A Kerboodle highlight for this lesson is **Maths skills: Nuclear reactions**. Refer to the **Content map** on Kerboodle for a full list of resources and assessment.

P7.4 More about alpha, beta, and gamma radiation

AQA spec Link: 4.2.1 The nuclear radiation emitted may be:
- an alpha particle (α) – this consists of two neutrons and two protons, it is the same as a helium nucleus
- a beta particle (β) – a high speed electron ejected from the nucleus as a neutron turns into a proton
- a gamma ray (γ) – electromagnetic radiation from the nucleus
- a neutron (n).

Required knowledge of the properties of alpha particles, beta particles, and gamma rays is limited to their penetration through materials, their range in air, and ionising power.

Students should be able to apply their knowledge to the uses of radiation and evaluate the best sources of radiation to use in a given situation.

4.2.4 Radioactive contamination is the unwanted presence of materials containing radioactive atoms on other materials. The hazard from contamination is due to the decay of the contaminating atoms. The type of radiation emitted affects the level of hazard.

Irradiation is the process of exposing an object to nuclear radiation. The irradiated object does not become radioactive.

Students should be able to compare the hazards associated with contamination and irradiation.

Suitable precautions must be taken to protect against any hazard that the radioactive source used in the process of irradiation may present.

Students should understand that it is important for the findings of studies into the effects of radiation on humans to be published and shared with other scientists so that the findings can be checked by peer review.

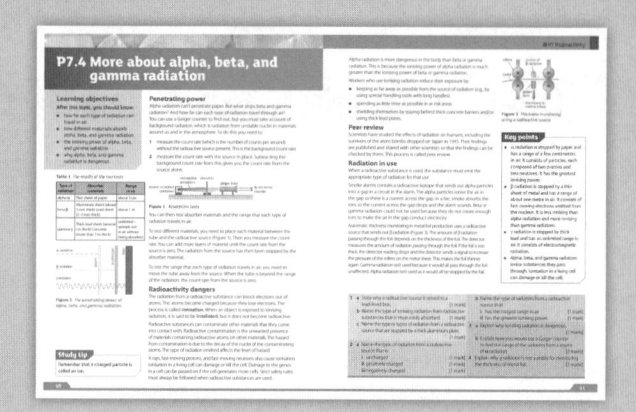

WS 1.4
MS 1c

Aiming for	Outcome	Checkpoint	
		Question	Activity
Aiming for GRADE 4	Rank the three types of nuclear radiation in order of their penetrating power.	1 End of chapter 2, 5	Main
	Rank the three types of nuclear radiation in order of their range through air.	1, End of chapter 2	Main
	State that all three types of nuclear radiation are ionising.	1	Main, Plenary 1
Aiming for GRADE 6	Describe how the penetrating powers of radiation can be measured.	4, End of chapter 5	Main
	Describe the path of radiation types through a magnetic field.	2, End of chapter 6	Main
	Describe the process of ionisation.	3	Main, Plenary 1, Plenary 2
Aiming for GRADE 8	Describe in detail how the thickness of a material being manufactured can be monitored by using a beta source.		Main
	Compare the ionisation caused by the different types of nuclear radiation.	3	Main, Plenary 2
	Evaluate in some detail the risks caused by alpha radiation inside and outside the human body.	1	Main, Plenary 1, Plenary 2

Maths
Students compare the distances through which the different types of nuclear radiation can travel in different materials.

Literacy
Students discuss the effects of radiation on living tissue.

Key words
ionisation, irradiated

90

■ P7 Radioactivity

Starter	Support/Extend	Resources
Too many symbols? (10 min) Scientists use a lot of symbols in their work. Students use the interactive to match some symbols they have met so far with what they represent (e.g., elements, equations, the names of things, etc.). Discuss the reasons that scientists use symbols. **X-ray flashback** (5 min) The students should explain why X-rays can be harmful and the precautions used to reduce exposure.	**Support:** Give some example symbols and ask students to say what they represent. **Extend:** Students should describe how X-rays are produced.	**Interactive:** Too many symbols?

Main	Support/Extend	Resources
Radiation in action (40 min) Describe how the penetrating power of radiation can be measured by using a Geiger counter. Discuss the safety measures that must be used when measuring radiation. Introduce the different penetrating powers of the three types of radiation – alpha, beta, and gamma. Students suggest how the penetrating power could be used to measure the thickness of a material and how this can be applied to controlling thickness. Students complete the Working scientifically sheet to examine the results from an investigation on beta radiation through cardboard and link it to the measurement and control of cardboard manufacture. Discuss the damage caused by ionisation and some of the precautions that can reduce exposure, emphasising that keeping the sources at a distance is one of the most effective methods. The concept of sharing data about radiation effects should be covered here.	**Support:** The students can fill in a partially completed flow chart showing how thickness is controlled. **Extend:** The deflection of charged particles by magnetic fields can be shown.	**Working scientifically:** Radiation in action

Plenary	Support/Extend	Resources
Local rules (10 min) The students should make a plan for a poster or booklet explaining how the radioactive sources should be stored and handled and explaining how these precautionary rules reduce harm. They can then produce this booklet as homework. **Protect and survive** (5 min) Ask students to suggest what would need to be done if one of the radioactive sources was dropped and lost.	**Support:** Show the students the rules and ask them to explain how each of the rules reduce risk or harm.	

Homework		
Ionising radiation can be detected by cloud and bubble chambers, spark detectors, and photographic films. The students could find out about these devices and why they are used.	**Support:** Each student is allocated one device to research and share their information in class.	

kerboodle

A Kerboodle highlight for this lesson is **Extension sheet: Radiation hunt!** Refer to the **Content map** on Kerboodle for a full list of resources and assessment.

P7.5 Activity and half-life

AQA spec Link: 4.2.1 Activity is the rate at which a source of unstable nuclei decays.

Activity is measured in becquerel (Bq).

Count-rate is the number of decays recorded each second by a detector (e.g., Geiger–Muller tube).

4.2.3 Radioactive decay is random.

The half-life of a radioactive isotope is the time it takes for the number of nuclei of the isotope in a sample to halve, or the time it takes for the count rate (or activity) from a sample containing the isotope to fall to half its initial level.

Students should be able to explain the concept of half-life and how it is related to the random nature of radioactive decay.

Students should be able to determine the half-life of a radioactive isotope from given information.

(H) Students should be able to calculate the net decline, expressed as a ratio, in a radioactive emission after a given number of half-lives.

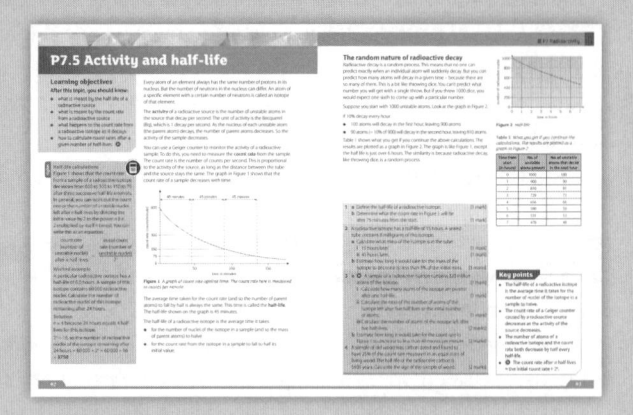

MS 1b, 1c, 3d, 4a

Aiming for	Outcome	Checkpoint	
		Question	Activity
Aiming for GRADE 4 ↓	State that the activity of a radioactive sample will fall over time.		Main 1
	Define half-life in simple terms such as 'the time it takes for half of the material to decay'.	1	Main 1
	Find the half-life of a substance from a graph of count rate (or nuclei remaining) against time with support.		Main 1
Aiming for GRADE 6 ↓	**(H)** Find the ratio of a sample remaining after a given number of half-lives.	2, 3, End of chapter 4	Main 2
	State that all atoms of a particular isotope have an identical chance to decay in a fixed time.		Main 1
	Plot a graph showing the decay of a sample and use it to determine half-life.	End of chapter 3	Main 1
Aiming for GRADE 8 ↓	Compare a physical model of decay with the decay of nuclei, noting the limitations of the model.		Starter 1, Starter 2, Main 1
	Outline how the age of organic material can be determined by using radioactive dating.	4, End of chapter 4	Main 2
	(H) Calculate the changes in count rate or nuclei remaining by using an exponential decay function.	2	Main 2

Maths
Students plot graphs of data and find half-life from them (1c, 4a). They also calculate changes in count rate by using exponential functions (1b, 3d).

Literacy
Students describe the random but predictable nature of decay.

Key words
activity, count rate, half-life

92

P7 Radioactivity

Practical

Title	A decay model
Equipment	set of 60 identical six-sided dice
Overview of method	The students roll the full set of dice, and after each roll, they remove the dice that landed showing one. They record the number of dice 'surviving' and then roll *only these dice*, and so on. They continue this process of elimination for 20 rolls or until no die survives. Plotting a graph of the number of dice remaining (y-axis) against roll number (x-axis) reveals that the dice behave like decaying atoms and a half-life can be calculated.
Safety considerations	Keep dice off the floor.

Starter	Support/Extend	Resources
An exponential decay puzzle (5 min) A farmer has a warehouse with two million corn cobs in it. Every day she sells exactly half of her remaining stock. How long before she has sold every last nugget (not cob) of corn? **An exponential growth puzzle** (10 min) A philosopher places a grain of rice on the first square of a chess board, two on the next, four on the next, and so on. How many go on the last (sixty-fourth) square?	**Support:** Use a calculator and just keep dividing by two to see how many steps this would take. **Support:** Limit the calculation to the first two rows and then show the graph to see what happens next.	
Main	**Support/Extend**	**Resources**
Activity and count rate (20 min) Recap decay and remind students that some sources seem more active than others. Discuss the concept of activity (decay rate) and then count rate. Students should then try the decay model with dice described in the practical, finding the half-life from a graph. **Half-life calculations** (20 min) 🄷 The students try some half-life calculations using the relationship shown. Discuss why the random behaviour of particles can be mathematically modelled whereas individual behaviour cannot. Outline radioactive dating briefly, linking to a decay curve graph.	**Extend:** The students should compare this model with the decay of nuclei, noting that the numbers of dice used is far smaller than the number of atoms in a typical sample. **Support:** Students can spend this time completing and analysing the graph from the practical. Decay simulations are useful here. Each student can try to guess which of the particles will survive to the end.	**Activity:** Activity and count rate **Extension:** Half-lives and radioactive decay
Plenary	**Support/Extend**	**Resources**
Activity and decay (5 min) Show the students a graph with three decay curves on it. Students use the interactive to put the three decay curves in order of longest half-life. **Coin toss** (10 min) If someone has 120 coins and tosses them all, removing all of the heads after each toss, how many tosses until there are only 15 left?	**Extend:** Students should find the half-lives of the three isotopes. **Extend:** Ask students to discuss why the real results can diverge from theoretical models.	**Interactive:** Activity and decay
Homework		
The students should find out how radioactive carbon dating works and report on one example of its use in dating an object.		

kerboodle

A Kerboodle highlight for this lesson is **Bump up your grade: Half life and the random nature of decay**. Refer to the **Content map** on Kerboodle for a full list of resources and assessment.

P7 Radioactivity

Overview of P7 Radioactivity

In this chapter the students have described how the structure of the nucleus was discovered by the radiation emitted during nuclear decay and how experimentation and developments in our understanding of sub-atomic particles have driven changes in the model used to describe the atom from the plum pudding model, through to the Rutherford model and then the Bohr model.

The students have described the changes in the nucleus which occur during alpha, beta, and gamma decay along with neutron emission in terms of atomic (proton) number and mass number using the appropriate nuclear notation for isotopes. The properties of alpha, beta, and gamma radiation have been demonstrated leading to a discussion of their use in thickness monitoring and then the safety measures required when using radioactive materials.

Students then moved on to discuss the concepts of activity, count rate, and the patterns in radioactive decay that explain half-life and the associated graphs despite the random nature of individual decays. Higher tier students have performed calculations involving the relationship between the initial activity, current activity, and half-life.

MyMaths

You can find additional support for the maths skills covered in this chapter on **MyMaths**, including making order of magnitude calculations, translating information between graphical and numeric form, visualising and representing 2D and 3D forms including two dimensional representations of 3D objects.

kerboodle

For this chapter, the following assessments are available on Kerboodle:

P7 Checkpoint quiz: Radioactivity
P7 Progress quiz: Radioactivity 1
P7 Progress quiz: Radioactivity 2
P7 On your marks: Radioactivity
P7 Exam-style questions and mark scheme: Radioactivity

Checkpoint follow up lesson

A student's route through this lesson can be determined using the Checkpoint assessment. Percentage pass marks are supplied in the Checkpoint teacher notes.

For each successive route through it is assumed that the student can perform to their current route as well as previous routes. For example, students working at Aiming for 6 are assumed to be secure in Aiming for 4 knowledge and understanding and working towards achieving all the learning outcomes for Aiming for 6.

	Aiming for 4	**Aiming for 6**	**Aiming for 8**
Learning outcomes	Describe the structure of the nucleus, how we show what is in a nucleus. The Thomson, Rutherford and Bohr models of the atom, and evidence that led to the model changing.	Describe the Thomson, Rutherford and Bohr models of the atom, the structure of the nucleus and evidence that led to the model changing.	Explain how and why the model of the atom has changed over time.
	Describe what alpha, beta, and gamma radiation is, and their different properties.	Describe what alpha, beta, and gamma radiation are, and their different properties and how to balance equations for nuclear decay.	Use ideas about radiation to balance nuclear equations.
	State what is meant by half-life.	Use ideas about half-life to solve problems.	Use a graph to determine half-life, calculate net decline, and solve problems involving half-life.
Starter	**Radioactive tennis (5 min)** Put students in groups of three. Two students take it in turns to say words relating to radioactivity and they keep going until one person can't go. The third student notes down the words. These are then fed back as a whole class. The words just need to be related to the topic not to each other (as in word association). Leave the words as a list for use in the plenary.		
Differentiated checkpoint activity	Aiming for 4 students use the Checkpoint follow-up sheet to complete one of two activities: • design a matching game to summarise alpha, beta, and gamma radiation • model half-life and radioactive decay using sweets. The follow-up sheet is highly structured and students should work in pairs with teacher support. If the lesson is conducted in a laboratory, marbles or other small objects should be used instead of sweets, or students should be told not to eat the sweets.	Aiming for 6 students use the Checkpoint follow-up sheet to complete one of two activities: • design a cartoon to explain the principles of radioactive decay • model half-life and radioactive decay using sweets. The follow-up sheet provides limited support and students should aim to work independently. If the lesson is conducted in a laboratory, marbles or other small objects should be used instead of sweets, or students should be told not to eat the sweets.	Aiming for 8 students use the Checkpoint follow-up sheet to complete one of two activities: • design a cartoon to explain the principles of radioactive decay • model half-life and radioactive decay using sweets. The follow-up sheet provides minimal support and students should work independently. If the lesson is conducted in a laboratory, marbles or other small objects should be used instead of sweets, or students should be told not to eat the sweets.
	Kerboodle resource P7 Checkpoint follow up: Aiming for 4; P7 Checkpoint follow up: Aiming for 6; P7 Checkpoint follow up: Aiming for 8		
Plenary	**Radioactivity mind map (5 minutes)** Display the words from the tennis starter. Give out a large sheet of paper to each group and ask them to put all the words on a mind map. Each student could be responsible for a separate section of the map (model of the atom, α, β, γ, nuclear medicine, fission/fusion, half-life) and then they can discuss the links between them. **What's the question? (10 minutes)** Give students A4 dry wipe boards, pens and an eraser. Ask or display a series of answers, such as: 'because most of the alpha particles went through but some of them came back', and ask them to write the question. Alternatively give out a list of answers that are tailored to the different levels at which students are aiming.		
Progression	Students should be able to describe the model of the atom that we use now, give some evidence for how the model of the atom has changed, and describe the radiation emitted by unstable isotopes. They should be able state what is meant by half-life.	Students should be able to give an account of the history of the model of the atom and describe evidence that led to the discovery of the nucleus, use nuclear equations to account for the emission of radiation from nuclei. They should be able to do calculations involving half-life.	Students should be able to account for changes to the model of the atom, balance nuclear equations and use ideas about half-life, types of radiation emitted and the effect on tissue to explain the choice of isotopes in nuclear medicine. They should be able to calculate the net decline in activity of an isotope, and do calculations using half-life in a range of situations.

3 Forces in action

Specification links

AQA specification section	Assessment paper
5.1 Forces and their interactions	Paper 2
5.2 Work done and energy transfer	Paper 2
5.3 Forces and elasticity	Paper 2
5.6 Forces and motion	Paper 2
5.7 Momentum	Paper 2

Required practicals

AQA required practicals	Practical skills	Topic
Investigate the relationship between force and extension for a spring.	AT1 – use appropriate apparatus to make and record length accurately. AT2 – use appropriate apparatus to measure and observe the effect of force on the extension of springs and collect the data required to plot a force–extension graph.	P10.5
Investigate the effect of varying the force on the acceleration of an object of constant mass, and the effect of varying the mass of an object on the acceleration produced by a constant force.	AT1 – use appropriate apparatus to make and record measurements of length, mass, and time accurately. AT2 – use appropriate apparatus to measure and observe the effects of forces. AT3 – use appropriate apparatus and techniques for measuring motion, including determination of speed and rate of change of speed (acceleration/deceleration).	P10.1

Maths skills

AQA maths skills	Topic
1a Recognise and use expressions in decimal form	P8.1, P8.2, P8.6, P9.1, P10.1, P10.2, P10.3, P10.4
1b Recognise and use expressions in standard form	P9.1
1c Use ratios, fractions, and percentages	P9.1
1d Make estimates of the results of simple calculations	P9.1
2a Use an appropriate number of significant figures	P8.1, P8.2, P8.6, P10.3, P10.4
2b Find arithmetic means	P10.3
2c Construct and interpret frequency tables and diagrams, bar charts, and histograms.	P10.2, P10.3
2f Understand the terms mean, mode, and median	P9.1, P10.3
2g Use a scatter diagram to identify a correlation between two variables.	P10.2
2h Make order of magnitude calculations	P8.1, P10.3
3a Understand and use the symbols: $=, <, \ll, \gg, >, \propto, \sim$	P8.1, P8.5, P9.1, P10.1, P10.2, P10.3, P10.4
3b Change the subject of an equation	P8.5, P9.1, P9.2, P9.3, P9.4, P10.1, P10.2, P10.3, P10.4, P10.5
3c Substitute numerical values into algebraic equations using appropriate units for physical quantities	P8.5, P8.6, P9.1, P9.2, P9.3, P9.4, P10.1, P10.2, P10.3, P10.4, P10.5
3d Solve simple algebraic equations	P8.5, P8.6, P9.2, P10.1, P10.2, P10.3, P10.4
4a Translate information between graphical and numeric form	P9.1, P9.2, P9.3, P9.4, P10.1
4b Understand that $y = mx + c$ represents a linear relationship	P9.1, P9.2, P9.3, P9.4
4c Plot two variables from experimental or other data	P9.2, P9.3, P9.4, P10.2
4d Determine the slope and intercept of a linear graph	P9.1, P9.2, P9.3, P9.4
4f Understand the physical significance of area between a curve and the x-axis and measure it by counting squares as appropriate	P9.2, P9.3, P9.4

P3 Forces in action

AQA maths skills	Topic
5a Use angular measures in degrees	P8.5
5b Visualise and represent 2D and 3D forms including two dimensional representations of 3D objects	P8.1, P8.5, P8.6

KS3 concept	GCSE topic	Checkpoint	Revision
Force is measured in newtons (N) using a newton-meter.	P8.2 Forces between objects	Ask students to describe how they would measure the force need to lift a chair.	Students can label a range of simple force diagrams using force arrows and approximate values for the forces.
An object is in equilibrium because the forces acting on it are balanced.	P8.3 Resultant forces	Ask students to draw a force diagram showing the forces acting on a car travelling at a constant speed.	Students can determine which objects are in equilibrium by analysing a set of diagrams of objects with a range of forces acting on them.
Speed is measured in metres per second.	P9.1 Speed and distance–time graphs	Ask students to estimate the speed that you walk around the classroom.	Students should use the speed equation to calculate the speed of some common objects in metres per second.
An object is accelerating if its speed is increasing.	P9.2 Velocity and acceleration	Ask the students to describe the motion of a drag car through the whole race.	Students label the speed–time graph of motion for a drag race noting acceleration and deceleration.
When objects interact, each one exerts a force on the other one.	P8.2 Forces between objects	Ask students to draw a force diagram for a ball falling directly downwards and a second force diagram showing what happens at the moment of impact.	Students should draw diagrams which match up pairs of forces such as the forces between an object and the Earth, a pair of magnets or a ship floating.
The force in a stretched object is called tension and it increases if the object is stretched more.	P10.8 Forces and elasticity	Ask students to describe the forces acting when a catapult is stretched.	Students plot a force–extension graph for a stretching spring and describe the relationship between these variables.
Assess risk in an experiment.	P10.8 Forces and elasticity	Ask students to preform a risk assessment for the spring constant investigation.	The students should assess each other's risk assessments after the experiment and determine which was the most suitable.
The pressure in a liquid acts in all directions.	P11.2 Pressure in a liquid at rest	Ask students to explain why a balloon full of water is stretched in all directions.	Place some tape over parts of a water filled balloon and pin-prick some small holes. Students discuss why the water is forced out and why the flow gradually decreases.

P 8 Forces in balance
8.1 Vectors and scalars

AQA spec Link: 5.1.1 Scalar quantities have magnitude only.

Vector quantities have magnitude and an associated direction.

A vector quantity may be represented by an arrow. The length of the arrow represents the magnitude, and the direction of the arrow the direction of the vector quantity.

5.1.2 Force is a vector quantity.

MS 1a, 2a

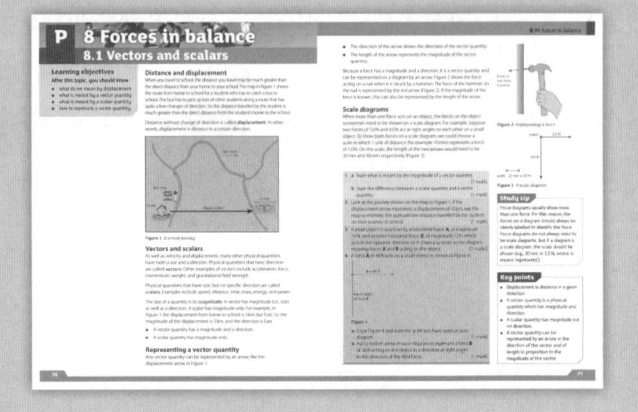

Aiming for	Outcome	Checkpoint	
		Question	Activity
Aiming for GRADE 4 ↓	Describe how scalars have size (magnitude) without direction.	1	Starter 1, Main 1
	Describe how vectors have both size (magnitude) and direction.	1	Main 1
	List some common scalars and vectors.		Main 1
Aiming for GRADE 6 ↓	Draw a scale diagram to represent a single vector.	3, 4	Main 2
	Categorise a wide range of quantities as either a vector or a scalar.		Main 1
	Compare a scalar and a similar vector and explain how these quantities are different.		Starter 2, Main 1
Aiming for GRADE 8 ↓	Interpret a scale diagram to determine the magnitude and direction of a vector.	2	Main 1, Main 2
	Translate between vector descriptions and vector diagrams and vice versa using a range of appropriate scales.	3, 4	Main 2
	Use a scale diagram to add two or more vectors.	4	Main 2, Plenary 2

Maths
Students will add and subtract both vector and scalar quantities including the use of SI prefixes.

Literacy
Students should translate between vector diagrams and accurate descriptions of the vectors shown and vice versa.

Key words
vectors, scalar, magnitude, displacement

Practical

Title	Measuring instruments
Equipment	wide range of measuring instruments such as: rulers, tape measures, trundle wheel, callipers, ammeter, voltmeter, resistance meter, force meter, top-pan balance, scales, measuring cylinder, thermometer, stopwatch, compass, light meter, joule meter, protractor
Overview of method	The students examine and discuss the instruments and how they are used. They note the type of measurements which can be made, including the appropriate units for this measurement. Students can also discuss how the instruments can be used in combination to measure quantities such as speed (a stopwatch and tape measure) which leads on to the idea of velocity (stopwatch, tape measure and compass or protractor).

■ P8 Forces in balance

Starter	Support/Extend	Resources
Measuring instruments (5 min) Students examine a range of measuring instruments and discuss their operation. **As the crow** (10 min) Interactive where students measure the direct distance between two places on a map. They then compare their value to the distance given from an Internet mapping service, choosing reasons for why there is a discrepancy.	**Extend:** Discuss the importance of measurement in physics and the fundamental quantities of length, mass, and time. **Extend:** Extend this discussion into much longer journeys, for example, How far away is Sydney? Should we measure in a straight line through the Earth?	

Main	Support/Extend	Resources
The difference between a vector and scalar quantity (15 min) Discuss the similarities and differences between a distance and a displacement. Use plenty of examples such as those in the Starter 2 and the student book. Ensure that the students understand the concepts of magnitude (size) and direction. Link back to the ideas in the first starter and discuss the quantities that the instruments measure in more depth. Discuss whether these quantities are scalar or vector in nature. Can some of the instruments be used to measure both? For example, a measuring cylinder will only measure volume (always scalar) whilst a ruler may be used with a protractor to measure displacement. **Representing vectors** (25 min) Introduce the idea of a scale diagram to discuss how vectors can be represented. Start with further examples of displacements before introducing forces. Students should attempt to draw several scaled vector diagrams from descriptive sentences (e.g., a force of 500 N acting to the left or a force of 3.2 N at an angle of 30 degrees to the horizontal). In addition, they should write a description of a vector by interpreting a diagram. Students can use the activity sheet to examine the relationship between displacement and distance in detail.	**Extend:** Ask the students to categorise all of the measurements they think can be made with the measuring instruments. Discuss the degree of measurement uncertainty associated with each measuring instrument. **Support:** Using squared paper will make drawing scale diagrams simpler. **Extend:** Students should use a scale diagram to represent a pair of vectors at right angles and then find the resultant. They should also use SI prefixes in their diagrams as appropriate.	**Activity:** Scalars and vectors

Plenary	Support/Extend	Resources
Vectors and scalars (5 min) Students complete the interactive where they choose the correct words to complete a summary of the key points from the lesson. **The shortest journey** (10 min) Use a local map and select six different locations. Ask the students to find the shortest journey that allows them to visit all six. They should estimate the total distance travelled, for example, using string and the appropriate scale.	**Extend:** Students should explain if any of these measurements are vector or scalar in nature. Are all of the properties *measureable* scientifically? **Support:** Limit the number of locations to five and provide a clear starting and end point. **Extend:** The students must select the best starting and end points to produce the shortest travel distance.	**Interactive:** Vectors and scalars

Homework		
Students should be asked to draw a range of scale diagrams showing vectors based on the description provided. For example, the forces acting on a moving car or directions on a map.	**Support:** Provide partial diagrams for the students to draw the vectors on. **Extend:** Students should also find the resultant of several vectors using diagrams.	

kerboodle

A Kerboodle highlight for this lesson is **Literacy sheet: Scalars and vectors**. Refer to the **Content map** on Kerboodle for a full list of resources and assessment.

P8.2 Forces between objects

AQA spec Link: 5.1.2 A force is a push or pull that acts on an object due to the interaction with another object. All forces between objects are either:

- contact forces – the objects are physically touching
- non-contact forces – the objects are physically separated.

Examples of contact forces include friction, air resistance, tension, and normal contact force.

Examples of non-contact forces are gravitational force, electrostatic force, and magnetic force.

Force is a vector quantity.

Students should be able to describe the interaction between pairs of objects which produce a force on each object. The forces should be represented as vectors.

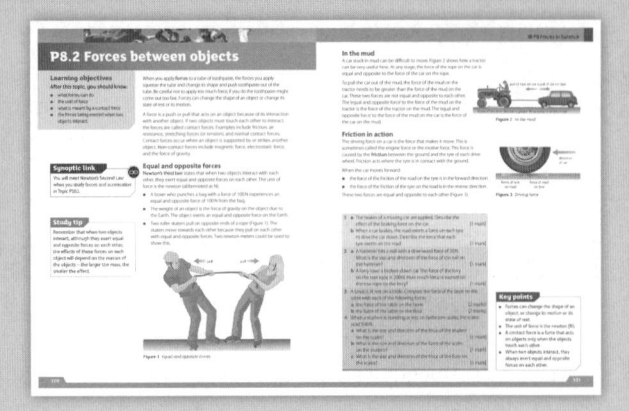

MS 1a, 2a

Aiming for	Outcome	Checkpoint	
		Question	Activity
Aiming for GRADE 4 ↓	Use arrows to represent the directions of forces.		Starter 2
	Give examples of contact and non-contact forces.	3	Starter 1
	Compare the sizes of forces using the unit newton (N).	2, 4	Plenary 1
Aiming for GRADE 6 ↓	Use scale diagrams to represent the sizes of forces acting on an object.		Starter 1, Main 1
	Describe the action of pairs of forces in a limited range of scenarios.	1, 2	
	Investigate the effect of different lubricants on the size of frictional forces.		Main 2
Aiming for GRADE 8 ↓	Use appropriate SI prefixes and standard form to describe a wide range of forces.		Plenary 1
	Explain the pairs of forces acting in a wide range of unfamiliar scenarios, including the nature (contact or non-contact), direction, and magnitude of the forces.	3	Main 2
	Evaluate force measurement techniques in terms of precision and accuracy.		Main 2

Maths
Students compare the size of forces that include SI multipliers.

Literacy
Students describe the action of forces, referring clearly to the objects.

Key words
force, friction, Newton's third law

P8 Forces in balance

Starter	Support/Extend	Resources
It's a drag (5 min) Show a video of a drag racer deploying a parachute to assist in braking. Ask the students to explain how the parachute helps to slow the car down. Try and draw out the key concepts of forces and friction. **Force diagrams** (10 min) Show a set of diagrams of objects and statements about their motion – standing still, at constant velocity or accelerating and ask the students to mark on all of the forces. Check that the students are using 'force arrows' and that they are marked clearly onto the point at which the force acts.	**Extend:** Show the start of the race, especially if a rocket booster is being used, and ask the students to discuss the forces acting during this part of the motion. **Extend:** Expect the students to compare the size of the forces by drawing scale diagrams.	

Main	Support/Extend	Resources
The nature of forces (15 min) Demonstrate the action of some forces by pushing and pulling some objects to show that there can be different sizes and that the direction of the force is significant. This will establish that forces are vector quantities. Students can drag a few items using a newton-meter to experience different sizes of forces. **Forces between objects** (25 min) Students read a passage on high diving describing the heights, times, and the potential risks involved. They use this passage to identify contact and non-contact forces, action and reaction pairs, and to explain changes in motion due to the action of forces.	**Support:** Students can visualise forces by attaching cardboard 'force arrows' to objects showing weight and reactions.	**Activity:** Forces between objects

Plenary	Support/Extend	Resources
Pulling power (5 min) Provide students with ten (or more) force strengths of players (50 N, 100 N, 150 N, 200 N, 250 N, 300 N, 350 N, 400 N, 450 N, 500 N). Students assign them to two tug-of-war teams so that the teams are balanced. There may be several solutions. **Forces between objects** (10 min) Students use the interactive to sort examples of contact and non-contact forces. They then identify the action and reaction pairs in the given scenario of a car driving at a constant speed.	**Support:** Start with only a small set of forces which can be balanced by placing three on each side. **Extend:** Use SI prefixes and/or standard form for some of the forces. **Support:** Limit the forces to simple examples. **Extend:** Use SI prefixes and/or standard form for some of the forces.	**Interactive:** Forces between objects

Homework		
Students analyse the forces acting in a scenario of their choice such as a particular sport or an engineering project. They should include ideas about the size and directions of the forces.	**Support:** Limit the scenarios appropriately. **Extend:** Students should produce a force diagram of a complex scenario such as the forces acting on a bridge with traffic travelling across it.	

kerboodle

A Kerboodle highlight for this lesson is **Go further: The effects of nuclear forces**. Refer to the **Content map** on Kerboodle for a full list of resources and assessment.

P8.3 Resultant forces

AQA spec Link: 5.1.1 A vector quantity may be represented by an arrow. The length of the arrow represents the magnitude, and the direction of the arrow the direction of the vector quantity.

5.1.2 Force is a vector quantity.

5.1.4 A number of forces acting on an object may be replaced by a single force that has the same effect as all the original forces acting together. This single force is called the resultant force.

Students should be able to calculate the resultant of two forces that act in a straight line.

H Students should be able to:
- describe examples of the forces acting on an isolated object or system
- use free body diagrams to describe qualitatively examples where several forces lead to a resultant force on an object, including balanced forces when the resultant force is zero.

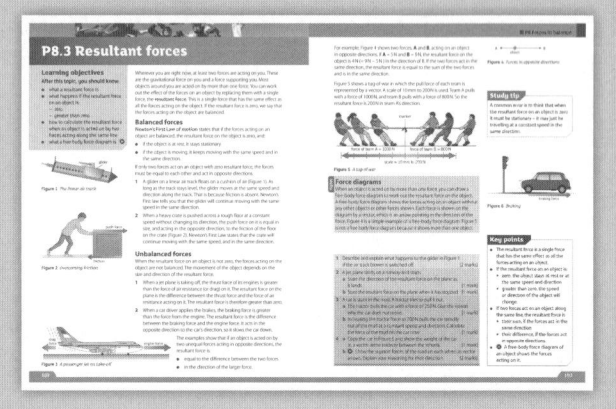

WS 1.2

Aiming for	Outcome	Checkpoint	
		Question	Activity
Aiming for GRADE 4	Label a diagram showing several forces acting on an object.		Starter 2
	Calculate a resultant force from two parallel forces acting in opposite directions.		Starter 1
	State that a non-zero resultant force will cause a change in motion and a zero resultant force will not (Newton's First Law of motion).	2	Starter 2
Aiming for GRADE 6	Draw a scaled diagram of the forces acting in a range of situations using arrows to represent the forces.	4	Main 1
	H Calculate resultant force produced by several forces acting on an object in coplanar directions.	3	Main 2
	Describe the effect of zero and non-zero resultant forces on the motion of moving and stationary objects.	1, 2	Main 1
Aiming for GRADE 8	**H** Draw a scaled free-body force diagram showing forces as vectors and find the resultant force vector.	4	Main 2
	H Calculate resultant forces from several forces acting in coplanar directions using a range of SI prefixes.		Main 2
	Create a detailed plan to investigate the factors that affect the acceleration of objects acted on by a non-zero resultant force.		Main 1

Maths
Students perform simple vector addition on coplanar vectors. These may be represented by positive and negative numbers.

Literacy
Students focus on the terminology for forces and the description of their effects.

Key words
resultant force, Newton's First Law of Motion

■ P8 Forces in balance

Starter	Support/Extend	Resources
Vector addition (5 min) Develop students' mathematical skills using addition sums that include negative numbers to check their understanding. Link this to the idea that forces are added together but ones in opposite directions are treated as negative. **Balanced forces** (10 min) Show the students a toy boat floating on water and ask them to draw a diagram of all of the forces on the boat. Add small masses, one at a time, until the boat sinks. Ask them to draw a diagram showing the forces at the time when the boat was sinking.	**Support:** Use force arrows lying in the same direction to show addition, and in the opposite direction to show subtraction. **Extend:** Ask the students why the upward thrust of the water increases as the load does.	

Main	Support/Extend	Resources
Resultant forces and their effects (25 min) Discuss with students how an object with zero resultant force will be either moving at a constant velocity or stationary. Focus on an object moving at a constant velocity, using the example of an aircraft cruising to demonstrate. Then show a video of a jet aircraft taking off and discuss the forces involved – the sound of the engines will give an indication of increasing and decreasing thrust. Emphasise the concept that unbalanced forces cause *acceleration*, which can be a change in speed or direction of motion. Students then complete the activity sheet where they apply their knowledge and understanding of zero and non-zero resultant (balanced and unbalanced) forces on three different objects – a motorbike, an aircraft, and a runner – and carry out calculations of resultant forces from forces applied on different objects. **Free-body force diagrams** (15 min) **H** The activity sheet also gives higher-tier students the opportunity to gain confidence in interpreting free-body diagrams and in describing the effects of force on different objects. They need to focus on individual objects and the forces acting on them when drawing free-body diagrams. Sketch some additional ones at this point, such as the forces acting on a boat resting on the ocean surface or a sprinter leaving the starting blocks. Two versions of each diagram can be drawn – one with all of the forces and one with just the resultant. Emphasise the term *vector* as opposed to *arrow* when describing the forces.	**Extend:** Students should be able to describe the forces acting in all of these situations using vector diagrams. **Support:** Pause at key moments and draw force arrows onto the still frame. Ask the students to describe what will happen to the motion at these key points. **Extend:** An extension sheet is available for further practice in drawing free-body diagrams.	**Activity:** Resultant forces and their effects **Extension:** Free-body diagrams

Plenary	Support/Extend	Resources
Resultant forces (10 min) Interactive where students identify true and false statements about the forces acting on a cyclist. **H** They then identify the correct free-body diagram for a submarine moving forward and descending. **An uphill struggle** (10 min) Challenge students to come up with some explanations about forces and link the ideas to energy transfer. For example, why is it harder to push a car uphill rather than on a flat road?	**Extend:** Students suggest how to correct the false statements. **Extend:** Calculations of work done (studied in KS3) can allow the students to find changes in the energy stores.	**Interactive:** Resultant forces

Homework		
Students can find the resultant forces in a range of situations both from prose questions and from simple diagrams. They should describe the effect of the forces on the motion of objects.	**Extend:** Use examples that involve a wide range of forces with SI prefixes.	

kerboodle

A Kerboodle highlight for this lesson is **Bump up your grade teacher: What is the resultant force?** Refer to the **Content map** on Kerboodle for a full list of resources and assessment.

P8.4 Centre of mass

AQA spec Link: 5.1.3 The weight of an object may be considered to act at a single point referred to as the object's 'centre of mass'.

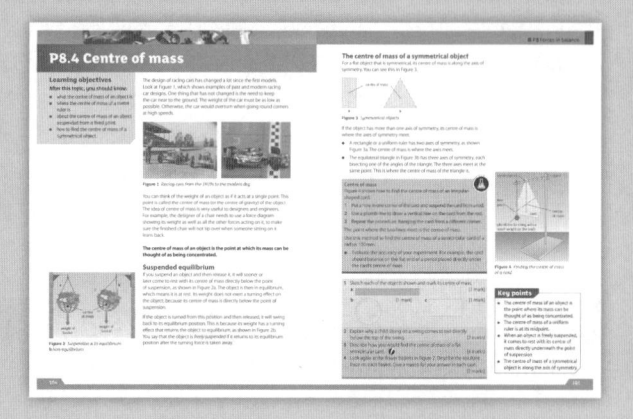

Aiming for	Outcome	Checkpoint	
		Question	Activity
Aiming for GRADE 4 ↓	Identify the approximate centre of mass of a range of simple shapes.		Main
	State that a suspended object will come to rest so that the centre of mass lies below the point of suspension.	1	Main
	Use lines of symmetry to identify the location of the centre of mass.	1	Main
Aiming for GRADE 6 ↓	Describe an experimental technique to determine the centre of mass of an object.	3	Main
	Explain why a suspended object comes to rest with the centre of mass directly below the point of suspension in terms of balanced forces.	2, 4	Main
	Compare the stability of objects to the position of their centre of mass.		Main
Aiming for GRADE 8 ↓	Evaluate an experimental technique to determine the centre of mass of an object, identifying the likely sources of error leading to inaccuracy.		Main
	Apply understanding of the particle model and moments to explain why objects have a point at which the mass seems to act.		Main
	Plan a detailed investigation into the stability of three-dimensional objects.		Homework

Maths
Students should apply the concept of symmetry when finding the centre of mass of regular objects.

Literacy
Students should describe why objects will rest with the centre of mass below the point of suspension.

Practical

Title	Centre of mass
Equipment	retort stands, bosses and clamps, string and pendulum bobs (plumb lines), corks, long pins, card, and scissors
Overview of method	Students cut out a range of shapes from the cards — rectangles, triangles, and irregular shapes. Hold the cork in the clamp, so that the pins can be pushed through the card into it. Wrap the plumb line around the pin and push it through a point near the edge of the card into the cork. Students gently press the line against the card (squeezing from both sides) and mark a point near the bottom of the shape. They then remove the card and draw a line from the mark to the pinhole.
Safety considerations	Protect feet, furniture, and the floor, from falling objects.

■ P8 Forces in balance

Starter	Support/Extend	Resources
Force diagrams (10 min) Students label the forces on a car moving at a steady speed along a horizontal road. Discuss why the students have drawn the weight where they have. Does their force arrow show the force coming from the bottom of the car or the middle? Show that the arrows should be coming from the centre of the car, and explain that the lesson will deal with what this centre is. **Fearful symmetry** (5 min) Give students a set of shapes (rectangle, square, equilateral triangle, isosceles triangle, circle) and ask them to draw on the shapes the lines of symmetry. Discuss whether the point at which these lines cross is the centre.	**Support:** To reduce the complexity, the car can be stationary. **Extend:** Expand the discussion to include the parts of the car – why is only one arrow for the weight used when each individual part has a weight? **Extend:** Ask the students to discuss how to balance the flat shapes. Do not provide any clues about symmetry and centres.	

Main	Support/Extend	Resources
Centre of mass (40 min) Discuss the concept of the 'middle' of objects in terms of where the mass of an object seems to be. This is a simplification of all of the individual masses of the particles within the object. Demonstrate suspending some objects to show that they align themselves in particular ways and that there is a point that is always directly below the suspension point. Secure a clamp to a desk, and students suspend the objects from the stand using string. Suspend the same object from several different points to show roughly where the centre of mass is. Show the students, or allow them to find, the position of the centre of mass of symmetrical objects by drawing the lines of symmetry and lifting the objects at this point. Students then test various objects to find their centre of mass. Start with simple geometric shapes to confirm that the centre of mass is where they expect, and then move on to irregular shapes.	**Extend:** Discuss the nature of a centre of mass as result of the individual particles within an object. **Extend:** Students use some objects for which the centre of mass is actually outside the physical object. Emphasise that this point will always be directly below a suspension point when the object hangs freely. **Support:** Provide cards with holes pre-cut and lines already drawn on them. **Extend:** Students describe the types of error that lead to inaccuracy in the experiment.	**Practical:** Centre of mass

Plenary	Support/Extend	Resources
Centre of mass (10 min) Interactive where students decide where the centre of mass is in a series of images, and then decide which item will topple over. **Topple** (10 min) Students draw a table, listing some objects designed to topple over and some objects designed to be stable. They sketch these shapes and try to describe where the centre of mass is in each of them.	**Extend:** Use complex shapes with portions cut out. **Support:** Look at simple shapes such as bowling pins. **Extend:** Looking at chairs, tables, and non-symmetrical objects.	**Interactive:** Centre of mass

Homework		
Students complete the WebQuest to research stability, the centre of mass, equilibrium, and when objects topple. They use their research to produce a presentation on two or three examples of objects/situations where stability is important.	**Extend:** Students should provide a qualitative measurement which indicates stability for the objects.	**WebQuest:** Stability

105

Higher tier

P8.5 The parallelogram of forces

AQA spec Link: 5.1.4 Students should be able to:
- use free-body diagrams to describe qualitatively examples where several forces lead to a resultant force on an object, including balanced forces when the resultant force is zero.

A single force can be resolved into two components acting at right angles to each other. The two component forces together have the same effect as the single force.

WS 1.2
MS 5a, 5b

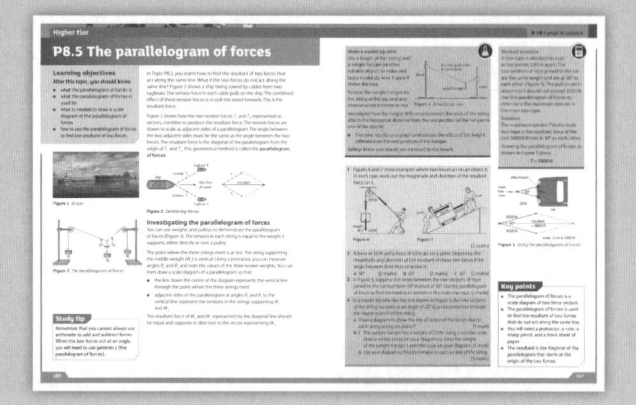

Aiming for	Outcome	Checkpoint	
		Question	Activity
Aiming for GRADE 6	Find the resultant of two forces at an acute angle by drawing a scale diagram.	1, 2, 4	Main
	Describe a system in equilibrium in which non-parallel forces are acting.		Main
	Calculate the component of a force using scale diagrams and ratios.		Main
Aiming for GRADE 8	Find the resultant of two forces at an obtuse angle by drawing a scale diagram.	End of chapter 5	Main
	Investigate non-parallel forces acting on a system in equilibrium to verify the parallelogram of forces.		Main
	Analyse a wide range systems of non-parallel forces using a parallelogram technique.	End of chapter 5	Plenary 2, Main, Homework

Maths
The students use scale diagrams to find the resultants of forces. Some may also use trigonometric and geometric approaches to find the resultant forces (5a, 5b).

Literacy
Ensure accurate descriptions of the forces with clear references to direction and magnitude.

Key words
parallelogram of forces

Practical

Title	Making a model zip wire
Equipment	two retort stands with bosses, string, mass holder and masses, protractors, ruler, two G-clamps
Overview of method	Tie the string securely between the retort stands. One side of the string should be lower than the other. Hang the mass onto the top end of the string and release. Observe where it comes to rest. Investigate how the height difference between the ends of the string affects the horizontal distance from the rest position of the hanger to one of the stands.
Safety considerations	The retort stands can be clamped to the desk for additional stability.

■ P8 Forces in balance

Starter	Support/Extend	Resources
Resultant recap (5 min) Provide the students with a few resultant force questions to refresh their understanding of adding forces. Move on to a final question where the two forces are perpendicular (e.g., 4 N at right angles to 3 N) and ask how they would find a resultant in this case. **Shape up** (5 min) Provide written descriptions of some shapes and ask the students to draw them using a ruler and protractor. The final shape should be a parallelogram.	**Support:** Use the force arrows technique to model forces. **Extend:** The final question can be solved using trigonometry (Pythagoras' theory). **Support:** Simpler shapes can be described.	

Main	Support/Extend	Resources
Parallelogram of forces (40 min) Recap on the idea that forces are vectors – they have magnitude and direction – by working through a few examples of parallel forces such as the tug of war. The students place a pair of force arrows head to tail so that the second arrow is at an angle to the first. They find the resultant of the two arrows using the metre rule (and the protractor if required). Students then investigate the parallelogram of forces using a zip wire. Ask student to draw force diagrams for their experiment and discuss the changes in the sizes of these forces for differences in height between the ends of the wire.	**Extend:** This activity can be extended by examining the resultant of forces at obtuse angles. **Support:** Each mass can be assumed to represent 1 N and be drawn to a scale of 1 cm to simplify the diagrams.	**Practical:** Parallelogram of forces

Plenary	Support/Extend	Resources
Finding the resultant force (10 min) Interactive where students order instructions for finding the resultant of two forces. **Force chain** (10 min) Two students call out forces with directions, and the teacher (or nominated student) must find the resultant by drawing a scale diagram on the board. After this, another force is added onto the end, and the new resultant is found. Continue until time runs out. Restart if the resultant goes off the board.	**Extend:** Challenge the students to draw scale diagrams at the same time and find the resultant.	**Interactive:** Finding the resultant force

Homework		
Use additional questions involving finding resultants of a set of forces. This may include the use of graph paper to find components of vectors drawn on the paper and the drawing of resultant vectors from descriptions of their components.	**Support:** Limit the analysis to a single vector at a time. **Extend:** Students should find the perpendicular components of a set of forces, add them, and then find the overall resultant.	

kerboodle
A Kerboodle highlight for this lesson is **Extension sheet: Force vector diagrams**. Refer to the **Content map** on Kerboodle for a full list of resources and assessment.

Higher tier

P8.6 Resolution of forces

AQA spec Link: 5.1.4 Students should be able to:
- use free-body diagrams to describe qualitatively examples where several forces lead to a resultant force on an object, including balanced forces when the resultant force is zero.

A single force can be resolved into two components acting at right angles to each other. The two component forces together have the same effect as the single force.

WS 1.2
MS 5b

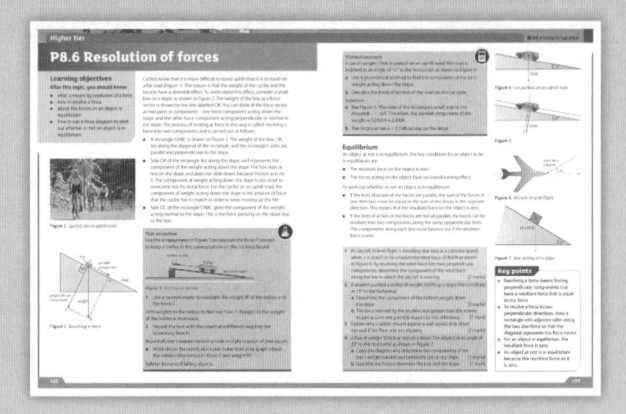

Aiming for	Outcome	Checkpoint	
		Question	Activity
Aiming for GRADE 6 ↓	Resolve a single force into two perpendicular components.	1, 2	Main 1
	Determine if an object is in equilibrium by considering the horizontal and vertical forces.	3	Main 3
	Investigate the effect of increasing the weight of an object on a slope on the component of the weight acting along the slope.		Main 1
Aiming for GRADE 8 ↓	Resolve a pair of forces into the overall perpendicular components.	End of chapter 5	Main 1, Plenary 2
	Determine if an object is in equilibrium by considering the horizontal and vertical components of forces.	3	Main 3
	Plan a detailed investigation into the effect of increasing the gradient of a slope on the component of the weight acting along the slope.		Main 1

Maths
Students will need to resolve vectors into two components using diagrams (5b). Some students may move on to find components using sine and cosine functions.

Literacy
The focus should be on terms used to describe directions such as 'along the line of the slope' and 'perpendicular to the slope'.

Practical

Title	Testing an incline
Equipment	dynamics trolley (or other low-friction toy car), a set of 50 g masses, newton-meter, string, adjustable slope
Overview of method	The students measure the force required to keep the empty trolley stationary, and then gradually increase the weight of the trolley by adding masses and noting the effect on this force.
	To extend the students the angle of the slope can be gradually increased instead of the weight. In this version the students could be provided with the suggestion that the force is proportional to either the sine or the cosine of the slope angle, and the students determine which is more likely.
Safety considerations	Prevent the trolley from rolling off the edge of the desk.

■ P8 Forces in balance

Starter	Support/Extend	Resources
Slide (5 min) Show some video footage of various slides, and ask the students to explain the motion of the people on them. Look for explanations about why the people are accelerating (unbalanced forces) and why they reach constant speeds (balanced force) or end up stuck.	**Support:** Pause the video at important points and mark on the forces to allow discussion of the effects.	
Direction sense (10 min) Students should translate prose descriptions of forces (e.g., 'a 20 N force acting at 30 degrees to the horizontal') into figures and vice versa to develop their ability to describe forces precisely.	**Support:** Provide descriptions and figures for the students to match up.	

Main	Support/Extend	Resources
Resolving vectors (10 min) Demonstrate the idea of breaking down a force into components by showing that any one force can be represented by two forces acting at right angles. Cardboard force arrows can assist with this. Apply this technique to the forces acting on an object on a slope emphasising that the components act at right angles.	**Support:** Limit the discussion to horizontal and vertical components initially. **Extend:** The fraction of the force acting in particular directions can be discussed.	
Testing an incline (20 min) Students can try this experiment to see that the force increases with the weight of the trolley. A simple mathematical model should show that doubling the weight doubles the force. It is likely that this will not be exactly true because frictional effects increase with the weight of the trolley.	**Extend:** Students can investigate the effect of changing the angle of the slope instead of the weight.	**Practical:** Testing an incline
Equilibrium (10 min) Students analyse a system at equilibrium in detail, as shown in the student book, to ensure they are aware of the conditions required for equilibrium. This needs to be a methodical treatment of this demanding situation.	**Extend:** It is possible to discuss the additional condition for moments around any point to be equal as a more formal definition of equilibrium.	

Plenary	Support/Extend	Resources
Resolving a force (10 min) Interactive where students resolve components of forces acting in different directions.		**Interactive:** Resolving a force
How long is a piece of string? (5 min) Give each student a length of string and ask the student to stick it on to a sheet of squared paper in a random diagonal direction. The students then resolve the string into horizontal and vertical components, writing down these values.	**Extend:** Students place separate two pieces of string head to head and find the components of the resultant.	

Homework		
Students should produce a summary poster of all of the content from this chapter, including a range of figures showing the key ideas.	**Support:** A partially completed template can be provided. **Extend:** The poster must show examples of all of the types of calculation required in this topic.	

P8 Forces in balance

Overview of P8 Forces in balance

In this chapter students have compared vectors and scalars using the examples of distance and displacement along with the nature of forces. Representations of vectors using scale diagrams led to descriptions of the forces acting in a wide variety of situations and the identification of Newton's third law.

The concept of balanced and unbalanced forces was used to determine the behaviour of objects and the application of Newton's first law of motion. Higher-tier students have produced free body diagrams demonstrating the forces acting on an isolated object. Students also determined the centre of mass of an object experimentally.

Higher-tier students have analysed the forces acting on an object in additional depth using a parallelogram of forces approach to determine the resultant force or a 'missing force' when an object is in equilibrium. In addition, the students have resolved forces at right angles to analyse systems and determine if a system is in equilibrium.

MyMaths

You can find additional support for the maths skills covered in this chapter on **MyMaths**, including substituting numerical values into algebraic equations, using appropriate units for physical quantities, and using angular measures in degrees.

kerboodle

For this chapter, the following assessments are available on Kerboodle:

P8 Checkpoint quiz: Forces in balance
P8 Progress quiz: Forces in balance 1
P8 Progress quiz: Forces in balance 2
P8 On your marks: Forces in balance
P8 Exam-style questions and mark scheme: Forces in balance

Checkpoint follow up lesson

A student's route through this lesson can be determined using the Checkpoint assessment. Percentage pass marks are supplied in the Checkpoint teacher notes.

For each successive route through it is assumed that the student can perform to their current route as well as previous routes. For example, students working at Aiming for 6 are assumed to be secure in Aiming for 4 knowledge and understanding and working towards achieving all the learning outcomes for Aiming for 6.

	Aiming for 4	**Aiming for 6**	**Aiming for 8**
Learning outcomes	Describe what is meant by a resultant force.	Calculate resultant forces.	Use the parallelogram of forces to find a resultant force.
	State how the centre of mass is linked to stability.	Describe why some objects are stable and others topple.	Explain why some objects are stable and others topple.
Starter	**Make the force! (5 min)** Give out diagrams with arrows showing forces on them. The arrows should be recognisably 1 unit, 2 units, and 3 units in length. Call out a force and ask them to hold up two arrows that produce that resultant force.		
	How stable? (5 min) Give out a selection of diagrams of objects that are stable, unstable, and have neutral stability. In small groups, ask students to put them in order of most to least stable. Pair groups together and ask them to compare their orders, and discuss the best explanation for the order.		
Differentiated checkpoint activity	Aiming for 4 students use the Checkpoint follow-up sheet to investigate adding forces to produce a resultant force and to investigate how the stability of a box depends on the mass inside a box. The follow-up sheet provides structured tasks and questions to help them complete these activities and check their understanding of resultant forces and stability.	Aiming for 6 students use the Checkpoint follow-up sheet to investigate how the stability of a box depends on the mass inside a box. The Aiming for 6 Checkpoint follow-up sheet provides tasks and questions to help them complete these activities and check their understanding of moments, stability, and resolving forces.	Aiming for 8 students use the Checkpoint follow-up sheet to model the stability of a lorry on a slope, and to model removing a fence post from the ground using a tractor. The Aiming for 8 Checkpoint follow-up sheet provides tasks and questions to help them complete these activities and check their understanding of moments, stability, resolving forces, and the parallelogram of forces.
	Kerboodle resource P8 Checkpoint follow up: Aiming for 4, P8 Checkpoint follow up: Aiming for 6, P8 Checkpoint follow up: Aiming for 8		
Plenary	**Make the forces again (10 min)** Use the same arrows from the starter activity. Aiming for 4 students should find as many different resultant forces as they can from the arrows they are given.		
	Against the wall! (5 min) Students should work in pairs. One student should stand against the wall so that they are close enough that their back and legs are touching it. The other student should place a chair in front of them, and ask them to reach down and pick it up. They swap, and then discuss why it is not possible. Discuss the ideas with the class, and the link between moments and stability.		
Progression	Encourage students to review a series of objects and describe their stability.	Encourage students to calculate the components of a force using trigonometry and check their results using a scale diagram.	Encourage students to practise using the parallelogram of forces to find resultant forces.

P 9 Motion
9.1 Speed and distance–time graphs

AQA spec Link: 5.6.1.1 Distance is how far an object moves. Distance does not involve direction. Distance is a scalar quantity.

5.6.1.2 Speed does not involve direction. Speed is a scalar quantity.

The speed of a moving object is rarely constant. When people walk, run, or travel in a car their speed is constantly changing.

The speed at which a person can walk, run, or cycle depends on many factors including: age, terrain, fitness, and distance travelled.

Typical values may be taken as: walking ~ 1.5 m/s, running ~ 3 m/s, cycling ~ 6 m/s.

For an object moving at constant speed the distance travelled in a specific time can be calculated using the equation:

distance travelled = speed × time

$[s = v\,t]$

distance s in metres, m

speed v in metres per second, m/s

time t in seconds, s

5.6.1.4 If an object moves along a straight line, the distance travelled can be represented by a distance–time graph.

The speed of an object can be calculated from the gradient of its distance–time graph.

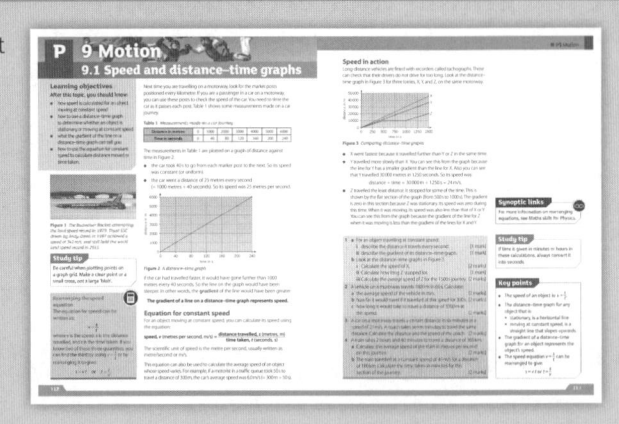

MS 1a, 1b, 1c, 1d, 3b, 3c, 4a, 4b, 4d

Aiming for	Outcome	Checkpoint Question	Checkpoint Activity
Aiming for GRADE 4	Describe how the gradient of a distance–time graph represents the speed.	1	Starter 1
	Estimate typical speeds for walking, running, and cycling.		Main
	Calculate the distance an object at constant speed will travel in a given time.	2	Main
Aiming for GRADE 6	Use the gradients of distance–time graphs to compare the speeds of objects.	End of chapter 4	Main
	Describe the motion of an object by interpreting distance–time graphs.		Starter 1, Main
	Calculate the speed of an object and the time taken to travel a given distance.	2, 3, 4, End of chapter 1	Main
Aiming for GRADE 8	Calculate the speed of an object by extracting data from a distance–time graph.	End of chapter 2	Main
	Extract data from a distance–time graph to calculate the speed of an object at various points in its motion.		Main
	Perform calculations of speed, distance, and time which involve conversion to and from SI base units.		Main

Maths
Students will calculate speed using the appropriate relationship (3b, 3c). Some students will extract the necessary data from a distance–time graph (4a, 4b, 4d).

Literacy
The students will describe the movement of an object based on information extracted from a graph.

Key words
gradient

P9 Motion

Starter	Support/Extend	Resources
Speed, velocity, and acceleration graphs (10 min) Ensure the students can interpret a simple graph of motion by matching data with a graph. They should identify the gradient and note that it is constant when the distance is changing by a fixed amount each second. **Speedy start** (5 min) Give students different moving objects, and ask them to put the objects in order from fastest to slowest. Provide data on the objects so that the students can actually work out the speed of the objects using the speed equation. Examples could be a worm (0.5 cm/s), human walking (0.5 m/s), bicycle (5 m/s), car (20 m/s), passenger aircraft (200 m/s), and missile (1 km/s).	**Extend:** Students should discuss what would happen to the graph if the speed was not constant and how this relates to the gradient. **Support:** Focus on base units in the examples. **Extend:** Try some unusual units (e.g., mm/year for continental drift).	**Interactive:** Speed, velocity, and acceleration graphs

Main	Support/Extend	Resources
Distance–time graphs (40 min) Students try a few example speed calculations based on the equation. Use examples that lead to typical walking (1.5 m/s), running (3 m/s), and cycling speeds (6 m/s) as students are expected to recall these values. Students then complete the activity sheet where they analyse a distance–time graph of a motorbike, describing when it was travelling at the slowest speed, and extracting simple data from the graph to find speed in different phases of motion.	**Support:** A simple calculation frame should be used, especially for rearrangement of the equation. **Extend:** Use examples which require changes to SI base units. **Support:** Students make a set of rules about what different features of the graph represent (e.g., steeper = faster). **Extend:** Ask the students to describe a graph that shows acceleration and deceleration rather than sudden speed changes.	**Activity:** Distance–time graphs

Plenary	Support/Extend	Resources
Timetable (5 min) Provide the students with a graph and ask them to describe the motion of the object in prose and calculate the speed of the object during each stage of the motion. **A driving story** (10 min) Provide students with a paragraph describing the motion of a car through a town, including moving at different speeds and stopping at traffic lights, and so on. Ask them to sketch a graph of the described motion.	**Extend:** Students use bus timetables and a map to estimate speeds between different stops. **Support:** Give students a graph of the motion and ask them to convert it into prose. **Extend:** Provide numerical information for the students to use in accurately plotting a graph.	

Homework		
Students analyse data about the 100 m sprint records (or other records such as swimming). They can try to find out if there appears to be a continuous improvement in running speeds or if there are leaps where the records change suddenly.	**Extend:** Students should discuss the resolution implied by the measurements and link this to improvements in timing technology.	

kerboodle

A Kerboodle highlight for this lesson is **Extension sheet: Distance–time gradient calculations**. Refer to the **Content map** on Kerboodle for a full list of resources and assessment.

P9.2 Velocity and acceleration

AQA spec Link: 5.6.1.3 The velocity of an object is its speed in a given direction. Velocity is a vector quantity.

Students should be able to explain the vector–scalar distinction as it applies to displacement, distance, velocity, and speed.

H Students should be able to explain qualitatively, with examples, that motion in a circle involves constant speed but changing velocity.

5.6.1.4 If an object moves along a straight line, the distance travelled can be represented by a distance–time graph.

The speed of an object can be calculated from the gradient of its distance–time graph.

H If an object is accelerating, its speed at any particular time can be determined by drawing a tangent and measuring the gradient of the distance–time graph at that time.

Students should be able to draw distance–time graphs from measurements and extract and interpret lines and slopes of distance–time graphs, translating information between graphical and numerical form.

Students should be able to determine speed from a distance–time graph.

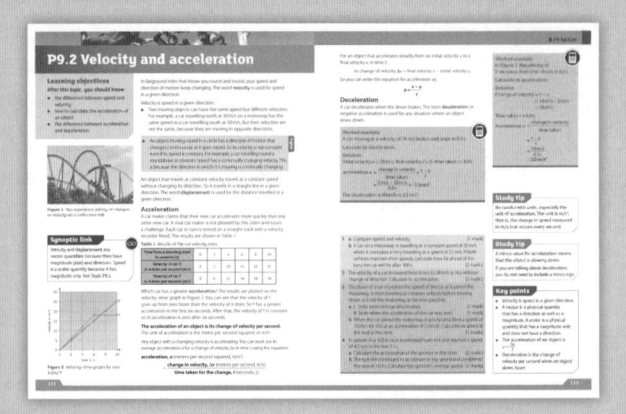

MS 3b, 3c, 3d, 4a, 4b, 4c, 4d, 4f

Aiming for	Outcome	Checkpoint	
		Question	Activity
Aiming for GRADE 4	Describe the difference between speed and velocity using an appropriate example.	1, 3	Starter 1, Main 1
	Give the equation relating velocity, acceleration, and time.	2	Main 3
	Calculate the acceleration of an object using the change in velocity and time.	2, End of chapter 4	Main 3
Aiming for GRADE 6	Identify the features of a velocity–time graph.		Plenary 1
	Rearrange the acceleration equation in calculations.	3	Main 3
	Calculate the change in velocity for an object under constant acceleration for a given period of time.	3	Main 3
Aiming for GRADE 8	Compare and contrast the features of a distance–time, displacement–time, and velocity–time graph.	End of chapter 4	Plenary 1
	Combine equations relating to velocity and acceleration in multi-step calculations.	3	Main 3, Plenary 2
	Calculate a new velocity for a moving object that has accelerated for a given period of time.	3	Main 3

Maths
The students will be performing a series of calculations based on velocity and acceleration equations (3b, 3c, 3d).

Literacy
There are many terms with fine distinctions between them (e.g., *distance* and *displacement*), which the students need to use correctly throughout this lesson.

Key words
displacement, velocity, acceleration, deceleration

114

■ P9 Motion

Starter	Support/Extend	Resources
Getting nowhere fast (5 min) A racing driver completes a full circuit of a 3 km racetrack in 90 seconds. Ask what is his average speed? Why aren't they 3 km away from where they started? Use this idea to explain the difference between distance travelled and displacement. **Treasure island** (10 min) Provide the students with a scaled map with a starting point, hidden treasure, protractor, and ruler. At first, only give them the times they have to walk for, then the speeds they must go at, and finally the matching directions. See which group can find the treasure first. This shows how important direction is when describing movement.	**Support:** Show an overhead map of the track and discuss the difference between direction and displacement at different points along it. **Extend:** Ask the students to produce a set of instructions to get to a treasure chest whilst avoiding a set of obstacles such as the 'pit of peril'.	

Main	Support/Extend	Resources
Defining velocity (15 min) Use plenty of examples involving the description of the direction of motion as students can struggle with the difference between speed and velocity. 🄷 For higher-tier students you will need to discuss circular motion. Showing a conical pendulum, bolas, or a lasso can assist with this. **Acceleration** (25 min) Students will understand acceleration to mean *getting faster*. Use this as a starting point and move towards the idea that it is possible to find out how much faster each second. This leads to the formal equation. The students will need to try several example calculations at this point. Ensure they can identify starting or end velocities of zero in the questions (e.g., at rest, stopped, stationary). Students use the term deceleration in a description of an object slowing down to make sure they understand it.	**Support:** Show partially complete calculations and a methodical method for the students to follow. **Extend:** Students should tackle multi-step calculations where they need to find speeds from distance and time values, and then acceleration using these speeds. **Extend:** Consider an object which is moving backwards and slowing down, and discuss which term would describe this motion best.	**Activity:** Acceleration

Plenary	Support/Extend	Resources
Comparing graphs (10 min) Ask the students to make a comparison of what a distance–time graph and a velocity–time graph show. They should produce a chart/diagram highlighting the distinctions between what the features of these graphs represent. **Accelerated learning** (10 min) The students should try a few additional acceleration questions. Differentiate these so that there are several stages of calculation in some of the questions.	**Support:** Provide a pair of simple example graphs for the students to use. **Extend:** Ask the students to sketch a pair of graphs which show the motion of the same object, matching up important points. **Support:** Use more structure in questions to guide students through them.	**Interactive:** Accelerated learning

Homework		
Ask the students to find data on vehicle accelerations (e.g., 0–60 mph in 10 s) and to show this data as a graph. Expand this beyond the typical cars, and ask them to look at sprinters, animals, rockets, and so on.	**Extend:** Ask the students to convert the data into SI units. They need to find how many metres are in 1 mile (1609 metres).	

kerboodle

A Kerboodle highlight for this lesson is **Working scientifically: Acceleration of a trolley**. Refer to the **Content map** on Kerboodle for a full list of resources and assessment.

P9.3 More about velocity–time graphs

AQA spec Link: 5.6.1.5 An object that slows down is decelerating.

The acceleration of an object can be calculated from the gradient of a velocity–time graph.

Ⓗ The distance travelled by an object (or displacement of an object) can be calculated from the area under a velocity–time graph.

MS 3b, 3c, 4a, 4b, 4c, 4d, 4f

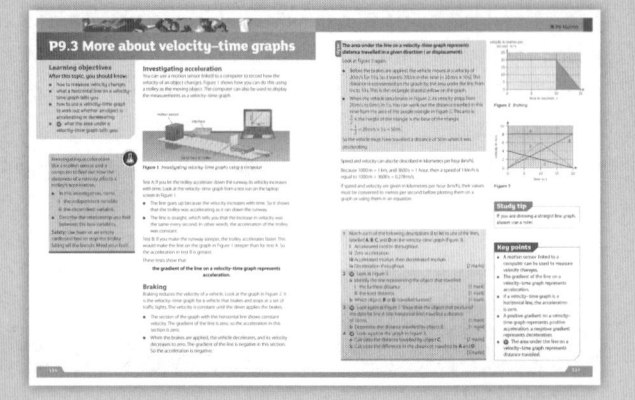

Aiming for	Outcome	Checkpoint	
		Question	Activity
Aiming for GRADE 4	Identify the feature of a velocity–time graph that represents the acceleration [the gradient], and compare these values.	1, 3	Main 2
	Identify the feature of a velocity–time graph that represents the distance travelled [the area beneath the line], and compare these values.		Main 2
	Measure the acceleration of an object as it moves down a ramp.		Main 1
Aiming for GRADE 6	Describe sections of velocity–time graphs, and compare the acceleration in these sections.	3, End of chapter 6	Main 2
	Calculate the distance travelled using information taken from a velocity–time graph for one section of motion.	3, End of chapter 4	Main 2
	Use a series of repeat measurements to find an accurate measurement of the acceleration of a moving object.		Main 1
Aiming for GRADE 8	Calculate the acceleration of an object from values taken from a velocity–time graph.		
	Calculate the total distance travelled from a multi-phase velocity–time graph.	2, 4, End of chapter 5, 6	Main 2
	Evaluate an experiment into the acceleration of an object in terms of precision based on the spread of repeat measurements.		Main 1

Maths
Students will interpret graphs to extract numerical information (4a, 4d) to use in calculations of distance and acceleration (3b, 3c).

Literacy
Specific scientific language is required to compare displacement, distance, velocity, and speed. The students should ensure that they apply these terms correctly.

Practical

Title	Investigating acceleration
Equipment	dynamics trolley, adjustable slope, protractor, data-logging equipment including a velocity sensor
Overview of method	Set up the equipment so that the angle of the ramp can be adjusted and easily measured. Make sure that the sensor is pointing along the path of the slope as otherwise the velocity will not be measured accurately. The students activate the sensor and then release the trolley. Repeating this for a range of slope angles should give the result that the steeper the slope, the greater the acceleration.
Safety considerations	Make sure the trolley does not shoot off the end of the runway. Protect feet and bench.

P9 Motion

Starter	Support/Extend	Resources
Late again? (5 min) Give the students the distance from their last class to where they are now and ask them to work out their speed on the journey to you, using the time it took them to arrive. Provide some example distances from other likely rooms if students have no idea about how far it is between places. **Finding areas** (10 min) Ask the students to calculate the total area of a shape made up of rectangles and triangles or circles.	**Support:** Provide simple data for the calculations. **Extend:** Supply data which requires conversions to SI base units (e.g., distance in km and time in minutes). **Support:** Provide the equation for the area of a triangle, rectangle, and circle as required. **Extend:** Use shapes with cut-out sections (e.g., a square with a circular hole in it).	

Main	Support/Extend	Resources
Investigating acceleration (25 min) After a brief recap of the concept of acceleration, the students can carry out this investigation depending on the equipment available. **Braking** (15 min) In this activity the students look at what the features of the velocity–time graph represent. They need to clearly identify the acceleration and distance travelled as separate concepts. Summary questions 1 to 4 in the student book will provide additional examples.	**Support:** The motion sensor apparatus provides the simplest method. **Extend:** The light-gate method requires additional calculations to find the speed of the trolley from which acceleration is calculated. **Support:** Limit the complexity of the graphs to two phases at most (and acceleration or deceleration, and a constant velocity section). **Extend:** Students can find accelerations and distance travelled on more complex graphs with several discrete phases of motion.	**Practical:** Investigating acceleration

Plenary	Support/Extend	Resources
Rushed off your feet (5 min) Wear a pedometer throughout the lesson, calculate your average step distance, and then ask the students to work out how far you have moved and your average speed. A typical example stride distance is 0.5 m with somewhere between 400 and 600 paces per lesson. **Matching motion** (10 min) Students match velocity–time graphs with the descriptions of a car's motion. They then interpret a velocity–time graph of an athlete during a training session.	**Extend:** The students could find their average daily speed, based on sensible estimations. **Support:** Take students through the provided examples step by step. **Extend:** Ask the students to read data from the graphs (such as starting speed and final speed) and attempt to calculate the acceleration.	**Interactive:** Matching motion

Homework		
The students can analyse a photocopy of a tachograph disc and describe the motion of the vehicle it was used in.	**Extend:** Students can also research the need for these devices and the replacement technology being introduced (based on GPS).	

kerboodle

A Kerboodle highlight for this lesson is **Bump up your grade: Using motion graphs to decide how things move**. Refer to the **Content map** on Kerboodle for a full list of resources and assessment.

P9.4 Analysing motion graphs

AQA spec Link: 5.6.1.4 The speed of an object can be calculated from the gradient of its distance–time graph.

(H) If an object is accelerating, its speed at any particular time can be determined by drawing a tangent and measuring the gradient of the distance–time graph at that time.

5.6.1.5 The acceleration of an object can be calculated from the gradient of a velocity–time graph.

(H) The distance travelled by an object (or displacement of an object) can be calculated from the area under a velocity–time graph.

The following equation applies to uniform acceleration:

(final velocity)^2 − (initial velocity)^2 = 2 × acceleration × distance
[$v^2 - u^2 = 2\,a\,s$]

final velocity v in metres per second, m/s
initial velocity u in metres per second, m/s
acceleration a in metres per second squared, m/s^2
distance s in metres, m

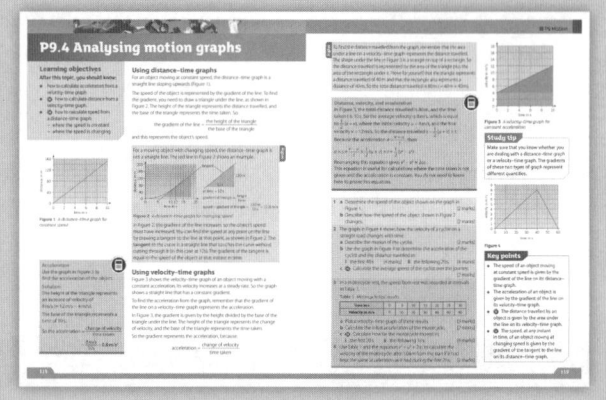

MS 3b, 3c, 4a, 4b, 4c, 4d, 4f

Aiming for	Outcome	Checkpoint	
		Question	Activity
Aiming for GRADE 4	Identify a change in speed on a distance–time graph using change in gradient.	2	Starter 1, Main 1
	Identify a change in acceleration on a velocity–time graph using change in gradient.	2	Main 2
	Calculate the distance travelled by an object at constant velocity using data extracted from a graph.		Main 3
Aiming for GRADE 6	Calculate the speed of an object by extracting data from a distance–time graph.	1	Main 3
	(H) Use a tangent to determine the speed of an object from a distance–time graph.		Main 2
	Use the equation $v^2 - u^2 = 2as$ in calculations where the initial or final velocity is zero.	4	Main 3
Aiming for GRADE 8	Calculate the acceleration of an object by extracting data from a velocity–time graph.	3	Main 2
	Use the gradient of a velocity–time graph to determine the acceleration of an object.	3	Main 2
	Apply transformations of the equation $v^2 - u^2 = 2as$ in calculations involving change in velocity and acceleration where both velocities are non-zero.	4	Main 3

Maths
The students will be using tangents of lines to determine gradients leading to speed or acceleration (4a, 4e). They will find the area of shapes to determine the distance travelled (4f). Students will also use equations describing the motion of objects under constant acceleration (3b, 3c).

Literacy
Conversion between graphs and descriptions of graphs is crucial in this lesson, and scientific language development should be focused in this area.

P9 Motion

Practical

Title	Cardboard graphs
Equipment	cardboard pieces in rectangles, triangles, and squares (cut from card with a grid pattern printed on)
Overview of method	Students can construct graphs from the cut-out shapes, placing them together in different combinations onto a grid background. This will allow them to analyse the area of the graph, leading to distance travelled for velocity–time graphs.
Safety considerations	None applicable.

Starter	Support/Extend	Resources
Graph matching (5 min) The students have to match the description of the movement of objects with distance–time and velocity–time graphs. Provide three different descriptions of journeys and three graphs that represent the movement for the students to match them with. **Plot** (10 min) Give the students a set of velocity–time data for a moving object, and ask them to plot a graph of displacement against time. Check the graphs for accuracy of plotting and clear labelling of the axes.	**Extend:** Use similar graphs and ensure the descriptions contain similar numerical values. **Support:** Provide partially completed graphs to add points to.	

Main	Support/Extend	Resources
Using distance–time graphs (15 min) 🄷 Lead the students through the process of determining the gradient of a line using tangents. Ensure the students can identify when the object is speeding up and when it is slowing down clearly. Students should find some velocities from example graphs to ensure they have mastered the technique.		
Velocity–time graphs (15 min) Discuss finding acceleration from velocity–time graphs, making sure that students are aware of the difference between this type of graph and the earlier distance–time graph. Ask the students to analyse a few graphs and find acceleration using the gradient.	**Extend:** 🄷 The tangent techniques can be used to find the acceleration when objects are not accelerating uniformly.	**Activity:** Velocity–time graphs
Velocity–time graphs and distance travelled (10 min) Recap the idea that the area beneath the line on the graph represents the distance travelled. This can now be linked to the mathematical equations which find the area of the shapes, noting that these are a product of the velocity and the time. Then discuss the origin of this equation of motion ($v^2 = u^2 + 2as$). Adding the area of the triangle and the rectangle together will lead to the expression.	**Extend:** The students can be led through the derivation, and this can reinforce their understanding of it.	

Plenary	Support/Extend	Resources
Dynamic definitions (10 min) The students should provide detailed definitions of speed, velocity, distance, displacement, and acceleration, including how they are represented on graphs.	**Support:** Students should be provided with definitions to match up with the key terms.	
Using graphs (10 min) Students answer true or false statements on velocity, then identify velocity–time graphs.	**Extend:** Students correct the false statements.	**Interactive:** Using graphs

Homework		
The students have completed their look at graphs of motion and so should attempt a series of more formal questions to check their progress and identify areas to develop.	**Support:** Select appropriate levels of questions for the students.	

kerboodle

A Kerboodle highlight for this lesson is **Extension sheet: Non-uniform motion**. Refer to the **Content map** on Kerboodle for a full list of resources and assessment.

P9 Motion

Overview of P9 Motion

In this chapter the students have analysed the motion of objects in depth starting from a recap of the concept of speed and this relationship to distance travelled and time taken. The representation of motion using distance-time graphs representing single and multiple objects has been analysed to give detailed descriptions of the movement of the objects.

The students have defined acceleration in terms of changes in velocity before analysing it graphically and mathematically. Higher tier students have also outlined circular motion in terms of constant acceleration but with constant speed. All students have then investigated acceleration caused by an unbalanced force on ramp, linking acceleration to the gradient of a line on a velocity-time graph.

Students have continued to analyse graphs representing motion by looking at the area beneath the line on a velocity-time graph and its relationship to the distance travelled by an object. Students have used the gradient of a distance-time graph to determine the speed of an object. In addition, higher tier students have used the tangent of a line on a distance-time graph to determine the speed. All students have then applied these techniques to analyse a range of graphs to extract all of the possible information from them.

MyMaths

You can find additional support for the maths skills covered in this chapter on **MyMaths**, including changing the subject of an equation, translating information between graphical and numeric form, understanding that $y = mx + c$ represents a linear relationship, and determining the slope and intercept of a linear graph.

kerboodle

For this chapter, the following assessments are available on Kerboodle:

P9 Checkpoint quiz: Motion
P9 Progress quiz: Motion 1
P9 Progress quiz: Motion 2
P9 On your marks: Motion
P9 Exam-style questions and mark scheme: Motion

Checkpoint follow up lesson

A student's route through this lesson can be determined using the Checkpoint assessment. Percentage pass marks are supplied in the Checkpoint teacher notes.

For each successive route through it is assumed that the student can perform to their current route as well as previous routes. For example, students working at Aiming for 6 are assumed to be secure in Aiming for 4 knowledge and understanding and working towards achieving all the learning outcomes for Aiming for 6.

	Aiming for 4	**Aiming for 6**	**Aiming for 8**
Learning outcomes	Plot a distance-time graph.	Plot and interpret a distance-time graph.	Plot and interpret a distance-time graph and a speed-time graph.
	Make calculations of speed.	Make calculations of speed using a range of units.	Make calculations of velocity.
	Interpret data on speed.	Plot and interpret a speed-time graph.	Make calculations of acceleration using tangents drawn to a curve on a velocity time graph.
Starter	**Faster or slower? (5 minutes)** Give out some statements, such as 'A car that travels 10 miles in half an hour is going faster than a bus that travels at 30 mph', and ask students to sort them into true and false statements.		
	Walking the graph (10 minutes) Give students A4 dry wipe boards, pens and an eraser. Ask student to sketch distance time graphs of you walking. Try a variety of motions – steady speed, steady speed, stopping, steady speed. Ask them to explain how they knew how to draw each graph. You can extend the activity to speed-time graphs for Aiming for 6 students, and velocity-time graphs for Aiming for 8 students.		
Differentiated checkpoint activity	Aiming for 4 students use the Checkpoint follow-up sheet to make measurements of a ball on a track, and to do some calculations based on a 100-metre race. The follow-up sheet provides structured tasks and questions to help them complete these activities and check their understanding of speed, distance-time graphs, and velocity-time graphs.	Aiming for 6 students use the Checkpoint follow-up sheet to make measurements of a ball on a track, and to do some calculations based on a 100-metre race. They also investigate the stability of a box on a ramp. The follow-up sheet provides tasks and questions to help them complete these activities and check their understanding of speed and acceleration, and how to interpret distance-time and velocity-time graphs.	Aiming for 8 students use the Checkpoint follow-up sheet to investigate the speed and acceleration of a ball on a track. The follow-up sheet provides tasks and questions to help them complete these activities and check their understanding of speed and acceleration, how to interpret distance-time and velocity-time graphs, and how to calculate acceleration from a graph where the speed is changing.
	Kerboodle resource P9 Checkpoint follow up: Aiming for 4, P9 Checkpoint follow up: Aiming for 6, P9 Checkpoint follow up: Aiming for 8		
Plenary	**Are they right? (10 minutes)** Organise students into groups of four or five and pair groups together. Give students A4 dry wipe boards, pens and an eraser. Ask each group to draw a distance-time graph that has three sections on it. They should label the axes with numbers/units, and write on the sections what the object is doing, and the speed/acceleration. Half the information should be correct, and half incorrect. The groups swap boards and use two different coloured pens to circle the correct information and the incorrect information. They swap back and evaluate the conclusions of the other group.		
Progression	Encourage students to think about speed as the distance travelled in each second, so distance accumulates with speed and time.	Encourage them to think about acceleration as the change in speed in each second, so speed accumulates with acceleration and time.	Encourage them to think about acceleration as the change in speed in each second, so you can calculate it using a gradient.

P 10 Forces and motion
10.1 Force and acceleration

AQA spec Link: **H** 5.6.2.1 The tendency of objects to continue in their state of rest or of uniform motion is called inertia.

5.6.2.2 Newton's Second Law:

The acceleration of an object is proportional to the resultant force acting on the object, and inversely proportional to the mass of the object.

As an equation:

resultant force = mass × acceleration

$[F = m\ a]$

force F in newtons, N

mass m in kilograms, kg

acceleration a in metres per second squared, m/s^2

H Students should be able to explain that:

- inertial mass is a measure of how difficult it is to change the velocity of an object
- inertial mass is defined by the ratio of force over acceleration.

Students should be able to estimate the speed, accelerations, and forces involved in large accelerations for everyday road transport.

Students should recognise and be able to use the symbol that indicates an approximate value or answer ~.

Required practical: investigate the effect of varying the force on the acceleration of an object of constant mass, and the effect of varying the mass of an object on the acceleration produced by a constant force.

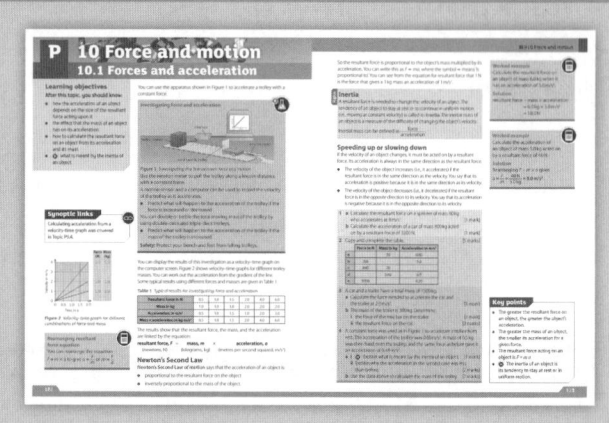

MS 1d, 3a 3b, 3c

Aiming for	Outcome	Checkpoint	
		Question	Activity
Aiming for GRADE 4	State the factors that will affect the acceleration of an object acted on by a resultant force.		Starter 1, Main 1
	Calculate the force required to cause a specified acceleration on a given mass.	1, 3	Main 2
	Investigate a factor that affects the acceleration of a mass.		Main 1
Aiming for GRADE 6	Describe the effect of changing the mass or the force acting on an object on the acceleration of that object.	4	Main 1
	Perform calculations involving the rearrangement of the $F = ma$ equation.	2, End of chapter 3	Main 2
	Combine separate experimental conclusions to form an overall conclusion.		Main 1
Aiming for GRADE 8	**H** Define the inertial mass of an object in terms of force and acceleration.		Main 2, Plenary 2
	Calculate the acceleration of an object acted on by several forces.	3, End of chapter 3	Main 2
	Evaluate an experiment by identifying sources of error and determining uncertainty in the resulting data.		Main 1

Maths

Students will investigate factors that are proportional or in inverse proportion (3a). Some will combine these factors to form an overall expression.

Literacy

Students discuss results, combining two different concepts together to produce an overall statement about acceleration, force, and mass.

Key words

Newton's Second Law of Motion inertia

122

■ P10 Forces and motion

Required practical

Title	Investigating force and acceleration
Equipment	dynamics trolley, track, string, masses (similar to trolley mass), stopwatch, and possibly motion sensor or light gates
Overview of method	Pull the trolley along a track of known distance, attempting to use a constant force by watching the newton-meter. Measure the acceleration. Repeat with at least three different constant forces. Add a mass to the trolley and pull along at a constant force. Measure the acceleration. Add another mass to the trolley and pull along at the same constant force, measuring the acceleration. Repeat for at least three different masses.
Safety considerations	Ensure a clear working area for the trolleys to be dragged.

Starter	Support/Extend	Resources
Accelerator (5 min) Ask the students to describe the function of the accelerator in a car. **Lift off** (10 min) Interactive where students complete a description on the changes in energy stores during the launch of a chemical rocket, and link the ideas to the action of forces.	**Support:** Animations of the process can be found with an Internet search.	**Interactive:** Lift off

Main	Support/Extend	Resources
Investigating force and acceleration (25 min) Students carry out two investigations. First they investigate the effect that changing the force on an object has on the acceleration. They then investigate the effect that changing the mass of the object has on the acceleration when a constant force is applied. Students use the investigations to reach two conclusions that can then be combined into a mathematical relationship.	**Extend:** Students should evaluate the data and discuss why the relationships are not exact. Ensure the students are familiar with sources of error and uncertainty.	**Practical:** Investigating force and acceleration
H Inertial mass and acceleration (15 min) Discuss the relationships $a \propto F$ and $a \propto \frac{1}{m}$ and combine them to reach the expression $a \propto \frac{F}{m}$, which leads to the more familiar $F = ma$. Analyse some scenarios involving resultant forces acting on objects to find the acceleration or the force required to cause particular accelerations. Focus on the idea that both the force and the acceleration are vectors in the same direction.	**Support:** Students should try questions that do not require rearrangement of the equation. Limit the calculations to finding the force when the equation is expressed as $F = ma$. **Extend:** Questions should involve rearrangements and some SI prefixes for values.	**Maths skills:** Force, mass, and acceleration.

Plenary	Support/Extend	Resources
What's wrong? (5 min) Students consider the common misconception *Objects always move in the direction of the resultant force* and write a corrected version. **I'm snookered** (10 min) Students draw a series of diagrams showing the forces involved in getting out of a snooker. They draw each of the stages of the movements, showing the forces as the white ball is first hit and the collisions with the cushions.	**Support:** Give examples of where a moving object is decelerating to show why this statement is wrong. **Support:** A snooker or pool simulation game can make this more interactive and fun for the students.	

Homework		
Students evaluate the experiment and suggest improvements, explaining why they would make the results more convincing. This should focus on the removal of forces that cause the results to be inaccurate, such as friction.	**Extend:** Expect at least one idea for reduction of friction, for example, compensated (tilted) track.	

kerboodle

A Kerboodle highlight for this lesson is **Maths skills: Force and acceleration**. Refer to the **Content map** on Kerboodle for a full list of resources and assessment.

P10.2 Weight and terminal velocity

AQA spec Link: 5.1.3 Weight is the force acting on an object due to gravity. The force of gravity close to the Earth is due to the gravitational field around the Earth.

The weight of an object depends on the gravitational field strength at the point where the object is.

The weight of an object can be calculated using the equation:

weight = mass × gravitational field strength

$[W = m\,g]$

weight W in newtons, N

mass m in kilograms, kg

gravitational field strength g in newtons per kilogram, N/kg (In any calculation the value of the gravitational field strength (g) will be given.)

The weight of an object may be considered to act at a single point referred to as the object's 'centre of mass'.

The weight of an object and the mass of an object are directly proportional.

Weight is measured using a calibrated spring-balance (a newton-meter).

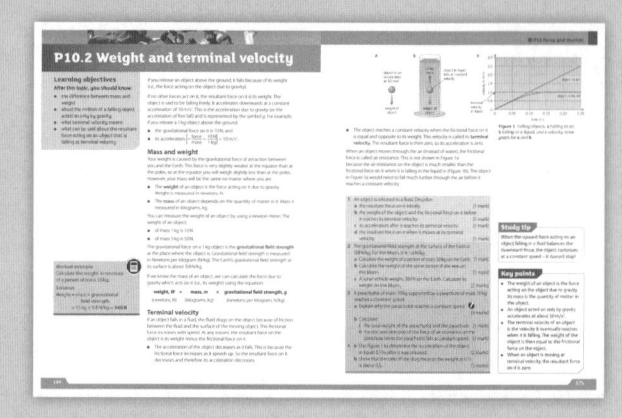

MS 2c, 2g, 3a, 3b, 3c, 4c

Aiming for	Outcome	Checkpoint	
		Question	Activity
Aiming for GRADE 4 ↓	State the difference between the mass of an object and its weight.		Main
	Describe the forces acting on an object falling through a fluid.	1	Starter 2, Main
	Investigate the motion of an object when it falls.		Main
Aiming for GRADE 6 ↓	Calculate the weight of objects using their mass and the gravitational field strength.	2, End of chapter 2	Main
	Apply the concept of balanced forces to explain why an object falling through a fluid will reach a terminal velocity.	3	Main, Homework
	Investigate the relationship between the mass of an object and the terminal velocity.		Main
Aiming for GRADE 8 ↓	Apply the mathematical relationship between mass, weight, and gravitational field strength in a range of situations.	2, End of chapter 2	Main
	Explain the motion of an object falling through a fluid by considering the forces acting through all phases of motion.	3, 4	Main
	Evaluate the repeatability of an experiment by considering the spread of each set of repeat results.		Main

Maths
Students plot a graph of experimental data (4c); this may be a simple bar chart or a scatter graph depending on the experiment (2c, 2g).

Literacy
Students describe the action of forces and their effect on the motion of an object. Explanations link together resultant forces, weight, frictional forces, and acceleration.

Key words
weight, mass, gravitational field strength, terminal velocity

Practical

Title	Investigating falling
Equipment	two small and different sized masses, string or cotton thread, scissors, approximately 15 × 15 cm square of cloth

P10 Forces and motion

Overview of method	Drop the mass from a set height. Then use the string or thread to tie the small mass to the cloth to make a basic parachute. Drop the parachute from the same height.
	The higher the parachutes are dropped from, the more effective they are, so use somewhere with sufficient height. A wide stairwell can be good if proper supervision can be arranged.
	Repeat the experiment using a different mass.
Safety considerations	Do not stand on desks or ladders. Drop the object from a safe point. It may be safer to pick one responsible student to perform the dropping, rather than the whole class.

Starter	Support/Extend	Resources
Fluid facts (5 min) Interactive where students match up information (including diagrams) about the physical properties of solids, liquids, and gases with explanations in terms of particle behaviour. This will help them revise the states of matter and the particle theory in particular.		**Interactive:** Fluid facts
Air resistance (10 min) Students use their understanding of particles and forces to suggest what causes air and water resistance. They should sketch the movement of objects, label the forces on them, and then try to show the particles being pushed out of the way and pushing back.	**Extend:** Draw out the idea that moving faster through a fluid will require a greater force as more particles will need to be pushed out of the way each second.	

Main	Support/Extend	Resources
Investigating falling (40 min) Demonstrate the acceleration caused by the weight of an object when there is no supporting force by dropping some objects. Discuss the unbalanced forces acting whilst they fall and when they stop.	**Support:** Limit the scope of the calculations to just finding the weight on Earth.	**Extension:** Getting to grips with gravitational field strength.
Spend a few minutes ensuring that the students are clear on the distinction between these two with some calculations of weight for different masses. Ensure the students are aware that the weight of the objects is due to a gravitational field surrounding masses.	**Extend:** Students work through the extension sheet that uses the gravitational field strength on some different planets in calculations.	**Practical:** Investigating falling
Continue with the discussion of forces focusing on drag and how this changes as the velocity increases. Students should realise that, when the drag force matches the weight, then the object stops accelerating and so reaches terminal velocity.	**Support:** Use simple force diagrams to show the relative sizes of the forces at each stage of motion.	**Animation:** Sky diver
Use the animation to describe the changes in the forces experienced by a sky diver. Then carry out the practical to investigate falling using a model parachute. Students should investigate the effect of different masses on the time for descent. If time is limited, individual groups could investigate one mass, and then collate results as a class. As there will be considerable variability in the results, the students should focus on repeat measurements to find mean values, reducing the effects of random error.	**Extend:** Students find the range of each repeat set of results and use this to evaluate the precision of the experiment. They may also use this to draw error bars on any graphs.	

Plenary	Support/Extend	Resources
Top speed (5 min) Show the students a list of top speeds for cars along with some other information such as engine power and a photograph. They can discuss why the cars have a maximum speed.	**Extend:** Provide data on the power of engines of sports cars and their maximum speeds.	
Falling forces (10 min) The students draw a comic strip with stick figures showing the forces at various stages of a parachute jump. This should summarise the concepts and demonstrate the changing size of the forces.	**Support:** Provide the images in the correct order and label them.	
	Extend: Students should draw the force arrows to scale.	

Homework		
Students can identify aerodynamic design features of vehicles that allow them to reach higher speeds. This can be a study of an individual car or a comparison of several.	**Support:** Provide stimulus material such as images of both older and more modern sports cars.	

kerboodle

A Kerboodle highlight for this lesson is **Bump up your grade: Getting to grips with gravitational field strength**. Refer to the **Content map** on Kerboodle for a full list of resources and assessment.

P10.3 Forces and braking

AQA spec Link: 5.6.3.1 The stopping distance of a vehicle is the sum of the distance the vehicle travels during the driver's reaction time (thinking distance) and the distance it travels under the braking force (braking distance). For a given braking force the greater the speed of the vehicle, the greater the stopping distance.

5.6.3.2 Reaction times vary from person to person. Typical values range from 0.2 s to 0.9 s.

A driver's reaction time can be affected by tiredness, drugs, and alcohol. Distractions may also affect a driver's ability to react.

Students should be able to:

- explain methods used to measure human reaction times and recall typical results
- interpret and evaluate measurements from simple methods to measure the different reaction times of students
- evaluate the effect of various factors on thinking distance based on given data.

5.6.3.3 The braking distance of a vehicle can be affected by adverse road and weather conditions and poor condition of the vehicle.

Adverse road conditions include wet or icy conditions. Poor condition of the vehicle is limited to the vehicle's brakes or tyres.

Students should be able to:

- explain the factors which affect the distance required for road transport vehicles to come to rest in emergencies, and the implications for safety
- estimate how the distance required for road vehicles to stop in an emergency varies over a range of typical speeds.

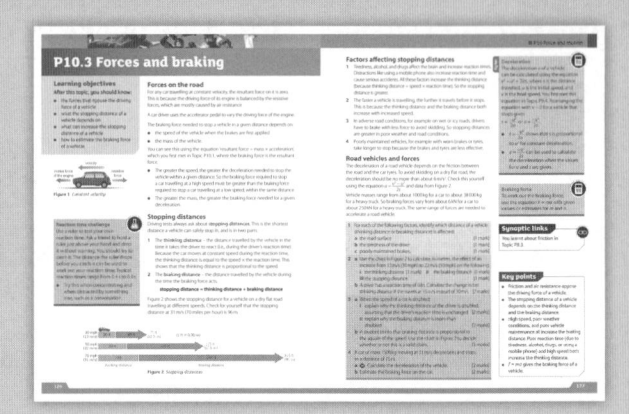

5.6.3.4 When a force is applied to the brakes of a vehicle, work done by the friction force between the brakes and the wheel reduces the kinetic energy of the vehicle and the temperature of the brakes increases.

The greater the speed of a vehicle the greater the braking force needed to stop the vehicle in a certain distance.

The greater the braking force the greater the deceleration of the vehicle. Large decelerations may lead to brakes overheating and/or loss of control.

Students should be able to:

- explain the dangers caused by large decelerations
- **H** estimate the forces involved in the deceleration of road vehicles in typical situations on a public road.

WS 1.5, 2.2

MS 1a, 1c, 1d, 2c, 2f, 2h, 3b, 3c

Aiming for	Outcome	Checkpoint	
		Question	Activity
Aiming for GRADE 4 ↓	List the factors which affect the stopping distance of a car.	1, End of chapter 1	Starter 2, Main
	Calculate the thinking distance for a car from the initial speed and reaction time.	2	Main
	Estimate the relative effects of changing factors which affect the stopping distance of cars.	1	Starter 2
Aiming for GRADE 6 ↓	Categorise factors which affect thinking distance, braking distance, and both.	1, End of chapter 1	Main
	Calculate the braking distance of a car.	4	Main
	Describe the relationship between speed and both thinking and braking distance.	3	Main
Aiming for GRADE 8 ↓	Calculate acceleration, mass, and braking force of vehicles.	4, End of chapter 3, 5	Main
	Calculate total stopping distance, initial speed, reaction time, and acceleration.	4	Main
	Explain the relative effects of changes of speed on thinking and stopping distance.	3	Main

Maths
Students calculate stopping distances and thinking distances (1a, 3b, 3c).

Literacy
Students discuss factors which affect the stopping of a car; working together to reach conclusions.

Key words
stopping distance, thinking distance, braking distance

P10 Forces and motion

Practical

Title	Reaction time challenge
Equipment	ruler
Overview of method	Students work in pairs. One student holds a ruler just above the other's hand. They drop the ruler suddenly and the other student has to catch it. The distance the ruler falls before it is caught can be used to work out your reaction time. Repeat multiple times, both when concentrating and when distracted by something else, such as a conversation.

Starter | Support/Extend | Resources

Safety first (10 min) Use information from government safety websites about car collisions in the local area to identify accident hotspots. Link these results to the idea of speed restrictions in the area, especially around primary schools.

Stop! (5 min) To support students in understanding the wide range of factors that can affect the stopping distance of cars, provide students with a list of factors to sort according to whether they will affect stopping distances or not.

Support: Research and simplify the statistics in advance to make them more accessible.

Extend: The students should discuss and describe how the factor affects the stopping distance and construct well-formed descriptions.

Main | Support/Extend | Resources

Reaction time challenge (40 min) Discuss the forces acting on a car whilst it is moving at constant velocity. Reinforce the idea that the forces must balance. Identify the resistive forces clearly.

The students should understand the factors affecting overall stopping distance, but they need to be clear which affect the thinking distance and which affect the braking distance.

H For higher-tier students, the braking distance should be linked closely to the decelerating forces using $F = ma$ with a few example car masses and maximum braking forces. From this acceleration and the initial speed, the braking distance should be calculated.

Formally introduce stopping distance to all students, ensuring that any misconceptions are corrected.

Students then carry out the practical to investigate how distractions can affect your reaction times to demonstrate how using a mobile phone whilst driving can affect stopping distances. They should appreciate that the times improve with practice and when they are fully concentrating on the clock. In a real car situation, the driver would not be able to focus on one simple task, so the times would be significantly greater.

Extend: Discuss the nature of the force driving the car forwards. This must be a frictional force between the road and tyres.

Support: Help students with the multiple equations.

Extend: Students should find total stopping distances. They should discuss the relative effects of changes of speed on thinking and stopping distance.

Extend: Students complete the Extension sheet where they investigate the circumstances in a fake car collision to identify if the driver was distracted.

Practical: Reaction time challenge

Extension: Finding the stopping distance of a vehicle

Plenary | Support/Extend | Resources

Stopping distances and motive forces (10 min) Interactive where students consolidate their understanding of stopping distances. Students link together parts of sentences on braking distance, identify true and false statements on stopping distance, reaction time, and braking distance, and put a description of the forces involved as a car stops in the correct order.

Interactive: Stopping distances and motive forces

Homework

Students complete the WebQuest where they research factors that affect stopping distance. They classify these as factors that affect either thinking distance or braking distance. They use their research to select one particular factor and produce a leaflet on their chosen factor.

Extend: Students must include graphical information in their reports such a pie charts.

WebQuest: Safe driving

kerboodle

A Kerboodle highlight for this lesson is **Extension sheet: Stop that bike!** Refer to the **Content map** on Kerboodle for a full list of resources and assessment.

Higher tier

P10.4 Momentum

AQA spec Link: 5.7.1 Momentum is defined by the equation:

momentum = mass × velocity

$[p = m\,v]$

momentum, p, in kilograms metre per second, kg m/s

mass, m, in kilograms, kg

velocity, v, in metres per second, m/s

5.7.2 In a closed system, the total momentum before an event is equal to the total momentum after the event.

This is called conservation of momentum.

Students should be able to use the concept of momentum as a model to:

- describe and explain examples of momentum in an event, such as a collision.

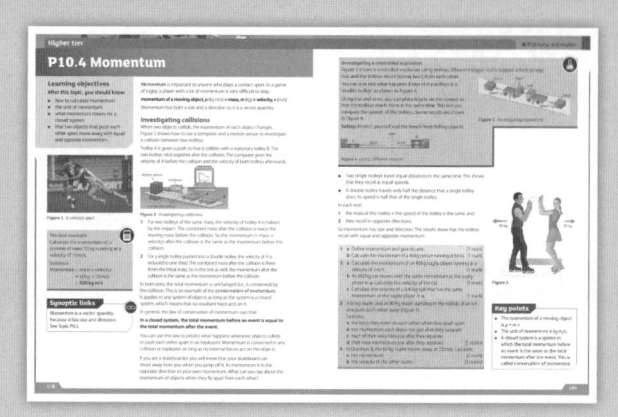

WS 1.2
MS 3b, 3c

Aiming for	Outcome	Checkpoint	
		Question	Activity
Aiming for GRADE 6	Apply the equation $p = mv$ to find the momentum, velocity or mass of an object.	1, 2, 4	Main 1
	Describe how the principle of conservation of momentum can be used to find the velocities of objects.	3	Main 1
	Investigate the behaviour of objects during explosions to verify the conservation of momentum.	3, 4	Main 2
Aiming for GRADE 8	Fully describe the motion of objects after an explosion accounting for any frictional effects.	3, 4	Main 2
	Apply the principle of conservation of momentum to a range of calculations involving the velocities of objects.	3, 4	Main 1, Main 2, Plenary 1
	Evaluate the data produced from an investigation and compare this to a theoretical framework.		Main 2

Maths
The students will perform a range of calculations to find momentum (3b, 3c).

Literacy
The students work in teams to discuss the results of their investigations building clear conclusions.

Key words
momentum, conservation of momentum

Practical

Title	Investigating a controlled explosion
Equipment	two trolleys (one with a trigger and bolt), runway, two wooden blocks
Overview of method	Set the two trolleys on the runway between the two blocks. Press the trigger on the trolley so the bolt springs out. Observe the movement of the two trolleys, then use trial and error to place the blocks on the runway so that the trolleys reach them at the same time.
Safety considerations	Protect feet and bench from falling trolleys.

■ P10 Forces and motion

Starter	Support/Extend	Resources
Trying to stop (5 min) Ask students to explain why it takes a container ship several kilometres to stop but a bicycle can stop in only a few metres, even when they are travelling at the same speed. **Stopping power** (10 min) Students use the interactive to put a list of sport balls (e.g., golf ball, cricket ball, rugby ball, and football) in order of difficulty to stop. They then complete a paragraph to explain what properties make it more difficult for the balls to stop. They should be able to link the stopability to the speed and mass of the balls.	**Extend:** The students should also discuss the forces acting in the two scenarios. **Support:** Provide typical masses and velocities for the balls.	**Interactive:** Stopping power

Main	Support/Extend	Resources
Calculating momentum (15 min) Introduce the concept of momentum and the equation for it by discussing a wide range of examples. The students should calculate the momentum of several objects and also the velocities of some objects when given the mass and momentum.	**Support:** Limit calculations to finding momentum without any rearrangement of the equation. **Extend:** Use SI prefixes and standard form in the examples.	**Support:** Understanding conservation of momentum **Extension:** Understanding conservation of momentum **Practical:** Investigating a controlled explosion
Investigating a controlled explosion (25 min) The students should refine the details of the practical, explaining how it will demonstrate the conservation of momentum in explosions. This will involve an explanation of the different velocities of the trolleys after the collision and hence the distance they will travel in the same time. Once the data is gathered they should compare it to their predictions and suggest explanations for any differences.	**Extend:** Students evaluate their data to see if it supports the law of conservation of momentum and provide reasons why it may not be an exact fit.	

Plenary	Support/Extend	Resources
The skate escape (5 min) Two people are trapped on a perfectly friction-free surface (e.g., an ice rink) just out of reach of each other. They are both 10 m from the edge and all that they have to help them escape is a tennis ball. Ask: how do they both escape? [Throw something from one to the other, this will give them momentum in opposite directions and they will slowly drift to the sides.]	**Support:** Students answer using diagrams. **Extend:** Students estimate the change in momentum when the ball is thrown. This may be conceptually linked to exchange particles in a discussion.	
Boating (10 min) Discuss what happens when somebody steps on to or off of a boat but falls in the water because the boat moves away from the land. Ask the students to explain what happened, perhaps with diagrams. They should understand that the person is actually pushing the boat away. When they move left, the boat will always be forced to the right as a consequence of the conservation of momentum.	**Support:** Students should use diagrams to show the forces involved. **Extend:** Students should provide explanations linked to forces acting and changes in momentum.	

Homework
Students try some additional momentum calculations for reinforcement and preparation for the next lesson.

kerboodle

A Kerboodle highlight for this lesson is **Working scientifically: Momentum in action**. Refer to the **Content map** on Kerboodle for a full list of resources and assessment.

P10.5 Forces and elasticity

AQA spec Link: 5.3 Students should be able to:

- give examples of the forces involved in stretching, bending, or compressing an object
- explain why, to change the shape of an object (by stretching, bending, or compressing), more than one force has to be applied – this is limited to stationary objects only
- describe the difference between elastic deformation and inelastic deformation caused by stretching forces.

The extension of an elastic object, such as a spring, is directly proportional to the force applied, provided that the limit of proportionality is not exceeded.

force = spring constant × extension

$[F = k\,e]$

force F in newtons, N

spring constant k in newtons per metre, N/m

extension e in metres, m

This relationship also applies to the compression of an elastic object, where 'e' would be the compression of the object.

A force that stretches (or compresses) a spring does work and elastic potential energy is stored in the spring. Provided the spring is not inelastically deformed, the work done on the spring and the elastic potential energy stored are equal.

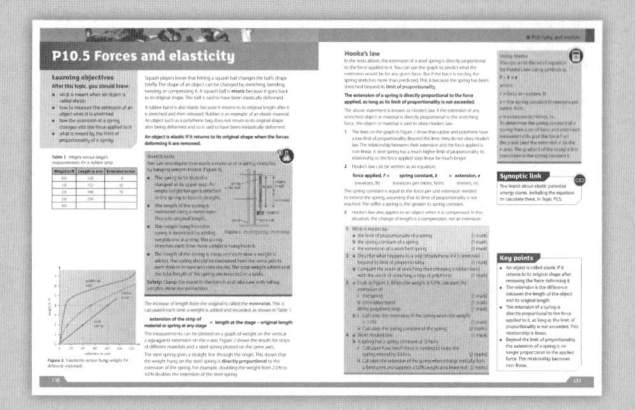

Students should be able to:

- describe the difference between a linear and non-linear relationship between force and extension
- calculate a spring constant in linear cases
- interpret data from an investigation of the relationship between force and extension.

Students should be able to calculate relevant values of stored energy and energy transfers.

Required practical: investigate the relationship between force and extension for a spring.

MS 3b, 3c, 4a, 4b

Aiming for	Outcome	Checkpoint	
		Question	Activity
Aiming for GRADE 4 ↓	State Hooke's law.	1, 4	Main
	Calculate the extension of a material using its length and original length.	End of chapter 4	Main
	Compare materials in terms of elastic and non-elastic behaviour.	2	Main
Aiming for GRADE 6 ↓	Explain the limitations of Hooke's law including the limit of proportionality.	4	Main
	Calculate the force required to cause a given extension in a spring using the spring constant.	3	Main
	Compare the behaviour of different materials under loads in terms of proportional and non-proportional behaviour.		Main
Aiming for GRADE 8 ↓	Find the spring constant of a spring using a graphical technique.	End of chapter 4	Main, Plenary 1
	Apply the Hooke's law equation in a wide range of situations.	3, 4	Main
	Evaluate an investigation into the extension of materials in terms of the precision of the data.		Main

Maths
Graphical skills are emphasised in this lesson along with the tabulated recording of data (4a, 4b).

Literacy
Students organise information in tables and describe the behaviour of materials under load during group work.

Key words
elastic, extension, directly proportional, limit of proportionality

■ P10 Forces and motion

Required practical

Title	Stretch tests
Equipment	set of masses (50 g) and holder, retort stand, clamp, spring, elastic band, strips of plastic, rulers (30 cm, 50 cm, and 1 m are likely to be needed), G-clamp (to hold the retort stand on the bench if needed)
Overview of method	Students set up the equipment as shown in Figure 1 from the student book. The initial length is measured, and then the spring is loaded by placing 50 g masses on it. Students measure the length and find the extension. The results should indicate the relationship for Hooke's law. Students should also investigate elastic (fishing-pole elastic is ideal). Finally, other materials such as strips of plastic can also be investigated.
Safety considerations	Eye protection should be worn in case the spring or elastic snaps.

Starter	Support/Extend	Resources
Distortion (5 min) Get the students to list the basic things that forces can do (cause acceleration, change the shape of the object). Concentrate on the forces in the diagrams that cause objects to compress or stretch, and use these to discuss whether these changes are permanent or can be reversed. **In proportion** (10 min) In this lesson the students will find a relationship that is proportional, so start the lesson by asking the students to use the interactive to compare some graphs and the relationship between them. They then complete a description on the idea of proportionality.	**Support:** Students can draw diagrams showing forces acting on objects that cause these things to happen. **Support:** Use a simple graph such as one showing the amount of money earned compared with hours worked to show an easily identifiable proportional relationship.	**Interactive:** In proportion

Main	Support/Extend	Resources
Stretch tests (40 min) Demonstrate a simple elastic band to show a material returning to its original shape showing elastic behaviour. Show the similar behaviour for a spring and then the plastic behaviour of polythene or something similar whilst also stretching a spring beyond the elastic limit to show permanent deformation. Students then test the behaviour of materials under load using the practical. They should focus on accurate measurement of length, well organised recording of the data, and calculation of extension. When the data for the practical has been collected, graphs can be plotted to show the relationships. Identify areas where the relationship is directly proportional, ensuring the students can identify this, and the limits to the behaviour. Use the data for the spring tests to explain Hooke's law and the associated equation. The students should find the spring constant for the spring they tested.	**Support:** Provide a results table, and support students in the calculation of extension. **Extend:** Students should use repeat tests to find ranges for the data, helping to evaluate it. **Support:** Provide simplified data for the graph plotting if required. **Extend:** Use data from the repeat tests to find the possible range of the spring constant. **Extend:** The energy changes can be linked to work done by the force stretching the spring.	**Required practical:** Stretch tests

Plenary	Support/Extend	Resources
Graphical analysis (5 min) Give the students a graph showing the extension of different springs and ask them to describe the differences. They should look at the limit of proportionality and the spring constants. **Catapult** (10 min) Students can explain how a catapult operates or plan an investigation measuring the energy stored in it.	**Extend:** Provide just the raw data and ask the students to plot the graphs.	

Homework		
Students can research the uses of springs for cushioning and support in seats, cars, and beds.		

kerboodle

A Kerboodle highlight for this lesson is **Working scientifically: Unbreakable laws and powerful theories**. Refer to the **Content map** on Kerboodle for a full list of resources and assessment.

131

P10 Forces and motion

Overview of P10 Forces and motion

Students began this chapter by experimentally determining the relationships between a force acting on an object and the acceleration, and the mass of the object and the acceleration. The results led to the formulation of Newton's second law of motion and its application. Higher-tier students have also defined the inertial mass of an object.

The students have then compared the concepts of mass and weight, linking them through the idea of a gravitational field before looking at the forces acting on an object as it falls through a fluid and the resulting terminal velocity. The forces acting during stopping a car have been analysed; identifying two phases of the motion; thinking and braking distance and the effects of a wide range of factors on both of these distances. Students have calculated the size of the accelerations experienced during braking with higher tier students deriving an appropriate equation involving the stopping distance.

The higher-tier students have investigated the concept of momentum and its conservation.

Finally, all of the students have investigated the effect of forces on the stretching of a range of materials identifying both linear and non-linear relationships between the force and extension. Students have applied Hook's law as appropriate and identified its limitations.

MyMaths

You can find additional support for the maths skills covered in this chapter on **MyMaths**, including translating information between graphical and numeric form, substituting numerical values into algebraic equations using appropriate units for physical quantities, determining the slope and intercept of a linear graph.

kerboodle

For this chapter, the following assessments are available on Kerboodle:

P10 Checkpoint quiz: Forces and motion
P10 Progress quiz: Forces and motion 1
P10 Progress quiz: Forces and motion 2
P10 On your marks: Forces and motion
P10 Exam-style questions and mark scheme: Forces and motion

Checkpoint follow up lesson

A student's route through this lesson can be determined using the Checkpoint assessment. Percentage pass marks are supplied in the Checkpoint teacher notes.

For each successive route through it is assumed that the student can perform to their current route as well as previous routes. For example, students working at Aiming for 6 are assumed to be secure in Aiming for 4 knowledge and understanding and working towards achieving all the learning outcomes for Aiming for 6.

	Aiming for 4	**Aiming for 6**	**Aiming for 8**
Learning outcomes	Describe the effect of force and mass on acceleration.	Explain the effect of force and mass on acceleration.	Explain the effect of force and mass on acceleration in unfamiliar situations.
	State factors that affect stopping distance.	Describe the factors that affect stopping distance.	Explain factors affecting stopping distance.
		Describe the behaviour of elastic materials.	Explain the behaviour of elastic materials.
Starter	**Safer cars (5 min)** Show images of a range of cars from different times in history, including the most recent and Formula 1, and ask students to come up with as many different reasons as possible for improvements in car safety.		
	Faster cars (5 min) Ask students to discuss what would happen if there was a race between a motorcycle, a car, and an aeroplane. Who would win? Why?		
Differentiated checkpoint activity	Aiming for 4 students use the Checkpoint follow-up sheet to model a car using a margarine tub and an elastic band, and to investigate the link between force, mass, and stopping distance. The follow-up sheet provides structured tasks and questions to help them complete these activities and check their understanding of the factors affecting stopping distance, and the link between force, mass, and acceleration.	Aiming for 6 students use the Checkpoint follow-up sheet to complete one of two activities: • model a car using a margarine tub and an elastic band, and investigate the link between force, mass, and stopping distance • investigate how the force on an elastic band affects the extension. The follow-up sheet provides tasks and questions to help them complete these activities and check their understanding of the link between force, mass, and acceleration and between force and extension.	Aiming for 8 students use the Checkpoint follow-up sheet to design an investigation into force, mass, and acceleration. The follow-up sheet provides tasks and questions to help them complete their plan and check their understanding of the relationship between force, mass, and acceleration.
	Kerboodle resource P10 Checkpoint follow up: Aiming for 4, P10 Checkpoint follow up: Aiming for 6, P10 Checkpoint follow up: Aiming for 8		
Plenary	**Stop the car (10 min)** Give students A4 dry wipe boards, pens, and an eraser. Read out a series of answers to questions about stopping distance and ask students to write the question, for example, 'because the friction between the wheels of the car and the road is less'.		
	Acceleration race (5 min) Group students by the level to which they are aiming, and give out a pack of cards. Each card should have a picture of an object with the force acting on it and the mass of the object. Include the motorbike, car, and aeroplane from the Starter. Aiming for 4 students should put them in order of fastest to slowest acceleration, and Aiming for 6/8 students should calculate the acceleration. Aiming for 8 students should also calculate the time that would produce the same force on each object if they are all travelling at 10 m/s.		
Progression	Encourage students to think about acceleration as affected by force and mass, rather than force affected by mass and acceleration.	Encourage students to think about acceleration as affected by force and mass, rather than force affected by mass and acceleration, and similarly to explain the effect of force and spring constant on extension.	Encourage students to think about acceleration and extension as the dependent variables.

4 Waves and electromagnetism

Specification links

AQA specification section	Assessment paper
6.1 Waves in air, fluids, and solids	Paper 2
6.2 Electromagnetic waves	Paper 2
7.1 Permanent and induced magnetism, magnetic forces and fields	Paper 2
7.2 The motor effect	Paper 2
8.2 Red-shift (physics only)	Paper 2

Required practicals

AQA required practicals	Practical skills	Topic
Make observations to identify the suitability of apparatus to measure the frequency, wavelength, and speed of waves in a ripple tank and waves in a solid and take appropriate measurements.	AT4 – make observations of waves in fluids and solids to identify the suitability of apparatus to measure speed/frequency/wavelength.	P11.4
Investigate how the amount of infrared radiation absorbed or radiated by a surface depends on the nature of that surface.	AT1 – use appropriate apparatus to make and record temperature accurately. AT4 – make observations of the effects of the interaction of electromagnetic waves with matter.	P12.2

Maths skills

AQA maths skills	Topic
1a Recognise and use expressions in decimal form.	P11.5
1b Recognise and use expressions in standard form.	P12.1, P12.2, P12.4
1c Use ratios, fractions, and percentages.	P11.2, P11.4, P12.1, P12.2, P12.3
3b Change the subject of an equation.	P11.2, P11.4, P12.1, P12.2, P12.3, P13.3
3c Substitute numerical values into algebraic equations using appropriate units for physical quantities.	P11.2, P11.4, P12.1, P12.2, P12.3, P13.3
4a Translate information between graphical and numeric form.	P13.2
5a Use angular measures in degrees.	P11.3
5b Visualise and represent 2D and 3D forms including two dimensional representations of 3D objects.	P11.3, P13.2

P4 Waves and electromagnetism

KS3 concept	GCSE topic	Checkpoint	Revision
Waves are vibrations that transfer energy.	P11.1 The nature of waves	Show the students footage of an earthquake and ask them to describe the energy transfers.	Demonstrate transverse and longitudinal wave motion with a slinky spring.
The top of a water wave is called a crest and the bottom is called a trough.	P11.2 The properties of waves	Students should be asked to label a diagram showing the appropriate parts of a transverse wave such as a ripple.	Students should compare a set of wave diagrams and describe differences in their amplitude and wavelength.
Waves can be reflected by smooth surfaces.	P11.3 Reflection and refraction	Ask students to describe how they can hear an echo of their own voices.	Students should describe the properties of an image reflected in a mirror with a suitable ray diagram.
Sound travels faster in solids than in liquids and faster in liquids than in gas.	P 11.4 Sound waves	Ask students to describe how they could compare the speed of sound in air to the speed of sound in a solid material.	Students should calculate the speed of sound in different materials using distance and time data.
Light waves travel much faster than sound waves.	P12.1 The electromagnetic spectrum	Ask students to explain why we see a flash of lightning before we hear the thunder clap.	Students use distance and speed data to calculate the time taken for a lightning flash and thunder clap to reach them.
The spectrum of white light is continuous from red to orange to yellow to green to blue to violet.	P12.2 Light, infrared, microwaves, and radio waves	Ask students to sketch a labelled diagram of a spectrum.	Demonstrate dispersion of white light by a prism or diffraction grating to produce a spectrum and discuss the colours produced.
A magnet lines up with the Earth's magnetic field.	P15.1 Magnetic fields	Ask students to find magnetic north using a magnet.	Students should describe how the magnetic poles of the Earth differ from the rotational poles.
An electric motor is used to turn objects. An electric generator produces an electric current when it turns.	P15.3 The motor effect	Ask students to describe the uses of a small electric motor.	Ask the students to match up the factors which affect the voltage output of a generator with their effects as well as the factors which affect the power of a motor.

P 11 Wave properties
11.1 The nature of waves

AQA spec Link: 6.1.1 Waves may be either transverse or longitudinal.

The ripples on a water surface are an example of a transverse wave.

Longitudinal waves show areas of compression and rarefaction. Sound waves travelling through air are longitudinal.

Students should be able to describe the difference between longitudinal and transverse waves.

Students should be able to describe evidence that, for both ripples on a water surface and sound waves in air, it is the wave and not the water or air itself that travels.

6.2.1 Electromagnetic waves form a continuous spectrum and all types of electromagnetic wave travel at the same velocity through a vacuum (space) or air.

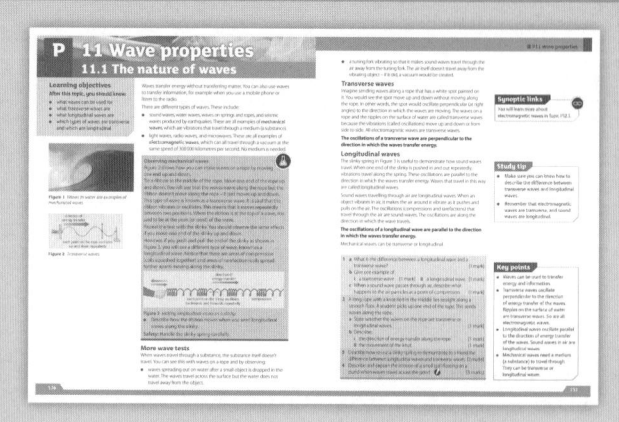

WS 1.2, 2.2

Aiming for	Outcome	Checkpoint	
		Question	Activity
Aiming for GRADE 4	State that waves can transfer energy and information without the transfer of matter.		Starter 1, Main
	Identify waves as either transverse or longitudinal.	1, 2	Main, Plenary 2
	Identify waves as either mechanical or electromagnetic.		Starter 1, Main
Aiming for GRADE 6	Investigate wave motion through a spring model.	3	Main
	Compare transverse and longitudinal waves in terms of direction of vibration and propagation.	1, 2, End of chapter 1	Main, Plenary 2
	Compare electromagnetic and mechanical waves in terms of the need for a medium.	1	Main, Plenary 2
Aiming for GRADE 8	Explain the features of a longitudinal wave in terms of compressions and rarefactions by using a particle model.	3	Main
	Discuss the features of a transverse wave in terms of particle or field behaviour.	4	Main
	Compare mechanical waves and their particulate nature with electromagnetic waves and their field oscillations.		Main

Maths
Students apply mathematical terminology such as parallel and perpendicular to describe wave motion.

Literacy
There is a focus here on careful descriptions and explanations of the behaviour and properties of waves. Students should question each other on these descriptions and refine them.

Key words
mechanical waves, electromagnetic waves, transverse waves, longitudinal waves, compression, rarefaction

Practical

Title	Observing mechanical waves
Equipment	slinky spring, piece of ribbon
Overview of method	Demonstrate longitudinal waves by stretching the spring out slightly and then move one end of the slinky spring in and out whilst keeping the other end still. The emphasis should be on the vibrations of the particles without them actually progressing. Sticking a bit of ribbon on a point on the spring can show this more effectively. Transverse waves can be produced by moving the spring from side to side, showing the particles vibrating at right angles to the direction of propagation of the wave.
Safety considerations	Make sure there is sufficient space, and do not move the spring violently.

P11 Wave properties

Starter	Support/Extend	Resources
Aftershock value (5 min) Use video clips of tsunami and recent earthquakes to demonstrate the power of an 'uncontrolled' wave. Point out the regular vibration in earthquakes – shaking buildings and so on. **Wave** (10 min) Ask students to list as many types of wave as possible. Check through a few lists with the class and then ask the students to explain what a wave actually does. Use some of the examples to get them to realise that waves transfer energy but not material.	**Extend:** Ask students to describe why these waves are not simple, by comparing them with the definition in the student book.	

Main	Support/Extend	Resources
Observing mechanical waves (40 min) Demonstrate mechanical waves in a wire and ripples in water to discuss the movement of particles. This will lead to the students exploring waves in a slinky spring through the practical. Use a light source to discuss electromagnetic waves. The waves act as a pathway to transfer energy (e.g., they can heat surfaces), but they are not transferring material and there are no particles vibrating. Discuss particle behaviour in springs, ropes, and ripples, ensuring that the students can visualise the movement of the particles clearly. Using the spring model again to discuss particle behaviour in longitudinal waves. Make sure that the students understand that forces are acting between the particles causing these vibrations.	**Support:** Provide diagrams so that the students can note the direction of oscillation in the waves. **Extend:** A model of oscillating electric and magnetic fields can be discussed. **Support:** Use the animation to help students with their understanding of longitudinal and transverse waves. **Support:** A support sheet is available to help students with the terminology of this topic.	**Practical:** Observing mechanical waves **Animation:** Transverse and longitudinal waves **Support:** Waves – knowing the words is half the battle

Plenary	Support/Extend	Resources
The same but different (5 min) Interactive where students match key words from the lesson to their definitions, complete a description of longitudinal and transverse waves, then identify true and false statements about longitudinal and transverse waves. **Mexican brain wave** (10 min) Put the students into three or four rows all seated. Select one student to be the questioner in each row and give them a set of questions and answers about waves. The student asks the first person in the row a question – if they get the answer right, then all of the people who have answered correctly so far stand up, wave, sit down, and the questioner moves on.	**Support:** Use foundation-level questions for appropriate groups. **Extend:** Involve higher-level questions.	**Interactive:** The same but different

Homework		
Students can explore the history of people's understanding of light, from particle models to wave models, and finally mixed models.	**Extend:** Students focus on the evidence that leads to a change in a model.	

kerboodle

A Kerboodle highlight for this lesson is **Bump up your grades: Transverse and longitudinal waves**. Refer to the **Content map** on Kerboodle for a full list of resources and assessment.

P11.2 The properties of waves

AQA spec Link: 6.1.2 Students should be able to describe wave motion in terms of their amplitude, wavelength, frequency, and period.

The amplitude of a wave is the maximum displacement of a point on a wave away from its undisturbed position.

The wavelength of a wave is the distance from a point on one wave to the equivalent point on the adjacent wave.

The frequency of a wave is the number of waves passing a point each second.

$$\text{period} = \frac{1}{\text{frequency}}$$

$$[T = \frac{1}{f}]$$

period T in seconds, s

frequency f in hertz, Hz.

The wave speed is the speed at which the energy is transferred (or the wave moves) through the medium.

All waves obey the wave equation:

$$\text{wave speed} = \text{frequency} \times \text{wavelength}$$

$$[v = f \lambda]$$

wave speed v in metres per second, m/s

frequency f in hertz, Hz

wavelength λ in metres, m

Students should be able to:
- identify amplitude and wavelength from given diagrams
- describe a method to measure the speed of sound waves in air
- describe a method to measure the speed of ripples on a water surface.

Required practical: make observations to identify the suitability of apparatus to measure the frequency, wavelength, and speed of waves in a ripple tank and waves in a solid and take appropriate measurements.

MS 1c, 3b, 3c

Aiming for	Outcome	Checkpoint	
		Question	Activity
Aiming for GRADE 4 ↓	Identify the wavelength and amplitude of a wave from a simple diagram.	1, 2	Main 1
	Describe how the frequency of a wave is the number of waves produced each second and is measured in hertz.		Main 1
	Measure the speed of a water wave.		Main 2
Aiming for GRADE 6 ↓	Outline the derivation of the wave speed equation.		Main 2
	Calculate the period of a wave from its frequency.		Main 1, Plenary 2
	Calculate the wave speed from the frequency and wavelength.	3, End of chapter 2	Main 2
Aiming for GRADE 8 ↓	Explain how the wave speed equation can be derived from fundamental principles.		Main 2
	Perform calculations involving rearrangements of the period equation and the wave speed equation.	4, End of chapter 2	Main 1, Plenary 2
	Perform multi-stage calculations linking period, frequency, wave speed, and wavelength.	4	Main 2

Maths
A wide range of calculations take place during this lesson using the wave speed equation and the relationship between frequency and period (1c, 3b, 3c).

Literacy
Students should work in small groups to discuss the movement of waves and the effect of changing frequency on wave speed.

Key words
amplitude, wavelength, frequency, speed

P11 Wave properties

Practical

Title	Measuring the speed of ripples
Equipment	ripple tank, stopwatch, ruler, tray, signal generator, loudspeaker, connecting leads
Overview of method	The practical is as described in the student book. Waterproof trays can be used as an alternative. The students fill the tray to about 1 cm depth – moving the ruler at one end should send a wave along the tray, and this can be measured. Alternatively, a sharp tap on the outside of the tray can initiate a good-quality wave pulse. Students can be extended by using this technique to see whether altering the depth of the water increases or decreases the wave speed. The changes to depth should only be by 1 mm at a time and between 1 and 2 cm overall.
Safety considerations	Clean up any water spills immediately.

Starter	Support/Extend	Resources
Up to speed (5 min) Students use the interactive to perform some simple speed calculations to remind them of this work from KS3. Make sure that they are using the correct units for speed, distance, and time. **Spotlight on knowledge** (10 min) Students need to list the properties of light and any other facts that they know about it. They should be able to produce a range of facts from KS3.	**Extend:** The students need to rearrange the equation and use more challenging data. **Support:** Students can confirm or refute a set of facts presented to them.	**Interactive:** Up to speed

Main	Support/Extend	Resources
Describing waves (20 min) Remind students of the basic shape of a transverse wave through a simple demonstration with a rope, and then each of the measureable or identifiable characteristics can be discussed. Particular attention should be paid to the amplitude because this is commonly mislabelled. Continue the analysis by looking at changing the frequency and showing the number of waves passing a fixed point per second on the rope. The relationship between frequency and period needs to be discussed, and the students should perform an example calculation. **Measuring the speed of ripples** (20 min) The wave speed equation can then be introduced, ideally using a ripple tank. Demonstrate that changing the frequency has an effect on the wavelength whilst the speed stays the same. Model a calculation and then ask students to try their own. The students can then use the ripple tanks to investigate the wave equation.	**Support:** Provide a diagram for the students to label and measure. Limit calculations to the $T = \frac{1}{f}$ arrangement. **Extend:** The amplitude of a longitudinal wave can be discussed in terms of maximum particle displacement. **Extend:** An extension sheet is available where students look at a wave diagram to calculate speed and frequency. **Extend:** Explain the derivation of the wave speed equation. Students may also investigate whether depth of water has an effect on wave speed.	**Practical:** Measuring the speed of ripples **Extension:** Waves

Plenary	Support/Extend	Resources
Wave taboo (5 min) Split the students into groups and assign each students a key word (e.g., transverse, longitudinal, reflect, speed) and a list of words they cannot use to describe it. Students take it in turns to describe their key word. How many can the group get in a set time limit? **Kinaesthetic maths challenge** (10 min) Provide students with cards labelled 'wavelength', 'wave speed', 'frequency', '×', and '='. Each card has a number on it too. The students must form themselves into 'living equations' by standing in groups of five to make a correct equation.	**Support:** Reduce the number of words in the 'banned words' list for each question. **Extend:** Provide students with more difficult numbers and questions that require rearrangement.	

Homework		
Students complete the calculation sheet to practise using the wave equation.		**Calculation sheet:** The wave equation

kerboodle

A Kerboodle highlight for this lesson is **Maths skills: The wave equation**. Refer to the **Content map** on Kerboodle for a full list of resources and assessment.

Higher tier

P11.3 Reflection and refraction

AQA spec Link: 6.2.2 Different substances may absorb, transmit, refract, or reflect electromagnetic waves in ways that vary with wavelength.

Some effects, for example refraction, are due to the difference in velocity of the waves in different substances.

Students should be able to construct ray diagrams to illustrate the refraction of a wave at the boundary between two different media.

Students should be able to use wave front diagrams to explain refraction in terms of the change of speed that happens when a wave travels from one medium to a different medium.

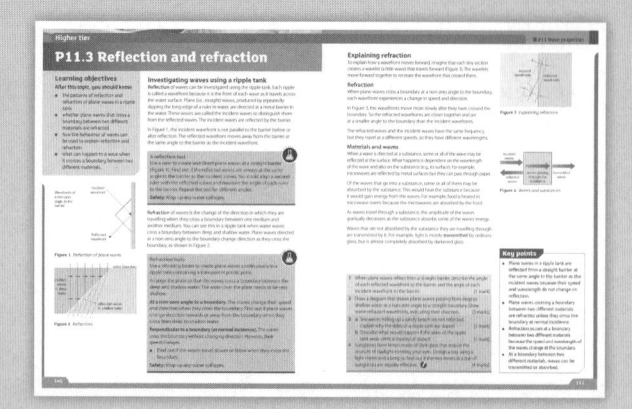

WS 1.2
MS 5a, 5b

Aiming for	Outcome	Checkpoint	
		Question	Activity
Aiming for GRADE 6	Describe refraction at a boundary in terms of wavefronts.	2, End of chapter 3	Main 2
	Describe refraction including the reflected rays.		Main 1
	Explain partial absorption as a decrease in the amplitude of a wave and therefore the energy carried.	4	Main 1
Aiming for GRADE 8	Use a wavefront model to explain refraction and reflection.		Main 2
	Describe the relationship between the angle of incidence and angle of refraction.	2, End of chapter 4	Main 1
	Explain refraction in terms of changes in the speed of waves when they move between one medium and another.	2, End of chapter 4	Main 2

Maths
Students measure and describe changes in angle when observing ray and wavefront paths (5a, 5b).

Literacy
The students discuss the wavefront model of reflection and refraction, forming and sharing explanations at different levels of understanding.

Key words
reflection, refraction, transmitted

Practical

Title	A reflection test
Equipment	ripple tank (or a plastic tray), ruler, solid obstacle, protractor
Overview of method	Students investigate the reflection of wave fronts using the ripple tank or water tray by sending a simple wave towards a barrier and measuring the angle of reflection.
Safety considerations	Clean up any water spills immediately.

Title	Refraction tests
Equipment	ripple tank, wave generator, block to alter depth of water
Overview of method	Students investigate the refraction of wave fronts using the ripple tank by allowing waves to pass over submerged obstacles.
	Simulations of ripple tanks are a simpler, safer, and cheaper alternative but these should be used alongside a demonstration of a real ripple tank to show the real scenarios.
Safety considerations	Clean up any water spills immediately.

■ P11 Wave properties

Starter	Support/Extend	Resources
It's just a broken pencil (5 min) Place a pencil in a beaker of water. Can the students produce an explanation of why the pencil looks broken? This is quite difficult – make sure that the students see the effect clearly (show a big photograph on the interactive whiteboard if needed). **Ray diagram** (10 min) Ask students to draw a ray diagram showing how they can see a non-luminous object such as the writing in their books. Make sure that the students are using a ruler to draw rays of light and that the rays are reflecting cleanly from the surface.	**Extend:** Ask students to draw a ray diagram explaining the effect. **Extend:** Ask students to critique each other's work and advise each other how to correct the work to make it the highest possible standard.	

Main	Support/Extend	Resources
Investigating reflection and refraction (25 min) Demonstrate the operation of the ripple tank focusing on reflection. The students can then introduce the barrier during the practical and find out about the reflection of the wavefronts at different angles. Link this to the simple light reflection experiments that students will have studied in KS3. Some students can also investigate the effect of changing the depth of water in a ripple tank and note the changes in speed of the wavefronts. Students should be able to see that speed changes during the refraction whilst the frequency does not change. **Explaining reflection and refraction** (15 min) Discuss the use of wavefronts and wavelets to explain reflection using a series of diagrams or a simulation. Use simulations or the ripple tank to show the behaviour of wavefronts during refraction, altering the angle of incidence to show the changing effect.	**Support:** Provide a visual set of instructions for the students to follow. **Extend:** Students can devise a method to verify the law of refection.	**Practical:** Investigating reflection and refraction **Bump up your grade:** Wave diagrams

Plenary	Support/Extend	Resources
Reflect or refract? (10 min) Interactive where students summarise the differences between reflection and refraction. They then identify correct ray diagrams showing reflection and refraction. **Mirror maze** (5 min) Check students' understanding of the law of reflection by asking them to add mirrors to a simple maze diagram so that a light ray can pass through it to the centre.		**Interactive:** Reflect or refract?

Homework		
Students complete question 4 from the student book where they design a test using a light meter and a lamp to find out if the two lenses in a pair of sunglasses are equally effective.		

kerboodle

A Kerboodle highlight for this lesson is **Working scientifically: Spectacle lens options**. Refer to the **Content map** on Kerboodle for a full list of resources and assessment.

P11.4 More about waves

AQA spec Link: 5.6.1.2 A typical value for the speed of sound in air is 330 m/s.

6.1.2 Required practical: Make observations to identify the suitability of apparatus to measure the frequency, wavelength, and speed of waves in a ripple tank and waves in a solid and take appropriate measurements.

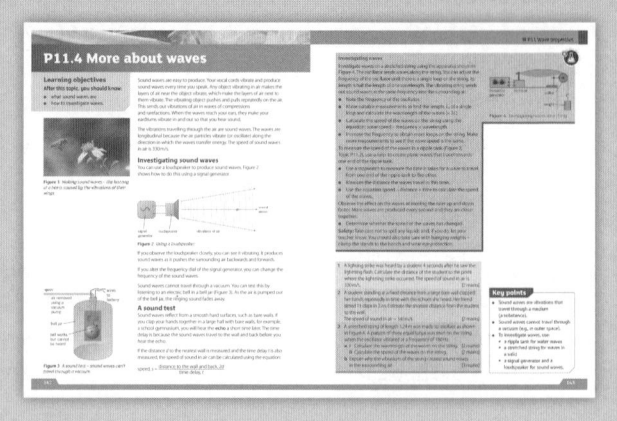

MS 1c, 3b, 3c

Aiming for	Outcome	Checkpoint	
		Question	Activity
Aiming for GRADE 4 ↓	Measure the speed of a wave in water.		Main
	Describe how sound waves travel more quickly in solid than they do in gases.		Main
	State that sound waves require a medium to travel in.		Main
Aiming for GRADE 6 ↓	Measure the speed of a wave in a solid (string).		Main
	Describe the effect that changing the frequency of a wave has on its wavelength in a medium.		Main
	Calculate the speed of waves using the wave speed equation.		Main
Aiming for GRADE 8 ↓	Evaluate the suitability of apparatus for measuring the frequency, wavelength, and speed of waves.		Main
	Explain why the wavelength of a wave in a particular medium changes as the frequency changes with reference to the wave equation.		Main
	Evaluate data from speed of sound experiments to discuss the range of uncertainty.		Main, Plenary 2, Homework

Maths
All students calculate the speed of sound, and some use speed and timing data to measure distances (1c, 3b, 3c).

Literacy
The reflection, absorption, and refraction of sound waves are used in descriptions of energy transfers.

Key words
echo

Required practical

Title	Investigating waves in a solid
Equipment	signal generator, vibration generator, pulley, masses on a mass holder, length of high quality string or wire (at least 1 m in length, preferably over 2 m), tape measure or meter rule
Overview of method	Test the apparatus in advance to ensure that stationary waves can be produced across its length using the vibrating motor. This depends on both the wire material and the tension in it. It may not be easy to set up a single half wave pattern as shown in the student book, therefore the students may need to start with a whole wave pattern depending on the wire and tension chosen.
Students set up stationary wave patterns measuring both the frequency (from the signal generator) and the wavelength (with the tape measure) trying to obtain at least four different patterns. They should discover that the wave speed is constant.
Safety considerations	The pulley should be clamped to the desk. Be careful of falling masses.

■ P11 Wave properties

Title	Investigating waves in a ripple tank
Equipment	ripple tank (or tray of water) and ruler, video camera, squared paper
Overview	Students measure the length of the tank and then produce ripples, timing how long they take to travel the length of the tank. This data is used to determine the wave speed. Placing squared paper beneath the tank and videoing the wave motion can make it easier to see that the wavelength decreases as the frequency increases.
Safety	Clear up any spilled water immediately.

Starter	Support/Extend	Resources
Sound facts (5 min) Give the students a set of 'facts' about sound and let them use traffic light cards to indicate whether they agree (green), don't know (amber), or disagree (red). **Good vibrations** (10 min) How do different instruments produce sound waves? Students should describe what is going on for five different ways of producing a sound. Demonstrate a drum, guitar, flute or recorder, loudspeaker, and singing. This should show that vibrations are needed to produce sound waves.	**Support:** Select simple 'facts' that are obviously true or false. **Extend:** Select 'facts' that are more open to debate and discussion. **Support:** Video clips can be used to illustrate the vibrations. **Extend:** The vibrations of key areas of acoustic instruments can be analysed.	

Main	Support/Extend	Resources
Investigating waves (40 min) Students should briefly examine the behaviour of sound waves in air and how a medium is required for these waves to travel. They then move on to investigate waves in solids and liquids using the two practical tasks as outlined. The practicals can be carried out simultaneously. The first practical relies on producing stationary waves which allow the wavelength to be measured. Students do not need to know the details of how these form; they only need to measure their wavelength. The second practical uses simple ripples which can be produced with a ruler or with a vibrating bar in a ripple tank.	**Support:** When investigating waves in a solid, provide students with approximate set of frequencies which will produce stationary waves. **Extend:** When investigating waves in a ripple tank, students can investigate whether changing the tension in the wire has any effect on the wave speed in it.	**Required practical:** Investigating waves

Plenary	Support/Extend	Resources
Oscilloscope solutions (5 min) Students use the interactive to match a set of problems encountered when using the oscilloscope to appropriate solutions, for example, a trace where the waves' peaks are too close together – the solution is to reduce the time base. **Let's hear your ideas** (10 min) Students need to design a simple experiment that will show that sound travels faster in solid materials than it does in air. This could be either a basic plan or a more detailed one.	**Extend:** Students should not be provided with potential solutions – they can produce their own. **Extend:** The plan must include procedures for measuring the speed.	**Interactive:** Oscilloscope solutions

Homework		
Students complete the WebQuest where they research the physics of Felix Baumgartner's skydive, where he broke the sound barrier.		**WebQuest:** Supersonic skydive

kerboodle

A Kerboodle highlight for this lesson is **Working scientifically: Measuring sound**. Refer to the **Content map** on Kerboodle for a full list of resources and assessment.

P11 Wave properties

Overview of P11 Wave properties

In this chapter the students have observed and described the properties of mechanical and electromagnetic waves in terms of energy transfer with or without the need for a transfer medium. They have compared transverse waves and longitudinal waves by examining the relationship between the direction of propagation and the direction of the oscillations.

The students have analysed wave properties such as wavelength, amplitude, and period leading to the relationships between period, frequency and wave speed, frequency, and wavelength. They have also measured the speed of sound in air and the speed of ripples on water.

Higher-tier students have investigated and described both the reflection and refraction of waves describing these effects in terms of wave fronts. The processes of absorption, transmission, and reflection of waves in terms of energy have also been described.

Required practical

All students are expected to have carried out the required practical:

Practical	Topic
Make observations to identify the suitability of apparatus to measure the frequency, wavelength, and speed of waves in a ripple tank and waves in a solid and take appropriate measurements.	P11.4

MyMaths

You can find additional support for the maths skills covered in this chapter on **MyMaths**, including recognising and using expressions in decimal form, using an appropriate number of significant figures, understanding and using the symbols: $=, <, \ll, \gg, >, \propto, \sim$, and changing the subject of an equation.

kerboodle

For this chapter, the following assessments are available on Kerboodle:

P11 Checkpoint quiz: Wave properties
P11 Progress quiz: Wave properties 1
P11 Progress quiz: Wave properties 2
P11 On your marks: Wave properties
P11 Exam-style questions and mark scheme: Wave properties

Checkpoint follow up lesson

A student's route through this lesson can be determined using the Checkpoint assessment. Percentage pass marks are supplied in the Checkpoint teacher notes.

For each successive route through it is assumed that the student can perform to their current route as well as previous routes. For example, students working at Aiming for 6 are assumed to be secure in Aiming for 4 knowledge and understanding and working towards achieving all the learning outcomes for Aiming for 6.

	Aiming for 4	**Aiming for 6**	**Aiming for 8**
Learning outcomes	Describe the nature and properties of waves.	Use equations for wave speed.	Recall and use the equations for wave speed and period.
	Describe what happens to waves when they hit a boundary.	Explain why waves are reflected and refracted.	Explain the behaviour of waves at boundaries.
Starter	**Articulate waves (10 min)** Give out cards with a wave property/key word on it and ask each student in the group in turn to pull out a card and explain the word to the group without using the word. The groups can keep score, and the student with the most correct answers can get a prize.		
	How fast? (5 min) Use cymbals or a fog horn make a short, loud sound. Give each student a piece of card, and ask students to write down: their name, the time for the sound to hit a wall and reach their ear, and the distance that a wall would need to be from them for them to hear an echo after 1 second. Students should put the cards in an envelope with the name of their group on it and give it to you.		
Differentiated checkpoint activity	Aiming for 4 students use the Checkpoint follow-up sheet to make a game about the nature and properties of waves, and practise using equations for wave speed and period.	Aiming for 6 students use the Checkpoint follow-up sheet to practise using equations for wave speed and period and model the reflection and refraction of waves.	Aiming for 8 students use the Checkpoint follow-up sheet to devise methods of modelling reflection and refraction.
	The follow-up sheet provides structured tasks and questions to help them complete these activities and check their understanding of the key words of this topic, use the wave equation correctly and calculate period.	The follow-up sheet provides tasks and questions to help them complete these activities and check their understanding of how to use the wave equation and what happens to waves when they interact with surfaces.	The follow-up sheet provides tasks and questions to help them complete these activities and check their understanding of the processes of reflection and refraction and how to explain refraction.
	Kerboodle resource P11 Checkpoint follow up: Aiming for 4, P11 Checkpoint follow up: Aiming for 6, P11 Checkpoint follow up: Aiming for 8		
Plenary	**Speed and structure (10 min)** Give students the task of working out the time using speed and distance, and distance using speed and time from the starter question. Work out which student/s were correct, and, if possible give out a small prize.		
	Aiming for 4 students can sort a set of cards with statements such as 'the period of a wave with a frequency of 10 Hz is 0.1 s into true statements and false statements.		
Progression	Encourage students to describe what happens to waves when they are reflected and refracted.	Encourage students to use changes of direction in refraction in terms of changes of speed.	Encourage students to think about changes of direction in refraction in terms of changes of speed and to link ideas of reflection and refraction to the production of the images of internal structure of people and the Earth.

P 12 Electromagnetic waves
12.1 The electromagnetic spectrum

AQA spec Link: 6.1.2 The wave speed is the speed at which the energy is transferred (or the wave moves) through the medium.

All waves obey the wave equation:

wave speed = frequency × wavelength

$[v = f\lambda]$

wave speed v in metres per second, m/s

frequency f in hertz, Hz

wavelength λ in metres, m

6.2.1 Electromagnetic waves are transverse waves that transfer energy from the source of the waves to an absorber.

Electromagnetic waves form a continuous spectrum and all types of electromagnetic wave travel at the same velocity through a vacuum (space) or air.

MS 1b, 1c, 3b, 3c

The waves that form the electromagnetic spectrum are grouped in terms of their wavelength and their frequency. Going from long to short wavelength (or from low to high frequency) the groups are: radio, microwave, infrared, visible light (red to violet), ultraviolet, X-rays and gamma rays.

Long wavelength ⟶ Short wavelength

| Radio waves | Microwaves | Infrared | Visible light | Ultraviolet | X-rays | Gamma rays |

Low frequency ⟶ Higher frequency

Our eyes detect visible light and so only detect a limited range of electromagnetic waves.

Students should be able to give examples that illustrate the transfer of energy by electromagnetic waves.

(H) 6.2.2 Different substances may absorb, transmit, refract, or reflect electromagnetic waves in ways that vary with wavelength.

Aiming for	Outcome	Checkpoint Question	Checkpoint Activity
Aiming for GRADE 4	State that electromagnetic (EM) waves transfer energy without transferring matter.		Starter 1, Main 1
	Identify the position of EM waves in the spectrum in order of wavelength and frequency.	2, 4	Main 1
	State that all EM waves travel at the same speed in a vacuum.	4	Starter 2, Main 1
Aiming for GRADE 6	Describe the relationship between the energy being transferred by an electromagnetic wave and the frequency of the wave.	1	Main 2
	Calculate the frequency and the wavelength of an electromagnetic wave.	3	Main 1, Plenary 2
	Explain why the range of wavelengths detected by the human eye is limited.		Main 1, Main 2
Aiming for GRADE 8	Apply the wave model of electromagnetic radiation as a pair of electric and magnetic disturbances that do not require a medium for travel.		Main 1
	Use standard form in calculations of wavelength, frequency, and wave speed.	3	Main 2, Plenary 2
	Explain the interactions between an electromagnetic wave and matter.	End of chapter 6	Main 2

Maths
Students calculate wave speed using the wave speed equation (3c). Some students rearrange this equation and use standard form in these calculations (1b, 1c, 3b).

Literacy
Students describe the discovery of different regions of the electromagnetic spectrum in a brief report (Homework).

Key words
wave speed

■ P12 Electromagnetic waves

Practical

Title	Introducing electromagnetic waves
Equipment	small radio, kitchen foil, microwave transmitter and receiver (if available), infrared remote control and device, sheet of paper, sheet of glass, UV source sheet of acetate or OHP sheet, sunscreen, white object
Overview of method	Radio waves: surround a small radio set with kitchen foil and see if it still picks up radio signals. Microwaves: Use a microwave transmitter and receiver. Infrared: Try using a remote control through paper, glass, and a human body. Ultraviolet: Investigate the effectiveness of sunscreen by smearing it onto acetate and seeing if it stops UV getting through and making a white object behind the acetate glow.
Safety considerations	Students must not touch the IR source or stare into the UV source.

Starter	Support/Extend	Resources
The visible spectrum (10 min) Ask students to outline their prior knowledge of the electromagnetic spectrum by asking them to show how light is reflected, transmitted, or refracted. **Light speed** (5 min) Ask the students to use the following data to determine the speed of light. It takes 1.3 s to travel from the Earth to the Moon, a distance of 390 000 km [300 000 km/s or 300 000 000 m/s].	**Extend:** Move on to see if they can explain reflection from coloured surfaces – this includes reflection and absorption. **Extend:** Use standard form for the numerical values.	

Main	Support/Extend	Resources
Introducing electromagnetic waves (25 min) Recap the nature of electromagnetic radiation compared with mechanical waves. Focus on the wide range of wavelengths of the waves, linking this to the effects. Show the link between frequency and wavelength. Students need to attempt a few calculations of wavelength and frequency. Outline the link between frequency and energy. Students then carry out the practical. They can either rotate through all of the experiments, or each group carries out one experiment and then they share and discuss results. **EM waves and matter** (15 min) 🄷 Recap absorption, reflection, and transmission using visible light as an example and ask students if this behaviour will be the same for all electromagnetic waves and materials.	**Extend:** Introduce the concept of oscillations in linked electric and magnetic fields to describe the waves. **Support:** Provide examples of how to deal with very large and small numbers which cannot be typed directly into a calculator. **Extend:** Discuss the effect on temperature when EM waves are absorbed.	**Practical:** Introducing electromagnetic waves **Maths skills:** Electromagnetic waves

Plenary	Support/Extend	Resources
RMIVUXG? (5 min) The students may know a mnemonic to give the order of the visible spectrum. Can they think up a method of remembering the regions of the electromagnetic spectrum? **EM calculations** (10 min) Students complete the interactive where they are given further calculations of wavelength or frequency for electromagnetic waves.	**Extend:** Speeds in other materials can be incorporated in examples.	**Interactive:** EM calculations

Homework		
Students can research the discovery of different regions of the EM spectrum to find out how each group of waves was discovered.	**Support:** Assign students a particular region to ensure all are covered.	

kerboodle
A Kerboodle highlight for this lesson is **Working scientifically: Unthinkably small, unimaginably large**. Refer to the **Content map** on Kerboodle for a full list of resources and assessment.

P12.2 Light, infrared, microwaves, and radio waves

AQA spec Link: 6.2.4 Electromagnetic waves have many practical applications. For example:
- radio waves – television and radio
- microwaves – satellite communications, cooking food
- infrared – electrical heaters, cooking food, infrared cameras
- visible light – fibre optic communications.

(H) Students should be able to give brief explanations why each type of electromagnetic wave is suitable for the practical application.

6.2.2 Required practical: Investigate how the amount of infrared radiation absorbed or radiated by a surface depends on the nature of that surface.

WS 1.4
MS 1b, 1c, 3b, 3c

Aiming for	Outcome	Checkpoint	
		Question	Activity
Aiming for GRADE 4 ↓	Describe how white light is a part of the electromagnetic spectrum and is composed of a range of frequencies.	End of chapter 1	Starter 2, Main 2
	List some simple examples of the uses of light, microwaves, and radio waves.	1, 3, End of chapter 1	Main 2, Plenary 1
	Measure the rate of cooling due to emission of infrared radiation.		Main 1
Aiming for GRADE 6 ↓	Describe how a range of electromagnetic waves are used in a variety of scenarios.	1, 3, End of chapter 6	Main 2
	(H) **Explain why a particular wave is suited to its application.**	2	Main 2
	Plan an investigation into the rate of cooling of infrared radiation.	4	Main 1
Aiming for GRADE 8 ↓	Determine the wavelength of radio waves in air.	3, End of chapter 2	Plenary 2
	Describe the interactions between a range of waves and matter, including the effect of absorption.	2, 4	Starter 2, Main 1, Main 2
	Evaluate an investigation into the rate of cooling of infrared radiation.	4	Main 1, Homework

Maths
Students compare waves in terms of wavelength and frequency and calculate the wavelength of some EM waves (1b, 1c, 3b, 3c).

Literacy
Students work in small groups identifying and discussing the properties of various EM waves and writing up an investigation.

Key words
white light

Required practical

Title	Absorption and emission of infrared radiation
Equipment	kettles or another way of heating water, two drink cans or two beakers (one painted silver and the other matt black), two thermometers (to 0.5°C), aluminium foil (if beakers are used), stopwatch, a measuring cylinder, ice cold water, infrared lamp or sunlight
Overview of method	Add the same volume of hot water to each of the containers and record the temperature every 30 seconds for 5 to 10 minutes as they cool. The containers can be filled with very cold water and placed in sunlight or under an infrared lamp to explore the absorption of infrared radiation.
Safety considerations	Avoid spills and scalds from hot water.

■ P12 Electromagnetic waves

Starter	Support/Extend	Resources
Radio gaga (5 min) Give the students a set of mixed-up sentences about radio waves and ask them to sort the words into the right order to produce correct sentences. **Colour filters** (10 min) Shine a bright white light through a series of filters and ask the students to explain what is happening with a diagram. Ask the students if they think that there will be a similar effect for the non-visible parts of the spectrum. This leads into the absorption of electromagnetic energy as it passes through materials.	**Support:** Remind students that white light is composed of bands of colours, and give an example of the effect of a filter before asking them to try some of their own.	

Main	Support/Extend	Resources
Absorption and emission of infrared radiation (20 min) Students investigate the absorption and emission of infrared radiation using the required practical task. **Electromagnetic radiation** (20 min) Remind students of the different parts of the electromagnetic spectrum. Then introduce the uses of IR radiation, microwaves, and radio waves. • IR radiation – emphasise the relatively low energy of the waves but explain that high intensity (relate to 'brightness') can mean that large amounts of energy can be delivered by electric heaters and so on. • Microwaves – describe the uses of microwaves, ideally with a phone and a microwave oven as props. Students should note that microwaves are absorbed by water and fat molecules, and this absorption produces the heating effect. • Radio waves – Demonstrate a radio to show that radio waves can penetrate walls. Bluetooth devices such as console game controllers can also be shown. Moving the device gradually further away from its partner will allow the students to check the maximum range. They should use the student book (and other resources if available) to produce a revision summary of the uses of the different parts of the electromagnetic spectrum.	**Extend:** Discuss the reduction in intensity with distance, leading to the idea of an inverse square law. **Extend:** The intensity of the microwaves can be discussed to explain why ovens cook food but mobile phones do not. Discuss the effect of absorption of radio waves in metal wires as part of an explanation about how antennae operate.	**Required practical:** Absorption and emission of infrared radiation

Plenary	Support/Extend	Resources
EM wave summary (10 min) Students produce a summary about all of the areas of the electromagnetic spectrum they have studied so far. **What's the frequency?** (5 min) Students use the interactive to calculate the wavelengths of some radio stations when given the frequency. They should then calculate the radio station frequency when given the wavelength. This recaps the calculations from earlier.	**Support:** Provide a table for the summary or a partially completed visual summary. **Support:** Use calculation templates to support students. **Extend:** Use standard form and SI prefixes.	**Interactive:** What's the frequency?

Homework		
Students can plan to investigate the penetrating power of microwaves, comparing the density of the material with the stopping power.	**Support:** Provide a framework for the students to use to make their plans.	

P12.3 Communications

AQA spec Link: (H) **6.2.2** Different substances may absorb, transmit, refract, or reflect electromagnetic waves in ways that vary with wavelength.

Students should be able to construct ray diagrams to illustrate the refraction of a wave at the boundary between two different media.

(H) **6.2.3** Radio waves can be produced by oscillations in electrical circuits.

When radio waves are absorbed they may create an alternating current with the same frequency as the radio wave itself, so radio waves can themselves induce oscillations in an electrical circuit.

6.2.4 Electromagnetic waves have many practical applications. For example:
- radio waves – television and radio
- microwaves – satellite communications, cooking food
- visible light – fibre optic communications.

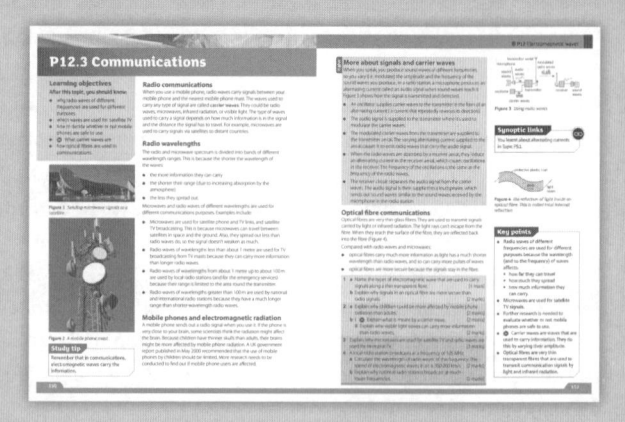

MS 1c, 3b, 3c

Aiming for	Outcome	Checkpoint	
		Question	Activity
Aiming for GRADE 4 ↓	State that radio waves and microwaves are used in communications through the atmosphere.	1	Main 1
	State that the higher the frequency of a wave, the greater the rate of data transfer possible.	1	Main 1, Main 2
	Describe the sub-regions of the radio spectrum.	3	Main 1
Aiming for GRADE 6 ↓	Compare the rate of information transfer through optical fibres and radio signals.	1	Main 1, Main 2
	Outline the operation of a mobile phone network and the waves used.	1	Main 1
	Discuss the evidence for mobile phone signals causing damage to humans.	2, End of chapter 3	Main 1
Aiming for GRADE 8 ↓	(H) Describe in detail how carrier waves are used in the transfer of information.		Main 2
	(H) Describe the structure of a radio communication system, including the effect of a radio wave on the current in the receiver.		Main 2
	Discuss the relationship between wavelength, data transmission, and range to explain why particular frequencies are chosen for particular transmissions.	3, 4	Main 1, Main 2

Maths
Students use the wave equation to calculate wavelength from frequency for electromagnetic waves (1c, 3b, 3c).

Literacy
A wide variety of communication systems can be discussed by the students.

Key words
carrier waves

Practical

Title	Optical fibres for communication
Equipment	length of optical fibre (2–10 m), bright light source (preferably one that can be switched on and off quickly)
Overview of method	Bend the fibre around several objects. Allow one student to observe the distant end whilst demonstrating the flash of a torch into the near end. Even with the thinnest of fibres, the transmitted light should be obvious.
Safety considerations	Ensure that there is adequate space for the activity.

■ P12 Electromagnetic waves

Starter	Support/Extend	Resources
Instant messaging (5 min) How does mobile phone messaging work? Students complete the interactive to explain how a message gets from one phone to another phone in the same room by putting the different stages in order. **Get the message across** (10 min) The students must think up as many ways as possible to communicate with each other and pass on a simple message such as 'I am hungry' or 'I am thirsty'.	**Support:** Provide the stages and ask students to place them into a flow chart. **Support:** Provide some unusual examples such as semaphore.	**Interactive:** Instant messaging

Main	Support/Extend	Resources
Radio waves and mobile phones (20 min) Discuss the various regions of the radio spectrum, with a particular emphasis on the position of microwaves within it. Link this to the rate at which data can be transmitted – microwaves provide the greatest rate. Discuss the transmission of signals, particularly the need for transmission towers – the phones do not communicate directly. An older, broken phone may be useful here to show the aerial. No link between mobile phone use and brain effects has so far been found – the intensity of the signals are very low and are unlikely to cause damage. Students then complete the Bump up your grade worksheet to consolidate their understanding of the electromagnetic spectrum and how microwaves and radio waves are used in communication. **Optical fibres for communication** (20 min) Demonstrate a simple transition of light pulsed through a fibre with a torch and convoluted path for the cable. Remind students that visible light and IR are much higher frequency than radio and so fibres will transmit data at a higher rate. Students can compare energy and information transfer through a fibre to that in radio transmissions. **(H)** Higher-tier students also need to discuss signals and carrier waves. The process here is quite complex and students need to be led through the stages carefully.	**Support:** A flow chart can simplify the explanation. **Extend:** Discuss the ray path within the fibre core, showing total internal reflection. **Support:** Foundation-tier students can spend this time discussing safety precautions for the use of mobile phones.	**Bump up your grade:** Communicate – Stay in touch **Activity:** Optical fibres for communication

Plenary	Support/Extend	Resources
Round the bend (5 min) Give the students a diagram of an optical fibre with a curved path and ask them to draw the path of a ray that is shown entering the fibre. **Broken signal** (10 min) Students design a leaflet from a satellite TV company explaining why the television signal has been poor recently. It should explain how the TV signal is transmitted to the house and what factors can affect it (rain, snow, sunspots).	**Extend:** Provide a more convoluted fibre diagram and insist on proper construction of the reflection.	

Homework		
Students complete the WebQuest where they research claims that radio waves from human technologies are making people ill. They use their research to create an information leaflet for people who are worried about this.		

kerboodle

A Kerboodle highlight for this lesson is **Working scientifically: Range of a Bluetooth dongle**. Refer to the **Content map** on Kerboodle for a full list of resources and assessment.

P12.4 Ultraviolet waves, X-rays, and gamma rays

AQA spec Link: 6.2.3 Changes in atoms and the nuclei of atoms can result in electromagnetic waves being generated or absorbed over a wide frequency range. Gamma rays originate from changes in the nucleus of an atom.

Ultraviolet waves, X-rays, and gamma rays can have hazardous effects on human body tissue. The effects depend on the type of radiation and the size of the dose. Radiation dose (in sieverts) is a measure of the risk of harm resulting from an exposure of the body to the radiation.

Ultraviolet waves can cause skin to age prematurely and increase the risk of skin cancer. X-rays and gamma rays are ionising radiation that can cause the mutation of genes and cancer.

6.2.4 Electromagnetic waves have many practical applications. For example:
- ultraviolet – energy efficient lamps, sun tanning
- X-rays and gamma rays – medical imaging and treatments.

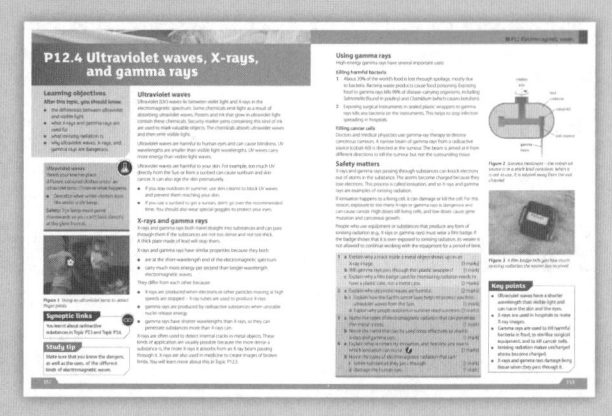

WS 1.5
MS 1b

Aiming for	Outcome	Checkpoint	
		Question	Activity
Aiming for GRADE 4 ↓	State that high-frequency electromagnetic radiation is ionising.		Main
	Describe the uses and dangers of ultraviolet (UV) radiation.	2	Starter 2, Main
	Describe the uses and dangers of X-rays and gamma radiation.	End of chapter 5	Starter 2, Main
Aiming for GRADE 6 ↓	Describe the penetrating powers of gamma rays, X-rays, and ultraviolet rays.	1, 2, 3	Main
	Compare X-rays and gamma radiation in terms of their origin.		Main
	Describe the ionisation of atoms in simple terms.	4, End of chapter 5	Main
Aiming for GRADE 8 ↓	Describe in detail the interaction between ionising radiation and inorganic materials.	End of chapter 6	Main
	Compare different regions of the electromagnetic spectrum in terms of their potential harmfulness.	4	Main
	Explain how the process of ionisation can lead to cell death or cancer through damage to DNA.	4, End of chapter 5	Main

Maths
Students may compare electromagnetic waves in terms of wavelength or frequency using standard form (1b).

Literacy
The students describe the effects of radiation on living cells and discuss the safety concerns.

Key words
ionisation

Practical

Title	Ultraviolet waves
Equipment	ultraviolet lamp, samples of different coloured clothing (or fabric)
	optional: cloths washed in biological washing powder, white paper, real paper money, other UV-responsive objects (e.g., nail-varnish beads)
Overview of method	Demonstrate the effect of UV light on the different clothing whilst explaining that they absorb the UV light and then emit visible light.
	Optional: demonstrate with the further suggested objects. Discuss the reaction of the paper money compared with that of the white paper.
Safety considerations	Ensure that students cannot look directly into the UV light source as this can cause eye damage.

■ P12 Electromagnetic waves

Starter	Support/Extend	Resources
Mutant mayhem (5 min) 'Mutants' with super powers caused by exposure to radiation are common in films and comics. Do students think that this radiation can have beneficial effects in reality? **Stellar imagery** (10 min) Show a range of images of the Sun, capturing the different parts of the EM spectrum (a visible light image, ultraviolet, infrared, and so on). Discuss how these images are captured and which parts reach the surface of the Earth.	**Extend:** A graph showing the transmission characteristics of the atmosphere can be used.	

Main	Support/Extend	Resources
UV, X-rays, and gamma rays (40 min) Start by demonstrating the effect of UV radiation on a range of materials to show that it exists using the practical outlined. Emphasise the damage it can cause, particularly to the eyes. Images of skin damage are readily available on the Internet. Move to higher-frequency/higher-energy waves, emphasising the penetrating power through different materials. A few simple non-medical X-ray photographs can be used to outline a use for X-rays, because medical photographs will be used in Topic P13.5. Outline the key uses of gamma radiation, all of which are linked to high energy causing ionisation and damage to living cells. Describe the process of ionisation and, in particular, the damage to DNA. The students should understand that the greater the exposure, the more damage is likely. Various control procedures should be discussed, including reducing exposure, protective clothing, and dose measurement. The students should be provided with some data about the risks associated with radiation exposure to analyse.	**Extend:** Discuss the difference in origin of X-rays and gamma radiation. **Support:** Simple descriptions, without example bacteria and radioactive sources, can be used. **Extend:** Describe the process of ionisation in more depth, mentioning the role of the freed electron in causing further damage.	**Activity:** UV, X-rays, and gamma rays

Plenary	Support/Extend	Resources
One world (5 min) Interactive where students complete a paragraph to briefly discuss the problem with the ozone layer discovered in the 1980s and the steps taken to reduce it, to show that global problems can be solved when countries work together. **Safety first** (10 min) Students design a safety notice for either a sunbed or an X-ray machine.	**Extend:** The timescale for recovery can be discussed – the damage will not be overcome until 2050 or later. **Support:** Provide key phrases and images that may be used for the notice.	**Interactive:** One world

Homework		
Students can plan an investigation into the effectiveness of UV sunscreen lotion using a UV detector.	**Extend:** Expect a fully formed plan that can be carried out within the laboratory, including any safety precautions needed.	

kerboodle

A Kerboodle highlight for this lesson is **Bump up your grade: Electromagnetic waves**. Refer to the **Content map** on Kerboodle for a full list of resources and assessment.

P12.5 X-rays in medicine

AQA spec Link: 6.2.3 X-rays can have hazardous effects on human body tissue. The effects depend on the type of radiation and the size of the dose. Radiation dose (in sieverts) is a measure of the risk of harm resulting from an exposure of the body to the radiation.

1000 millisieverts (mSv) = 1 sievert (Sv)

Students will not be required to recall the unit of radiation dose.

X-rays are ionising radiation that can cause the mutation of genes and cancer.

6.2.4 Electromagnetic waves have many practical applications. For example:
- X-rays – medical imaging and treatments.

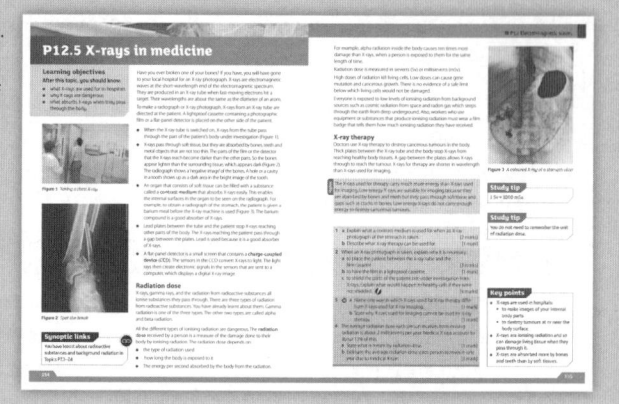

WS 1.5
MS 1a

Aiming for	Outcome	Checkpoint	
		Question	Activity
Aiming for GRADE 4	Describe some safety procedures that take place during the operation of devices that produce ionising radiation.		Main
	Describe the formation of an X-ray photograph in terms of absorption or transmission.	End of chapter 4	Starter 2, Main
	State that X-ray therapy can be used to kill cancerous cells in the body.		Main
Aiming for GRADE 6	Describe the operation of an X-ray machine.	2, End of chapter 4	Main
	Explain why contrast media can be used during X-rays.	1, End of chapter 4	Main
	Describe the factors that affect the radiation doses received by people.	4	Main
Aiming for GRADE 8	Compare the operation of a CT-scanner and that of a simple X-ray device.	3	Main
	Evaluate the doses of ionising radiation received in a variety of occupations or medical treatments.	4	Main
	Explain in detail how various safety features reduce exposure to ionising radiation.	End of chapter 4	Main

Maths
Students can compare radiation dose for different occupations using the appropriate units (1a).

Literacy
Students discuss the options for medical diagnosis in terms of costs, health benefits, and risks.

Key words
contrast medium, charged-coupled device (CCD), radiation dose

P12 Electromagnetic waves

Starter	Support/Extend	Resources
X-ray visions (10 min) Show a range of animal skeleton X-rays and ask students to identify the animals. At the same time, ask the students to discuss how the images were made. **Hand mit Ringen** (5 min) Show the very first medical X-ray image and ask the students what it shows and how it might have been made. It is an image of Wilhelm Röntgen's wife's hand with rings.	**Support:** Select simple images. **Extend:** X-rays of more complex objects can be used. **Extend:** The students can discuss whether taking this image was safe or necessary.	

Main	Support/Extend	Resources
Medical X-rays and CT scanners (40 min) Outline the process of making a medical X-ray, supporting this with some real images. Discuss the images in terms of absorption or transmission of the X-rays. Show some images that use contrast media to differentiate tissues. Recap ionisation and discuss the procedures used to reduce dose. The students should recognise the unit sievert and use it in comparisons – although they do not need to remember it. Then describe the operation of a CT scanner with a comparison to simple X-ray machines. Video clips of a CT scan can be found easily and show the advantage of 3D reconstruction. Make sure that students understand the improved soft-tissue differentiation. Link back to ionisation and the destruction of cells when discussing X-ray treatment.	**Support:** A simplified flowchart of the process can be produced. **Extend:** Students can compare photographic film, high resolution so greater image detail, with the convenience of CCD. Compare the exposure of a radiologist with that of a patient, and evaluate the relative risks. **Support:** A simplified table comparing the devices can be made for the students. **Extend:** Discuss the potential for causing new damage to cells.	**Activity:** Medical X-rays and CT scanners

Plenary	Support/Extend	Resources
Cost/benefit analysis (10 min) Interactive where students complete a paragraph to explain why all patients do not have CT scans instead of X-ray scans. They then sort statements according to whether they are benefits or disadvantages of these diagnostic technologies. **Organ identification** (5 min) Can the students identify particular organs from 3D CT scans or simple X-rays?	**Support:** Students can match up simple facts with the appropriate diagnostic technique. **Extend:** Include a comparison of ultrasound diagnosis.	**Interactive:** Cost/benefit analysis

Homework		
Students complete the WebQuest to research how X-ray and ultrasound scans work and consider their different uses and the risks associated with them. They use their research to create a short pamphlet aimed at a hospital patient who requires an X-ray or an ultrasound scan.		**WebQuest:** Ultrasound or X-ray?

kerboodle

A Kerboodle highlight for this lesson is **Working scientifically: Risks and benefits of using X-rays or gamma rays**. Refer to the **Content map** on Kerboodle for a full list of resources and assessment.

P12 The electromagnetic spectrum

Overview of P12 The electromagnetic spectrum

In this chapter the students have described the electromagnetic spectrum in terms of different regions related to wavelength. The speed of electromagnetic waves in a vacuum has been described as constant allowing the use of the wave equation to link wavelength and frequency which has then been tied to the energy carried by the wave.

Each of the regions of the electromagnetic spectrum has been described along with associated uses and students have investigated the relationship between surface colour, temperature, and the rate of emission of infra-red radiation. The use of radio waves in communications for television and mobile phones has been described along with outlining transmissions of signals through optical fibres. Higher tier students have also described the process of modulation of carrier waves to give a more complex picture of how information can be transmitted using waves.

All students have described the application of ultra violet waves in phosphorescence and the damage these waves can cause to skin and eyes before describing the uses of X-rays and gamma rays in medical applications. The process of ionisation has been outlined as well as the cause of tissue damage as a useful technique in killing bacteria or cancerous cells. Further details of the use of X-rays have been described including contrast media and detection devices such as the CCD and the concept of radiation dose. Higher tier students have compared the intensity of imaging and therapeutic X-rays.

Required practical

All students are expected to have carried out the required practical:

Practical	Topic
Investigate how the amount of infrared radiation absorbed or radiated by a surface depends on the nature of that surface.	B12.2

MyMaths

You can find additional support for the maths skills covered in this chapter on **MyMaths**, including recognise and use expressions in decimal form, use an appropriate number of significant figures, understand and use the symbols: $=, <, \ll, \gg, >, \propto, \sim$, change the subject of an equation.

kerboodle

For this chapter, the following assessments are available on Kerboodle:

P12 Checkpoint quiz: The electromagnetic spectrum
P12 Progress quiz: The electromagnetic spectrum 1
P12 Progress quiz: The electromagnetic spectrum 2
P12 On your marks: The electromagnetic spectrum
P12 Exam-style questions and mark scheme: The electromagnetic spectrum

Checkpoint follow up lesson

A student's route through this lesson can be determined using the Checkpoint assessment. Percentage pass marks are supplied in the Checkpoint teacher notes.

For each successive route through it is assumed that the student can perform to their current route as well as previous routes. For example, students working at Aiming for 6 are assumed to be secure in Aiming for 4 knowledge and understanding and working towards achieving all the learning outcomes for Aiming for 6.

	Aiming for 4	**Aiming for 6**	**Aiming for 8**
Learning outcomes	Recall all the main groupings of the electromagnetic spectrum and how they are different in terms of wavelength and frequency, and recall which waves our eyes detect.	Recall the electromagnetic spectrum, some of their uses and dangers, and calculate their frequencies and wavelengths.	Discuss in depth the uses and dangers of the electromagnetic spectrum, and calculate their frequencies and wavelengths.
	Describe some sources and detectors of electromagnetic waves and link them to their uses and dangers.	Compare the ways that we image the body with how we treat the body in terms of electromagnetic radiation.	Compare in detail the ways that we image the body with how we treat the body in terms of electromagnetic radiation.
	Describe how we use some of the waves in medicine and in communication.	Explain what is meant by radiation dose, and how you minimise risk.	Explain what is meant by radiation dose, and how you minimise risk.
	Write down the unit of radiation dose.	Describe how radio waves are produced and detected, and how they can be changed to carry information.	Explain how radio waves are produced and detected, and how they can be changed to carry information.
Starter	**What's the use? (10 min)** Give out cards for a pairs matching game that contains the names of waves of the electromagnetic waves on blue cards, with the same number of each card in yellow with a use on it. Students put the cards face down, and pick up pairs of different colours, keeping any pairs that match. When they have completed the game they sort the pairs into those used in communication and those used in medicine.		
	Good or bad? (5 min) Put a large 'Safe' sign on one side of the room and 'Dangerous' on the other. Ask students to stand in a place that shows what they think about electromagnetic radiation. Ask for some reasons for the choice of position.		
Differentiated checkpoint activity	Aiming for 4 students use the Checkpoint follow-up sheet to either create a matching game to summarise the main groupings of the electromagnetic spectrum or to produce a poster to summarise some of the uses of electromagnetic waves. Students will need access to scissors and A3 paper.	Aiming for 6 students use the Checkpoint follow-up sheet to either calculate typical wavelengths and frequencies of the waves of the electromagnetic spectrum and describe how radio waves were discovered or create a poster to describe some uses of electromagnetic waves.	Aiming for 8 students use the Checkpoint follow-up sheet to either calculate typical wavelengths and frequencies of the waves of the electromagnetic spectrum and describe how radio waves were discovered or create a poster to describe some uses of electromagnetic waves.
	The follow-up sheet is highly structured and provides simple questions to support students with consolidating their understanding from the tasks of the lesson.	Students will need access to large paper and a radio. The follow-up sheet provides some support and questions to consolidate students' understanding from the tasks of the lesson.	Students will need access to large paper and a radio. The follow-up sheet provides minimal support and more complex questions to consolidate students' understanding from the tasks of the lesson.
	Kerboodle resource P12 Checkpoint follow up: Aiming for 4, P12 Checkpoint follow up: Aiming for 6, P12 Checkpoint follow up: Aiming for 8		
Plenary	**Electromagnetic spectrum splat (5 min)** Write the names of all the electromagnetic waves on the board. Divide the class in two and have them line up on either side of the board. Read out a question about the waves of the electromagnetic spectrum, and each team member tries to find the word on the board and hit it with their hand (hence splat). Keep score to see which team wins.		
	Danger words (10 min) Use an online crossword maker to make a crossword using these words: DNA, radiotherapy, cancer, damage, treatment, dose, Sievert. Either give them the clues and ask them to solve the crossword, or give them the completed crossword and ask them to write the clues. They should swap with another student to check what they have done.		
Progression	Encourage students to think about finding a way of remembering the order of the waves, and the unit of radiation dose.	Encourage students to think about the balance of risk and benefit when using electromagnetic waves in medicine.	Encourage students to think about describing the use of electromagnetic waves in term of risk and benefit, and to remember broadly the range of wavelengths of the waves.

P 13 Electromagnetism
13.1 Magnetic fields

AQA spec Link: 7.1.1 The poles of a magnet are the places where the magnetic forces are strongest. When two magnets are brought close together they exert a force on each other. Two like poles repel each other. Two unlike poles attract each other. Attraction and repulsion between two magnetic poles are examples of non-contact force.

A permanent magnet produces its own magnetic field. An induced magnet is a material that becomes a magnet when it is placed in a magnetic field. Induced magnetism always causes a force of attraction. When removed from the magnetic field an induced magnet loses most/all of its magnetism quickly.

Students should be able to describe:
- the attraction and repulsion between unlike and like poles for permanent magnets
- the difference between permanent and induced magnets.

7.1.2 The region around a magnet where a force acts on another magnet or on a magnetic material (iron, steel, cobalt, and nickel) is called the magnetic field.

The force between a magnet and a magnetic material is always one of attraction.

The strength of the magnetic field depends on the distance from the magnet. The field is strongest at the poles of the magnet.

The direction of the magnetic field at any point is given by the direction of the force that would act on another north pole placed at that point. The direction of a magnetic field line is from the north (seeking) pole of a magnet to the south (seeking) pole of the magnet.

A magnetic compass contains a small bar magnet. The Earth has a magnetic field. The compass needle points in the direction of the Earth's magnetic field.

Students should be able to:
- describe how to plot the magnetic field pattern of a magnet using a compass
- draw the magnetic field pattern of a bar magnet showing how strength and direction change from one point to another
- explain how the behaviour of a magnetic compass is related to evidence that the core of the Earth must be magnetic.

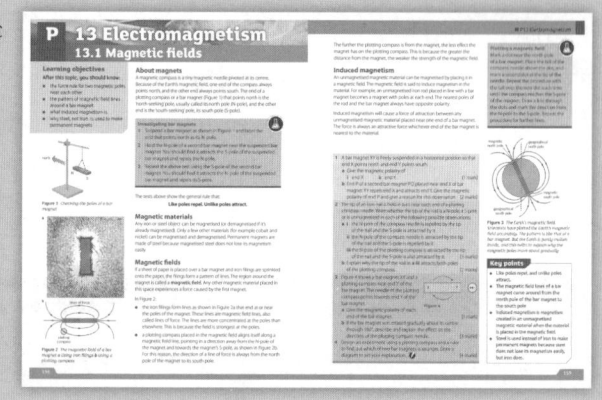

WS 2.2

Aiming for	Outcome	Checkpoint	
		Question	Activity
Aiming for GRADE 4 ↓	State the names of the poles of a magnet.	1	Main 1
	Describe the interaction of magnetic poles (attraction and repulsion).	1, 2	Starter 2, Main 1
	List some magnetic and non-magnetic metals.		Main 1
Aiming for GRADE 6 ↓	Sketch the shape of a magnetic field around a bar magnet.	End of chapter 1	Main 2
	Describe how the shape of a magnetic field can be investigated.	2	Main 2
	Compare the Earth's magnetic field to that of a bar magnet.		Main 1, Homework
Aiming for GRADE 8 ↓	Describe the regions in a magnetic field where magnetic forces are greatest using the idea of field lines.	4, End of chapter 1	Main 2
	Explain in detail how magnetism can be induced in some materials.		Main 2
	Plan in detail how the strength of a magnetic field can be investigated.	4	Plenary 1

Maths
Students use graphical representations of fields (field lines).

Literacy
Students describe the interactions of magnetic poles clearly and concisely.

Key words
magnetic field

158

P13 Electromagnetism

Practical

Title	Investigating bar magnets
Equipment	two bar magnets, cotton thread, retort stand and clamp
Overview of method	Suspend a bar magnet from a retort stand and clamp using string. Use a compass to identify the end of the magnet that points north, then hold the north pole of a second bar magnet near the suspended magnet. Finally hold the south pole of the second bar magnet to the suspended magnet.

Title	Plotting a magnetic field
Equipment	bar magnet, plotting compass, A4 paper
Overview of method	Place the bar magnet on an A4 sheet of paper. Mark a dot near the north pole of the bar magnet. Place the tail of the compass needle above the dot, and mark a second dot at the tip of the needle. Repeat the procedure with the tail over the new dot each time until the compass reaches the S-pole of the magnet. Draw a line through the dots and mark the direction from the N-pole to the S-pole.

Starter	Support/Extend	Resources
Force fields (10 min) Interactive where students categorise a list of the various forces they have studied into contact and non-contact forces. **Lost** (5 min) Show the students a compass (or a compass application for a mobile phone) and ask them how it works in terms of magnetic fields and poles.	**Extend:** Students should list the factors that affect the magnitude of the forces. **Extend:** Students describe other technology for finding their position and direction.	**Interactive:** Force fields

Main	Support/Extend	Resources
Investigating bar magnets (15 min) Students test the properties of magnets using the practical. Discuss the interaction of the bar magnet with the Earth's magnetic field, comparing the two. Demonstrate that only some metals are magnetic. **Plotting a magnetic field** (25 min) Demonstrate the existence of a magnetic field around a bar magnet using iron filings and then allow the students to plot the field pattern with the plotting compasses. Discuss regions where the field lines are closer together as regions where the force would be strongest. Show induced magnetism by lifting a paperclip with a strong bar magnet. A second clip will attach to the first even though the original clip was not magnetic. Explain the effect using the figure in the student book.	**Extend:** Discuss the naming of the poles of the magnets and the poles of the Earth's magnetic field. **Support:** Provide a list of the magnetic materials students are required to know from the specification. **Extend:** Use the idea of domains within the atoms in materials aligning to explain the effect.	**Practical:** Magnets and magnetic fields

Plenary	Support/Extend	Resources
Stronger fields (10 min) Show the students a horseshoe magnet and ask them to discuss the shape the field might be. **Applications** (5 min) Ask the students to list as many applications of permanent magnets as they can. Would these applications be improved if the magnetism could be turned off and on?	**Extend:** Students describe how the direction of the field lines can be found.	

Homework		
Students complete the WebQuest where they investigate the the scientific claims behind magnetic therapies, such as the magnetic healing bracelets sold by some retailers. They use their research to write a letter to a friend to recommend whether or not they should buy a product.		**WebQuest:** Magnetic therapies

kerboodle

A Kerboodle highlight for this lesson is **Bump up your grade: Magnets and magnetic fields**. Refer to the **Content map** on Kerboodle for a full list of resources and assessment.

P13.2 Magnetic fields of electric current

AQA spec Link: 7.2.1 When a current flows through a conducting wire a magnetic field is produced around the wire. The strength of the magnetic field depends on the current through the wire and the distance from the wire.

Shaping a wire to form a solenoid increases the strength of the magnetic field created by a current through the wire. The magnetic field inside a solenoid is strong and uniform.

The magnetic field around a solenoid has a similar shape to that of a bar magnet. Adding an iron core increases the strength of the magnetic field of a solenoid. An electromagnet is a solenoid with an iron core.

Students should be able to:
- describe how the magnetic effect of a current can be demonstrated
- draw the magnetic field pattern for a straight wire carrying a current and for a solenoid (showing the direction of the field)
- explain how a solenoid arrangement can increase the magnetic effect of the current.

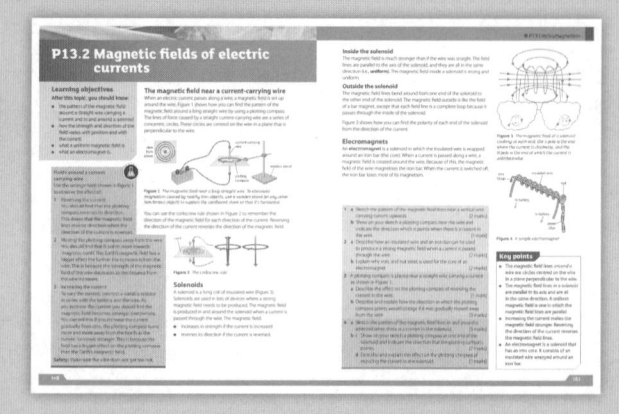

WS 2.2
MS 4a

Aiming for	Outcome	Checkpoint Question	Checkpoint Activity
Aiming for GRADE 4	State that the magnetic field produced by a current-carrying wire is circular.	1	Main 1
	Describe the effect of increasing the current on the magnetic field around a wire.	2	Main 1
	Describe the effect of reversing the direction of the current in the wire.	2	Main 1
Aiming for GRADE 6	Use the corkscrew rule to determine the direction of the field around a current-carrying wire.	2	Main 1
	Describe the shape of the field produced by a solenoid.	3	Main 2
	Describe the factors that affect the strength or direction of the magnetic field around a wire and solenoid.		Main 2, Plenary 1
Aiming for GRADE 8	Determine the polarity of the ends of a solenoid from the direction of the current.	3	Main 2
	Sketch the shape of the field surrounding a solenoid relating this to the direction of the current through the coil.	3, 4	Main 2
	Plan a detailed investigation into the factors that affect the strength of the magnetic field around a solenoid.		Main 2, Plenary 1

Maths
Students analyse graphical data to discuss the relationship between two factors (4a).

Literacy
Students describe the operation of a variety of devices in a structured way.

160

Practical

Title	Fields around a current-carrying wire
Equipment	thick copper wire passing through a cardboard or Perspex sheet, power supply or battery pack, plotting compass, iron filings, variable resistor
Overview of method	Suspend the wire from a wooden stand so that it passes through the card vertically (Figure 1 in the student book). Connect the wire to a power supply and pass a current through it. A compass placed near the wire should be deflected, or iron filings should form ring patterns.
Safety considerations	Limit the current through the wire with a variable resistor.

Starter	Support/Extend	Resources
Electricity and magnetism recap (10 min) Complete the interactive with a set of electricity questions to establish the students' prior knowledge. **Current effect** (5 min) Students should describe the factors which affect the current in a wire and the physical effects a current has in, and around, the wire.	**Support:** Differentiate the questions as appropriate. **Extend:** Students should describe the nature of a current in terms of charge movement.	**Interactive:** Electricity and magnetism recap

Main	Support/Extend	Resources
Fields around a current-carrying wire (20 min) Demonstrate the magnetic effect of a wire with the practical, or let the students find it. Discuss and then test the effect of reversing the current and/or increasing it. Ensure that students can apply the corkscrew rule (also known as the right-hand grip rule) to determine the direction of the field around the wire. **Fields around a solenoid** (20 min) Show a solenoid and compare it to a bar magnet. Connect it to a power supply and show the deflection on a plotting compass as the compass is moved around the coil. Students then plan an investigation into the factors which would affect the strength of this field.	**Support:** Diagrams of the corkscrew rule for current moving 'upwards' and downwards' are useful here. **Extend:** The students can discuss the shape of the field in more depth.	**Practical:** Fields around a current-carrying wire

Plenary	Support/Extend	Resources
More power (10 min) Ask the students to outline a test to see what affects the strength of the field around a solenoid. They should choose one possible factor (current, number of loops in coil, type of core) and form a plan to see if there is a qualitative or quantitative relationship that can be determined. **Space boots** (5 min) In space, astronauts are weightless but need some way of walking around the outer surface of a space station. Can the students describe a system to do this?	**Support:** Provide methods for the students to use in the investigation.	

Homework	Support/Extend	Resources
Students start or complete their plan to test what affects the strength of the field around a solenoid (from plenary 1).		

Higher tier

P13.3 The motor effect

AQA spec Link: 7.2.2 When a conductor carrying a current is placed in a magnetic field the magnet producing the field and the conductor exert a force on each other. This is called the motor effect.

Students should be able to show that Fleming's left-hand rule represents the relative orientation of the force, the current in the conductor, and the magnetic field.

Students should be able to recall the factors that affect the size of the force on the conductor.

For a conductor at right angles to a magnetic field and carrying a current:

force = magnetic flux density × current × length

$$[F = B\,I\,l]$$

force, F, in newtons, N

magnetic flux density, B, in tesla, T

current, I, in amperes, A (amp is acceptable for ampere)

length, l, in metres, m

7.2.3 A coil of wire carrying a current in a magnetic field tends to rotate. This is the basis of an electric motor.

Students should be able to explain how the force on a conductor in a magnetic field causes the rotation of the coil in an electric motor.

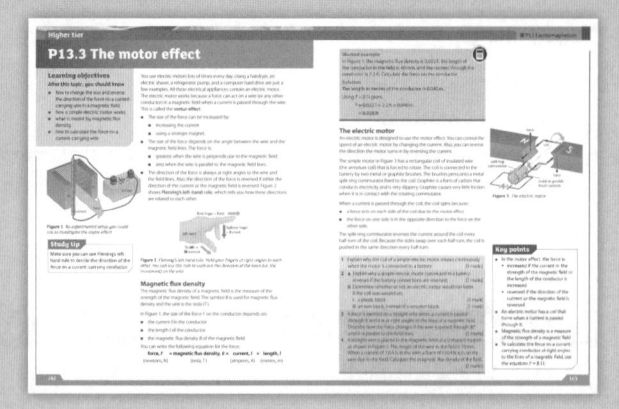

MS 3b, 3c

Aiming for	Outcome	Checkpoint	
		Question	Activity
Aiming for GRADE 6 ↓	Describe how the force acting on a wire due to the motor effect can be increased.	3	Main
	Apply Fleming's left-hand rule to determine the direction of the force acting on a conductor.	3	Main
	Calculate the force acting on a conductor when it is placed in a magnetic field.	4	Main
Aiming for GRADE 8 ↓	Describe and explain in detail the operation of a motor.	1, 2	Starter 2, Main, Plenary 2
	Perform calculations involving rearrangements of the equation $F = BIl$.	4	Main
	Investigate the factors that affect the rotation of an electric motor.		Main

Maths
Students calculate the force acting on a wire using the relationship $F = BIl$ (3c).

Literacy
Students describe the operation of a loudspeaker and a motor.

Key words
motor effect, Fleming's left-hand rule

P13 Electromagnetism

Practical

Title	The motor effect
Equipment	battery, length of wire (stiff wire works best), variable resistor, leads, two magnets mounted on U frame (or a U-shaped magnet)
Overview of method	Place the wire between the two magnets and pass a small current through it. The variable resistor allows control of the current to show its effect. Alternatively, as a simple demonstration of the effect, a wider strip of foil can be used instead of the stiff wire. This will deflect or bend when a current is passed through it, demonstrating that a force is experienced.
Safety considerations	Limit the current by using a variable resistor.

Starter	Support/Extend	Resources
Magnetic magic (5 min) Some magicians use magnetic effects to levitate objects. Show some footage of this levitation and ask the students to explain the 'magic' to see if they realise there is a scientific principle behind the mystery. **Motor demonstration** (10 min) Demonstrate an electric motor lifting a small load from the floor. Ask the students to explain what can be done to increase the force the motor can provide. They should be able to identify increasing the current.	**Extend:** Ask the students about the properties the levitated objects must have. **Extend:** Ask students to determine the power of the motor by giving them the load it lifts, the height it moves, and the time taken. Does this power match the electrical power provided ($P = VI$)? Why not?	

Main	Support/Extend	Resources
The motor effect (40 min) Demonstrate the motor effect and discuss the factors that affect the size and direction of the force. Show how Fleming's left-hand rule can be used to determine the direction of motion for the wire. Recap the idea of strong or weak magnetic fields and then introduce the equation, describing how this links to the earlier demonstration. The students should try some example calculations to embed the equation. Discuss how this force could be applied to produce continual movement. Allow the students to construct a motor or investigate the operation of one. If time permits, the students can construct small model motors from standard kits.	**Extend:** Ask the students to suggest a mathematical relationship between the factors. **Support:** Use calculation frames along with examples. **Support:** Provide constructed motors for the students to investigate. **Extend:** Discuss in detail the function of the split-ring commutator. **Extend:** Students complete the extension sheet to develop qualitative and quantitative understanding of the motor effect and some of its applications.	**Practical:** The motor effect

Plenary	Support/Extend	Resources
The motor effect (10 min) Students use the interactive to complete a paragraph to describe the motor effect. They then carry out some calculations using the equation $F = B\,I\,l$. **Motor competition** (5 min) The students should select the motor that is smoothest and most stable as the winner and give a prize.		**Interactive:** The motor effect

Homework		
Students can identify the differences in the sizes of loudspeakers used on different devices and explain why these are needed to produce a range of sounds.	**Extend:** Expect explanations in terms of mass, momentum, energy, and frequency.	

kerboodle

A Kerboodle highlight for this lesson is **Working scientifically: Current through a motor**. Refer to the **Content map** on Kerboodle for a full list of resources and assessment.

P13 Electromagnetism

Overview of P13 Electromagnetism

Students began this chapter by reinforcing their knowledge of magnetism by looking at the magnetic fields around permanent magnets and the concept of induced magnetism in some materials. The students have been reminded of the techniques used to plot a magnetic field and the shape of the Earth's field.

Students moved on to examine the magnetic field produced by a current and investigate the factors that affect the direction and strength of this field. They compared the field shape of a solenoid to that produced by a simple bar magnet.

Higher-tier students described how a current carrying wire placed in a magnetic field would experience the motor effect before going on to explain how this effect could be used to create an electric motor. The force produced on the motor was linked mathematically to the magnetic flux density of the magnetic field.

MyMaths

You can find additional support for the maths skills covered in this chapter on **MyMaths**, including recognising and using expressions in decimal form, using an appropriate number of significant figures, understanding and using the symbols: $=, <, \ll, \gg, >, \propto, \sim$, and changing the subject of an equation.

kerboodle

For this chapter, the following assessments are available on Kerboodle:

P13 Checkpoint quiz: Electromagnetism
P13 Progress quiz: Electromagnetism 1
P13 Progress quiz: Electromagnetism 2
P13 On your marks: Electromagnetism
P13 Exam-style questions and mark scheme: Electromagnetism

Checkpoint follow up lesson

A student's route through this lesson can be determined using the Checkpoint assessment. Percentage pass marks are supplied in the Checkpoint teacher notes.

For each successive route through it is assumed that the student can perform to their current route as well as previous routes. For example, students working at Aiming for 6 are assumed to be secure in Aiming for 4 knowledge and understanding and working towards achieving all the learning outcomes for Aiming for 6.

	Aiming for 4	**Aiming for 6**	**Aiming for 8**
Learning outcomes	Describe how to work out the shape of the magnetic field around a magnet.	Explain how the shape of a magnetic field explains why magnets attract or repel.	Explain how to investigate the shape of magnetic fields to explain why magnets attract or repel.
		Describe what affects the magnetic field pattern near a wire, and what affects the strength of a solenoid.	Explain what factors affect the magnetic field pattern near a wire, and the strength of a solenoid.
Starter	**Magnetic what? (10 min)** Give students A4 dry wipe boards, pens and an eraser. Display the word 'magnetic' on the board. Read out a description, like a crossword clue for words associated with 'magnetic', e.g. field, field lines, field strength, Earth's field, flux density. Students write the correct word or words on their white board and hold them up.		
Differentiated checkpoint activity	Aiming for 4 students use the Checkpoint follow-up sheet to complete one of two activities: • investigate magnetic fields around different magnets • suggest how to improve a plan for investigating electromagnets. The follow-up sheet is highly structured, and students could work in pairs for support. Simple questions are provided to support students with consolidating their understanding from the lesson.	Aiming for 6 students use the Checkpoint follow-up sheet to complete one of two activities: • investigate magnetic fields around different magnets • investigate electromagnets. The follow-up sheet provides structured support, and students could work in pairs for support. Questions are provided to support students with consolidating their understanding from the lesson.	Aiming for 8 students use the Checkpoint follow-up sheet to plot data on the strength of magnetic fields around a current carrying wire. The follow-up sheet provides questions to support students with consolidating their understanding from the lesson.
	Kerboodle resource P13 Checkpoint follow up: Aiming for 4, P13 Checkpoint follow up: Aiming for 6, P13 Checkpoint follow up: Aiming for 8		
Plenary	**What's the difference (5 min)** Students work in pairs to list the differences between a magnetic, a solenoid, and an electromagnet. They should attempt to suggest a use of each.		
Progression	Encourage students to think about the interaction of magnetic fields when explaining attraction and repulsion.	Encourage students to think about the interaction of magnetic fields when explaining the forces on objects, such as coils in motors.	Encourage students to think about giving explanations of forces in terms of the combination of magnetic fields, and to link these to the action of motors.

Answers

P1.1

1a loses GPE and gains KE, [1] some heat → surroundings due to air resistance [1]

b electrical energy → heat to heater element, [1] some heat → surroundings [1]

2a any two from: e.g., electric torch: chemical energy stored in battery → electric current transfers energy to lamp → light or heat energy → surroundings, [1] e.g., candle: energy from chemical reactions when candle burns → light or heat energy → surroundings [1]

b i candle [1]

ii electric torch [1]

3a energy transferred by electric current to train motor [1] → GPE to train [1]

b friction on train wheels due to brakes reduces KE of train to zero [1] → heat and sound to surroundings [1]

4 electrical energy supplied to oven used to generate microwaves, [1] microwaves → make food particles move faster so food becomes hot [1]

P1.2

1a brake pads become hot due to friction and energy transferred from brake pads to surroundings as heat, [1] braking → sound energy → surroundings [1]

b KE → GPE in roller coaster, [1] → KE in air going up, [1] GPE → KE going down [1]

2a descent: GPE → KE + heat to surroundings due to air resistance, [1] impact: KE → elastic energy of trampoline + heat to surroundings due to impact + sound, [1] ascent: elastic energy of trampoline → KE → GPE + heat to surroundings due to air resistance [1]

b less energy at top of bounce than at point of release [1]

c clamp metre ruler vertically over middle of trampoline, hold ball next to ruler with lowest point level with top of ruler, [1] release ball and observe highest level of bottom of ball after rebound, [1] repeat several times → average rebound position, [1] repeat with same ball for other two trampolines, [1] highest rebound position → bounciest [1]

3 elastic energy of rubber straps → KE of capsule, [1] KE → GPE as capsule [1]

4 rope not stretched as much so bungee jumper would not fall as far **or** rope stops jumper in shorter distance [1] so jumper experiences bigger (average) deceleration before ascent [1]

P1.3

1a i chemical energy stored in rower's muscles → KE of boat and water + heat to surroundings [1]

ii motor KE → GPE of barrier + thermal energy from friction and sound energy [1]

b 2000 N × 40 m = 80 000 J [1]

2a KE of car → brake pads by friction between brake pads and wheel discs [1] so brake pads become warm [1]

b 7000 N × 20 m = 140 000 J [1]

3a i 20 N × 4.8 m = 96 J [1]

ii 80 N × 1.2 m = 96 J [1]

b $\frac{1400\,\text{J}}{7.0\,\text{m}}$ [1] = 200 N [1]

4a 25 N × 12 m [1] = 300 J [1]

b chemical energy stored in student's muscles → KE in box, [1] when box moving KE + GPE of box does not change, [1] frictional force between box and floor transfers energy by heating from box to floor [1]

P1.4

1a descent: GPE of ball transferred by force of gravity → KE of ball, [1] + KE of air pushed aside by ball moving, [1] impact: KE of ball → elastic energy of ball + some elastic energy → KE as it rebounds, [1] after impact: KE of ball → GPE of ball as it rises → KE of air pushed aside by ball as it moves through the air [1]

b i mg = 1.4 N = 1.4 N × (2.5 m – 1.7 m) [1] = 1.1 J [1]

ii any two from: energy → surroundings due to air resistance as ball moves through air, [1] energy transfer due to heating of ball when it is deformed, [1] energy → surroundings by sound waves when ball hits floor [1]

2a 450 N × 0.20 m = 90 J [1]

b 50 × 90 J = 4500 J [1]

3a 25 kg × 10 N/kg × 1.8 m [1] = 450 J [1]

b ball falls 1.8 m – 0.3 m = 1.5 m [1]
$E_p = mgh$ = 25 kg × 10 N/kg × 1.5 m = 375 J [1]

4 energy supplied by blood system to biceps to keep muscle contracted, [1] no work done on object as it doesn't move, [1] energy supplied heats muscles → heat to surroundings [1]

P1.5

1a i 0.5 × 500 kg × (12 m/s)² [1] = 36 000 J [1]

ii 0.5 × 0.44 kg × (20 m/s)² [1] = 88 J [1]

b $E_K = \frac{1}{2}mv^2$ = 2 × 36 000 J so $\frac{1}{2}$ × 500 kg × v^2 = 72 000 J [1]
∴ $v^2 = \frac{72\,000\,\text{J}}{0.5 \times 500\,\text{kg}}$ [1] = 288 m²/s² ∴ v = 17 m/s [1]

2a i work done by muscles transfer chemical energy from muscles [1] → elastic PE of catapult [1]

ii elastic PE of catapult [1] → KE of object [1]

b i 2.0 N × 5.0 m [1] = 10 J [1]

ii mass = weight /g = 2.0 N ÷ 10 N/kg = 0.20 kg [1] assume all elastic energy → KE in object, $E_K = \frac{1}{2}mv^2$ = 10 J
so $\frac{1}{2}$ × 0.20 kg × v^2 = 10 J [1] ∴ $v^2 = \frac{10\,\text{J}}{0.5 \times 0.20\,\text{kg}}$ [1] = 100 m²/s² ∴ v = 10 m/s [1]

3a work done by brakes = energy transferred from kinetic store = 360 000 J [1] using $W = Fs$ → 360 000 J = F × 100 m [1]
∴ $F = \frac{360\,000\,\text{J}}{100\,\text{m}}$ = 3600 N [1]

b $\frac{1}{2} \times m \times (30\,\text{m/s})^2$ = 360 000 J [1] ∴ 0.5 × m × 900 (m/s)² = 360 000 J, rearranging → $m = \frac{360\,000\,\text{J}}{0.5 \times 900\,\text{m}^2/\text{s}^2}$ [1] = 800 kg [1]

4 elastic energy $E_e = \frac{1}{2}ke^2$ = 0.5 × 250 N/m × (0.21 m)² [1] = 5.5 J [1]

P1.6

1a i 0.5 × 500 kg × (12 m/s)² [1] = 36 000 J [1]

ii 0.5 × 0.44 kg × (20 m/s)² [1] = 88 J [1]

b 2 × 36 000 J so $\frac{1}{2}$ × 500 kg × v^2 = 72 000 J [1]
∴ $v^2 = \frac{72\,000\,\text{J}}{0.5 \times 500\,\text{kg}}$ [1] = 288 m²/s² ∴ v = 17 m/s [1]

Answers

2 a i WD by muscles transfers chemical energy from muscles [1] → elastic PE of catapult [1]
  ii elastic PE of catapult [1] → KE of object [1]
b i 2.0 N × 5.0 m [1] = 10 J [1]
  ii mass = 2.0 N ÷ 10 N/kg = 0.20 kg [1] assume all elastic energy → KE in object, $E_K = 10$ J so $\frac{1}{2} \times 0.20$ kg $\times v^2 = 10$ J [1]
  ∴ $v^2 = \frac{10 J}{0.5 \times 0.20 kg}$ [1] $= 100$ m²/s² ∴ $v = 10$ m/s [1]
3 a work done by brakes = energy transferred from kinetic store = 360 000 J [1] $W = 360 000$ J $= F \times 100$ m [1]
  ∴ $F = \frac{360 000 J}{100 m} = 3600$ N [1]
b $E_K = \frac{1}{2} \times m \times (30 m/s)^2 = 360 000$ J [1] ∴ $0.5 \times m \times 900$ (m/s)² = 360 000 J, rearranging → $m = \frac{360 000 J}{0.5 \times 900 m^2/s^2}$ [1] = 800 kg [1]
4 0.5×250 N/m $\times (0.21$ m$)^2$ [1] = 5.5 J [1]

P1.6

1 a wasted: sound, KE of air [1]
b useful: light and sound, wasted: heat [1]
c useful: boils water, wasted: heat lost through surfaces, sound [1]
d useful: sound, wasted: heat loss [1]
2 a any two from: gear box would heat up due to energy transfer through friction between the gears,[1] the hotter the gear box, the less efficient the gears, [1] if gear box becomes very hot, stops working as oil in it burns up and gear wheels wear away [1]
b inside of shoes heat up due to energy transfer (by conduction + infrared radiation) from feet which rub, [1] feet transfer less energy as shoes warm up so feet and athlete become hotter [1]
c drill heats up due to friction between rotating drill and wood, [1] if drill becomes very hot, it burns wood creating smoke [1]
d discs heat up due to energy transfer by friction between discs and brake pads, [1] KE of car decreases [1]
3 a as pendulum swings towards middle GPE decreases and KE increases, [1] as it moves from middle to highest position its KE → GPE, [1] air resistance causes some KE → heat to surroundings [1]
b as air resistance opposes motion KE from pendulum → air, [1] until pendulum stops moving and has no KE, [1] energy transferred to air dissipated to surroundings [1]
4 friction at wheel axles [1] and air resistance [1] reduces KE of cyclist and KE → heat to surroundings ,[1] sound might also be created and → energy to surroundings [1]

P1.7

1 a useful energy < energy supplied [1]
b i efficiency = useful energy delivered/input energy supplied, [1] a machine never > 100% efficient because useful energy delivered never > total energy supplied [1]
  ii useful energy always < total energy supplied, [1] due to electric currents in circuit wires/components [1] and friction between moving parts, [1] energy dissipated by transferring heat to surroundings [1]
2 a 60 J − 24 J [1] = 36 J [1]
b $\frac{24 J}{60 J}$ (× 100%) [1] = 0.40 (or 40%) [1]
3 0.25 × total energy supplied [1] = 0.25 × 3200 J = 800 J [1]
4 electric current supplied energy to fan heater → heat air and make air move, [1] air becomes hotter and gains KE, [1] energy wasted because sound waves transfer energy to surroundings [1] and friction between moving parts heats moving parts instead of air [1]

P1.8

1 a B [1]
b B [1]
c A [1]
2 a WD winding clockwork spring up [1] to store energy in spring [1]
b spring drives small electric generator in radio, energy → from spring to generator by force of spring when spring unwinds, [1] current from generator → energy to radio circuits [1]
c advantage: no replacement batteries needed [1] disadvantage: spring needs to be rewound after unwinding [1]
3 a heat water, [1] spray it and pump it out [1]
b hot water pumped from machine transfers energy to surroundings, [1] machine vibrations create sound waves → energy to surroundings [1]
4 a 80% × 60% [1] = 48% [1]
b (100% − 48%) = 52% [1]

P1.9

1 a i mains filament bulb [1]
  ii 10 000 W electric cooker [1]
b 2 million × 3 kW [1] = 6 million kW [1]
2 a 5000 W × 20 s [1] = 100 000 J [1]
b 12 000 J (× 100%)/100 000 J [1] = 0.12 (or 12%) [1]
3 a $\frac{1500 kJ}{50 s}$ [1] = 30 kW [1]
b $\frac{30 kW}{100 kW}$ [1] = 0.30 (or 30%) [1]
4 a current through heater → energy to heater raising temperature of water, [1] pump → energy to water to keep water moving enabling water to overcome resistive forces due to pipes, [1] energy → to surroundings by sound waves from pump [1]
b 12 000 W × 4800 s [1] = 960 000 J [1]

P2.1

1 a any two from: do not conduct by heating, [1] so handle not hot when pan hot, [1] steel handle becomes as hot as pan as steel is good conductor [1]
b felt: contains fibres that trap layers of air, [1] dry air good insulator [1]
2 a felt/synthetic fur, [1] trapped air good insulator [1]
b fair test e.g., wrapping each lining round can of hot water with same volume of water, [1] time temperature change in 5 minutes from same initial temperature, [1] smallest temperature decrease indicates best insulator [1]
3 any five from: fill beaker with measured volume hot water, measure initial temperature of water, place lid on beaker and measure temperature again after 300 s, [1] stir water before measuring temperature, [1] repeat test using two identical beakers, one inside the other, using same volume hot water at same initial temperature, [1] repeat test using three or more beakers, [1] should find temperature falls less the more beakers you use, [1] plot graph of temperature decrease vs number of beakers used [1]
4 C: glass has lowest thermal conductivity [1] so cool end heats up slower than A or B [1]

167

Answers

P2.3

1. small bucket [1] because mass of water much less than in large bucket [1]
2. a. lead has lower specific heat capacity, [1] for equal masses, less energy needed for a given temperature rise [1]
   b. i $0.20 \text{ kg} \times 900 \text{ J/kg} °C \times (40 - 15)°C$ [1] = 4500 J [1]
      ii $0.40 \text{ kg} \times 4200 \text{ J/kg} °C \times (40 - 15)°C$ [1] = 42 000 J [1]
      iii $\Delta E_{Al} = (mc\Delta\vartheta)_{Al} = 4500$ J (as in i) [1] $\Delta E_{water} = (mc\Delta\vartheta)_{water} = 42 000$ J (as in ii) [1] total energy = 4500 J + 42 000 J = 46 500 J [1]
   c. $\Delta E_{Cu} = 20 \text{ kg} \times 490 \text{ J/kg} °C \times (55 - 15)°C$ [1] = 392 kJ [1]
      $\Delta E_{water} = 150 \text{ kg} \times 4200 \text{ J/kg} °C \times (55 - 15)°C$ [1] = 25 200 kJ [1]
      total energy = 392 kJ + 25 200 kJ = 25 592 kJ = 25.6 MJ [1]
3. storage heater contains bricks/concrete heated by element, radiant heater does not, [1] storage heater gradually → heat to surroundings, radiant heater instantly [1]
4. any four from: measure mass m of empty beaker, fill two-thirds full with oil and measure mass of beaker and oil, calculate mass of oil, in beaker,[1] insulate beaker and use thermometer to measure initial temperature of oil, record initial joulemeter reading,[1] use heater and joulemeter to heat oil for 100 seconds then switch off power supply, [1] record final joulemeter reading, stir oil and measure its highest temperature, [1] calculate ΔE from the two joulemeter readings and temperature increase $\Delta\vartheta$ from the two temperature readings, use equation $\Delta E = mc\Delta\vartheta$ to calculate specific heat capacity of oil, [1] assuming negligible energy to heat polythene beaker [1]

P2.4

1. a. conducts much less energy than air, especially if air damp, [1] prevents energy transfer by radiation (and convection) across cavity [1]
   b. foil reflects infrared radiation from radiator [1] preventing absorption of radiation by surface of wall behind foil [1]
2. a. plastic = heat insulator, metal = good conductor, [1] ∴ more energy transferred through metal frame [1]
   b. air convects so energy transferred if space filled with air but not with vacuum [1]
3. wider gap transfers less energy, [1] air between panes insulates and the wider the air gap, the more effective the window is at reducing energy transfer through it [1]
4. a. 6 × £15 for the rolls + £90 to fit the insulation [1] = £180 [1]
   b. 6 × £10 [1] = £60 [1]
   c. £180 ÷ £60/year [1] = 3 years [1]

P3.1

1. a. i coal, oil and gas-fired power stations [1]
      ii nuclear power station [1]
   b. nuclear fuel → radioactive waste [1] which must be stored for many years until it becomes non-radioactive [1]
2. a. i advantage: no radioactive waste, disadvantage: produces greenhouse gases [1]
      ii advantage: starts quicker, disadvantage: gas supplies will run out before coal [1]
   b. 300 000 MJ ÷ 30 MJ/kg = 10 000 kg [1]
3. a. biofuel = any fuel obtained from living or recent organisms, [1] ethanol biofuel because obtained from fermented sugar cane [1]
   b. CO_2 released when burnt = C taken in as CO_2 from atmosphere [1] when it grows [1]
4. energy/person per year = 500 million million million J/6000 million [1] = 83000 MJ [1] energy/person per second = 83000 MJ/365 days × 24 × 3600) [1] = 2600 J/s [1]

P3.2

1. a. source of energy replenished by natural processes [1] at same rate as it is used [1]
   b. i tidal power [1]
      ii wind power [1]
2. a. i 1000 [1]
      ii 25 km [1]
   b. from top: hilly or coastal areas, estuaries, coastline, mountain areas (4 = [2] 3 =[1])
3. a. tidal: sea water flows through turbines in barriers built across estuaries, [1] hydroelectric: involve less construction because uses rainwater trapped in upland reservoirs [1] **or** tidal: sea water trapped by tidal flow in estuary by long barrier, periodic not constant, hydroelectric use water flowing continuously from upland reservoirs, [1] hydroelectric ∴ continuous, tidal power is produced for only part of each tidal cycle [1]
   b. i hydroelectricity [1]
      ii only possible where hilly not flat [1] with significant rainfall not dry [1]
4. a. HEP station that uses electricity from other power stations at off-peak time to pump water to upland reservoir, [1] when demand high, flow reversed and water in reservoir used to generate electricity [1]
   b. coal, oil and nuclear power stations run continuously as cannot be restarted quickly if demand rises suddenly, [1] water in reservoirs generates electricity when demand high [1]

P3.3

1. a. energy released by radioactive substances deep underground [1]
   b. solar energy not available at night whereas geothermal energy released all the time **or** output of solar panel reduced by cloud cover whereas geothermal energy unaffected [1]
2. a. 300 W/0.2 W per cell [1] = 1500 cells [1]
   b. to supply electricity when dark [1]
3. a. 200 kW × 48 hours [1] = 4800 kW [1]
   b. advantage: geothermal energy does not vary whereas wind energy depends on weather conditions, [1] disadvantage: geothermal power stations only operate where flow of geothermal energy from within the Earth is significant [1]
4. a. $0.010 \text{ kg/s} \times 4200 \text{ J/kg} °C \times (35 - 14)°C$ [1] = 880 J/s [1]
   b. 880 J/s = 0.017 kg/s × 4200 J/kg °C × $\Delta\theta$ [1] ∴ $\Delta\theta = \dfrac{880 \text{ J/s}}{0.017 \text{ kg/s} \times 4200 \text{ J/kg} °C}$ [1] = 30 °C [1] so output temperature = 44 °C [1]

P3.4

1. a. gas [1]
   b. increase of CO_2 in atmosphere, [1] acid rain [1]
   c. advantages: any two from: never run out, [1] do not release greenhouse gases/ CO_2 into atmosphere, [1] do not produce radioactive waste, [1] disadvantages: take up large areas, [1] affect habitats of plants and animals [1]

Answers

2 a A [1]
 b D [1]
 c C [1]
 d B [1]
3 a solar, [1] wave energy, [1] wind [1]
 b nuclear, [1] geothermal, [1] tidal [1]
4 discuss three types in terms of reliability (see **P3.2 to P3.4** for main points to include: each point requires an advantage and a disadvantage) [1] and environmental effects including use of land, [1] effect on natural habitats, [1] pollution, [1] and waste, [1]

P3.5

1 a gas-fired [1]
 b geothermal/hydroelectric/tidal [1]
 c wind, solar, wave [1]
 d hydroelectric [1]
2 a not enough electricity at night if no wind or waves [1]
 b more pumped storage schemes needed to store surplus electricity [1]
3 output power not increased quickly enough to meet sudden variations in demand [1]
4 HEP stations that use electricity at times of low demand [1] to pump water to uphill reservoir from lower level, [1] then reverse flow to generate electricity when high demand [1]
5 a gas without carbon capture storage [1]
 b i capital costs for wind and solar power much higher for same power output [1]
  ii nuclear and coal-fired power capital costs much higher for same power output, [1] when include carbon capture storage higher overall costs for gas-fired/oil power [1]
 c 4000 MW × 30 years = 4 × 10^6 kW × (30 × 365 × 24) = 1.05 × 10^{12} kWh [1] decommissioning cost per kWh = £1000 million/1.05 × 10^{12} ≈ 0.1 p/kWh [1]

P4.1

1 1 = cell, 2 = switch, 3 = indicator, 4 = fuse (all correct = [2], 3 correct = [1])
2 a circuit correct: diode at 2 with arrow pointing to 3 [1]
 b variable resistor [1]
 c 0.25 A × 60 s [1] = 15 C [1]
3 a measure electric current [1]
 b change current in the circuit [1]
4 a circuit with bulb, wires and cell (all correct = [2] one component incorrect = [1])
 b electron passing through battery gains energy from chemical reactions in battery, [1] electron transfers energy to filament bulb by colliding with atoms in filament as it passes through, [1] transfers some energy to atoms in wire in same way [1]

P4.2

1 a $\frac{4.0\,V}{0.5\,A} = 8.0\,\Omega$ [1]
 b suitable values read off graph and used [1] to give 10.0 Ω [1]
2 W 6.0 Ω [1]   X 80 V [1]   Y 2.0 A [1]
3 a $\frac{12.0\,V}{0.015\,A} = 800\,\Omega$ [1]
 b i 0.015 A × 1200 s = 18 C [1]
  ii 18 C × 12.0 V [1] = 216 J [1]
4 a suitable values read off graph and used [1] to give 10.0 Ω [1]
 b i $\frac{1.6\,V}{10\,\Omega}$ [1] = 0.16 A [1]
  ii 0.42 A × 10.0 Ω [1] = 4.2 V [1]

P4.3

1 a i thermistor [1]
  ii diode [1]
  iii filament bulb [1]
 b i $\frac{0.5\,V}{0.1\,A} = 5\,\Omega$ [1]
  ii $\frac{2.0\,V}{0.2\,A} = 10\,\Omega$ [1]
2 a $\frac{9.0\,V}{0.6\,A} = 15\,\Omega$ [1]
 b ammeter reading increases, [1] because resistance of thermistor decreases, [1] so total resistance decreases [1]
3 if LDR covered current decreases [1] as LDR resistance increases [1] and p.d. still 9.0 V [1]
4 a current = 0 until p.d. ≈ 0.7 V [1] then increases rapidly [1]
 b resistance very large until ≈ 0.7 V [1] then decreases rapidly [1]

P4.4

1 a 1.2 V – 0.8 V [1] = 0.4 V [1]
 b $I = \frac{1.0\,V}{5.0\,\Omega} = 0.20$ A [1], p.d. = 1.5 V – 1.0 V = 0.5 V [1]
2 a circuit with cell and 2 resistors in series correct [1]
 b i 3.0 Ω + 2.0 Ω = 5.0 Ω [1]
  ii $\frac{1.5\,V}{5.0\,\Omega}$ [1] = 0.3 A [1]
 c total $R = \frac{1.5\,V}{0.25\,A} = 6.0\,\Omega$ [1] $R_X = 6.0\,\Omega - 2.0\,\Omega = 4.0\,\Omega$ [1]
3 a i 2 Ω + 10 Ω = 12 Ω [1]
  ii 2 × 1.5 V = 3.0 V [1]
 b $\frac{3.0\,V}{12\,\Omega} = 0.25$ A [1]
 c $V_P = 0.25$ A × 2 Ω = 0.5 V [1] $V_Q = 0.25$ A × 10 Ω = 2.5 V [1]
 d i 2 Ω + 10 Ω + 5 Ω = 15 Ω [1]
  ii $\frac{3.0\,V}{15\,\Omega}$ [1] = 0.20 A [1]
  iii $V_P = 0.20$ A × 2 Ω = 0.4 V [1] $V_Q = 0.20$ A × 10 Ω = 2.0 V [1] $V_R = 0.20$ A × 3 Ω = 0.6 V [1]
4 any four from: same current through each resistor, [1] with additional resistor in series more resistors share total p.d., [1] so p.d. across each resistor less, [1] current through resistors less, [1] total p.d. unchanged so total resistance (= total p.d. ÷ current) > before [1]

P4.5

1 a 0.40 A – 0.10 A = 0.30 A [1]
 b 3 Ω resistor [1]
 c battery current = 10 A ∴ current same if R of single resistor = $\frac{6.0\,V}{10\,A}$ [1] = 0.60 Ω [1]
2 a circuit diagram: 6.0 V battery across 12 Ω and 24 Ω resistors in parallel [1]
 b i current = $\frac{6.0\,V}{12\,\Omega}$ [1] = 0.50 A [1]
  ii current = $\frac{6.0\,V}{24\,\Omega}$ [1] = 0.25 A [1]
 c cell current = 0.5 A + 0.25 A [1] = 0.75 A [1]
3 a i $I_1 = \frac{6.0\,V}{2\,\Omega} = 3.0$ A [1] $I_2 = \frac{6.0\,V}{3\,\Omega} = 2.0$ A [1] $I_3 = \frac{6.0\,V}{6\,\Omega} = 1.0$ A [1]
  ii 6.0 A [1]
 b I through R_3 6.0 V/4.0 Ω = 1.5 A [1] total I = 3.0 A + 2.0 A + 1.5 A = 6.5 A [1]
4 I through 2 Ω resistor = 3.0 A [1] total I = sum of currents in individual resistors so > 3.0 A [1] equivalent R = total p.d. across resistors (i.e. 6 V) ÷ total current [1] as total current > 3.0 A, equivalent R < 2 Ω [1] (**or** current through 2 Ω resistor < total current [1] as all resistors contribute to total current, [1] p.d. across 2 Ω

169

Answers

resistor = p.d. across combination, [1] so equivalent $R < 2\,\Omega$ as total current > current through $2\,\Omega$ resistor and p.d. is the same [1])

P5.1
1a 12 V [1]
b 230 V [1]
c 1.5 V [1]
d 325 V [1]
2a no. cycles increases, [1] waves same height [1]
b no. cycles decreases [1] waves twice as high [1]
3 each centimetre →10 ms so one cycle takes 80 ms [1] so $f = 1/0.080\,s = 12.5\,Hz$ [1]
4a d.c. in one direction only, a.c. repeatedly reverses direction [1]
b diode only allows current in one direction, (so it rectifies a.c. to d.c.) [1]
c i similar shape to P5.1, Figure 1 but when negative, current = 0 [1]
ii peaks not as high [1] horizontal spacing unchanged [1]

P5.2
1a live = brown , neutral = blue, earth = yellow and green [1]
b i so each appliance can be switched on and off [1] without affecting others [1]
ii brass doesn't oxidise but copper does, [1] brass harder than copper and doesn't deform as easily [1]
iii live wire could be exposed where cable is worn or damaged [1]
2a 1 = C, 2 = D, 3 = A, 4 = B (all correct =[2] 3 correct = [1])
b 1: flexible and insulator, [1] 2: insulator, doesn't wear and can't be squashed,[1] 3: good conductor and doesn't deteriorate, [1] 4: excellent conductor and wires bend easily [1]
3a each must be insulated to avoid dangerously large current in cable [1] due to very low resistance between live and other wires where they touch [1]
b earth is connected to terminal fixed to metal case, [1] other end of earth wire connected to earth pin, [1] so when plug connected to wall socket, metal case is connected via earth wire to the ground [1]
4a wall sockets: cables thicker so resistance lower and more current passes through them than through lighting cables [1] otherwise heating effect of current greater and cables would overheat [1]
b two-core cable has only live and neutral, three-core also has earth wire [1]
c any appliance with double-insulated plastic case can have two-core cable, [1] appliance with metal case must have three-core cable so metal case is earthed [1]

P5.3
1a 30 000 J/(8 hr × 3600 s) [1] ≈ 1 W [1]
b 5 A × 230 V [1] = 1150 W [1]
c $I = 0.4\,A$ (= 80 W/30 V) [1] $I > 0.4\,A$ would not melt 13 A fuse [1]
2a i 5 A × 12 V [1] = 60 W [1]
ii 12 A × 230 V [1] = 2760 W [1]
b i current is (50 W/12 V) = 4.2 A [1] so 5 A fuse should be used [1]
ii current is (800 W/230 V) = 3.5 A [1] so 5A fuse should be used [1]
3a in normal operation, current in oven = 3.5 A [1] so 3 A fuse would melt [1]
b i $\dfrac{12\,V}{4.0\,\Omega}$ [1] = 3.0 A [1]
ii 3.0 A × 12 V [1] = 36 W [1]
iii 36 W × 1200 s [1] = 43 200 J [1]

4a i 26 A × 0.25 Ω [1] = 6.5 V [1]
ii 26 A × 6.5 V [1] = 169 W [1] (or $26^2 \times 0.25\,\Omega = 169\,W$)
b $\dfrac{169\,W}{6000\,W} \times 100\%$) [1] = 2.8% [1]

P5.4
1a 3 A × 50 s [1] = 150 C [1]
b 30 C × 4 V [1] = 120 J [1]
c $P = 0.5^2 \times 12\,\Omega = 3.0\,W$ [1] $E = 3.0\,W \times 60\,s = 180\,J$ [1]
2a i 4 A × 20 s [1] = 80 C [1]
ii 0.2 A × 3600 s [1] = 720 C [1]
b i 20 C × 6 V [1] = 120 J [1]
ii 3 A × 20 s × 5 V [1] = 300 J [1]
3a 2 A × 60 s [1] = 120 C [1]
b 12 J/C from battery [1] 9 J/C to lamp + 3 J/C to variable resistor [1]
c 1440 J from battery [1] = 1080 J to lamp + 360 J to variable resistor [1]
4a 4.0 Ω + 8.0 Ω) [1] = 12.0 Ω [1]
b 6.0 V/12.0 Ω) [1] = 0.50 A [1]
c 4 Ω: 2.0 V (= 0.50 A × 4.0 Ω) [1] 8.0 Ω: 4.0 V (= 0.50 A × 8.0 Ω) [1]
d 4 Ω: 60 J (= 30 C × 2.0 V) [1] 8.0 Ω: 120 J (= 30 × 4.0 V) [1]
e 60 J + 120 J [1] = 180 J [1]

P5.5
1.a i 5 W × 3000 s [1] = 15 kJ [1]
ii 100 W × (24 × 60 × 60) s [1] = 8.64 MJ [1]
b i 3000 W × (6 × 5 × 60) s [1] = 5.4 MJ [1]
ii 1000 W × (30 × 60) s [1] = 1.8 MJ [1]
2a i 80 J (= 20% of 100 J) [1]
ii 5 J (= 20% of 25 J) [1]
b efficiencies very different, efficiency of each LED much > efficiency of halogen lamp [1] energy per second transferred by light from halogen lamp is 25 J (= 25% of 100 W) compared to 1.8 J (= 90% of 2 W) for each LED [1] so 14 LEDs (~ 25/1.8) give same light output as one 100 W lamp [1]
3a $\dfrac{36\,MJ}{4 \times 3600\,s}$ [1] = 2.5 kW [1]
b $\dfrac{36\,MJ}{2000\,W}$ [1] = 18 000 s **or** 5 hours [1]
4a 1.5 A × 230 V [1] = 345 W [1]
b 345 W × (130 × 60 × 60) s [1] = 161 MJ [1]

P6.1
1a 0.024 m³ (= 0.80 m × 0.60 m × 0.05 m) [1]
b $\dfrac{60\,kg}{0.024\,m^3}$ [1] = 2500 kg/m³ [1]
2a 136 g − 48 g [1] = 88 g [1]
b $\dfrac{88\,kg}{80\,cm^3}$ [1] = 1.1 g/cm³ [1]
3a i 0.000 40 m³ (= 0.10 m × 0.080 m × 0.05 m) [1]
ii $\dfrac{0.76\,kg}{0.000\,40\,m^3}$ [1] = 19 000 kg/m³ [1]
b $v = \dfrac{0.0015\,kg}{19\,000\,kg/m^3} = 7.9 \times 10^{-8}\,m^3$ [1] thickness $t = \dfrac{7.9 \times 10^{-8}\,m^3}{0.15\,m \times 0.12\,m}$ [1] = 4.4×10^{-6} m **or** 0.0044 mm [1]
4 Use top pan balance to measure mass of bolt, [1] fill measuring cylinder half-full of water and measure volume of water in it, [1] tie bolt on thread and gently lower fully into water, volume of bolt given by rise in level of water in measuring cylinder, [1] use density = mass/ volume to calculate density of bolt from its mass and volume [1]

170

Answers

P6.2
1 a i vaporisation [1]
ii freezing [1]
iii melting [1]
b same mass of ice cube and water in beaker after ice cube has melted, [1] density = mass per unit volume so if volume of ice cube > volume of melted water, density of ice < density of water [1]
2 a condensation [1]
b evaporation/vaporisation [1]
c melting [1]
d freezing [1]
3 a particles start to move about at random, [1] no longer in fixed positions [1]
b particles in water vapour move at random and not in contact with each other except when they collide, [1] when water vapour condenses on a cold surface, vapour particles lose energy when they collide with surface and stay on surface as a film of liquid, [1] particles in film move at random in contact with each other [1]
4 particles in gas much more energetic and move faster and spaced further apart than particles in solid or liquid, [1] for given mass of gas, particles occupy much greater volume than equal mass of same substance in liquid or solid state, [1] density = mass / volume, [1] density of gas much less than density of same substance as liquid or solid [1]

P6.3
1 boiling takes place at a certain temperature whereas evaporation occurs from a liquid at any temperature, [1] boiling takes place throughout liquid whereas evaporation from surface only, [1] evaporation can cause liquid to cool whereas boiling does not [1]
2 a i graph with suitable scales, [1] correctly plotted points, [1] best fit line with flat section from 150 s to about 240 s [1]
ii 79 °C [1]
b 60 °C: solid, [1] at 79 °C: begins to melt, [1] after 90 s all melted and liquid temperature then rises to above 90 °C [1]
3 any two from: salt and water form solution which will not freeze unless temperature drops below freezing point of solution, [1] so no ice forms on road unless temperature drops below this freezing point, [1] if solution does freeze, grit provides friction between tyres and ice to help stop vehicles sliding [1]
4 particles move randomly in contact with each other as temperature falls from 80 °C to 75 °C, [1] as temperature falls particles lose energy and move more slowly until at 75 °C they stop moving around and substance changes from liquid to solid, [1] at 75 °C particles become fixed in position and vibrate, [1] once all substance has changed state, temperature falls from 75 °C to 70 °C and vibrations of particles less vigorous [1]

P6.4
1 a particles in a gas move at high speed in random directions, [1] colliding with each other and with internal surface of container, [1] pressure on solid surface caused by force of impacts of gas particles with surface [1]
b when solid heated to its melting point particles gain KE and vibrate more about fixed positions, [1] at melting point, particles gain enough energy to break away from each other and move about, [1] molecules that break free are in liquid state as they move about in contact with each other [1]

2 a liquid: particles close together and move about, not in fixed positions [1]
b gas: particles far apart and move about [1]
c solid: particles vibrate about fixed positions and close together [1]
d does not exist: particles that vibrate about fixed positions are in solid and ∴ not far apart [1]
3 internal energy transferred to solid at its melting point gives molecules enough energy to overcome strong forces of attraction holding them together in solid structure, [1] PE increases as particles break free from each other [1]
4 heat energy transferred by heating from warm water to ice, [1] water cools and water particles move more slowly so they lose KE, [1] ice melts because it gains internal energy and particles in ice gain enough PE to break free from each other, [1] when ice melts, melted water from ice and warm water mix so molecules from the ice, on average, gain KE and molecules from warm water lose KE [1]

P6.5
1 a 0.068 kg − 0.024 kg [1] = 0.044 kg
b 15 000 J/0.044 kg) [1] = 340 kJ/kg [1]
2 m_w = 0.152 kg − 0.144 kg = 0.008 kg [1]
L = 18 400 J/0.008 kg [1] = 2.3 MJ/kg [1]
3 a E_1 = 0.120 × 4200 × (15 − 9) °C [1] = 3024 J [1]
b E_2 = 0.008 × 4200 × 9 [1] = 302 J [1]
c energy transferred to melt ice = 3024 − 302 = 2722 J [1] specific latent heat of fusion of water = $\frac{2722 J}{0.008 kg}$ [1] = 340 kJ/kg [1]
4 E = 0.100 kg × 2.25 MJ/kg = 225 000 J [1] $t = \frac{225\,000\,J}{3000\,W}$ [1] = 75 s [1]

P6.6
1 a increases [1]
b unchanged [1]
c increases [1]
2 smoke particles move at random due to random impacts of air molecules, [1] if gas temperature increases, gas molecules move faster on average so impacts are harder and number of impacts per second increases, [1] so smoke particles move faster [1]
3 gas pressure stops increasing (or decreases) when valve opens, [1] number of gas molecules in cylinder decreases, [1] so number of impacts they make per second on cylinder's internal surface decreases and gas pressure stops increasing (or decreases) [1]
4 a unless water is stirred, (hot water rises and so) temperature of water differs in beaker, [1] thermometer does not measure average temperature of water [1]
b air in flask before sealed at atmospheric pressure, [1] so pressure gauge reads atmospheric pressure before it is sealed [1]

P7.1
1 a radiation from U consists = particles, radiation from lamp = electromagnetic waves, [1] radiation from U is ionising, radiation from lamp is non-ionising [1]
b radioactive atoms have unstable nuclei whereas atoms in lamp filament do not, [1] decay of radioactive atom cannot be stopped whereas atoms in lamp filament stop emitting radiation when filament current switched off [1]
2 a i alpha [1]
ii beta or gamma [1]
b gamma [1]

171

Answers

3 atoms have unstable nuclei, [1] these nuclei become stable by emitting radiation [1]

4a substance emits (ionising) radiation [1] so radioactive [1]

b paper stopped most radiation from substance reaching Geiger counter, [1] paper absorbed radiation, [1] so must be alpha radiation [1]

P7.2

1 nucleus much smaller than atom, [1] nucleus positively charged, [1] mass of atom concentrated in nucleus [1] all positive charge of atom concentrated in nucleus [1]

2a B [1]

b A: attracted by nucleus [1] C: unaffected by nucleus [1] D: repelled in wrong direction by nucleus [1]

3a i atoms not indivisible, [1] atoms contain negatively charged electrons [1]

ii any two from: nuclear: all positive charge concentrated in nucleus much smaller than atom, plum pudding: positive charge spread out throughout atom, [1] nuclear: most mass concentrated in nucleus, plum pudding: mass spread out throughout atom [1] nuclear: most atom empty space, plum pudding: no empty space [1]

b nuclear model explains why some alpha particles scattered through large angles, [1] in plum pudding model such large-angle scattering should not be observed [1]

4a similarity: proton and neutron have about same mass (**or** both found in nucleus) [1] difference: proton is charged whereas neutron has no charge [1]

b He nucleus contains 4 (neutrons + protons) whereas H nucleus only contains one = a single proton, [1] 2 protons particles in He nucleus because He nucleus has twice as much charge as H nucleus, [1] ∴ other 2 particles in He nucleus are neutrons [1]

P7.3

1a 6 p + 6 n [1]

b 27 p + 33 n [1]

c 92 p + 143 n [1]

d 4 p [1] 10 n [1]

2a 92 p + 146 n [1]

b 90 p [1] + 144 n [1]

c 91 p [1] + 143 n [1]

3a $^{235}_{92}U \rightarrow ^{231}_{90}Th + ^{4}_{2}\alpha$ [2]

b $^{64}_{29}Cu \rightarrow ^{64}_{30}Zn + ^{0}_{-1}\beta$ [2]

4 $^{210}_{83}Bi$ [1] $\rightarrow ^{210}_{84}Po$ [1] $+ ^{0}_{-1}\beta$ [1]

P7.4

1a stops irradiation of nearby people or objects [1]

b alpha [1]

c α, β [1]

2a i gamma [1]

ii alpha [1]

iii beta [1]

b i gamma [1]

ii alpha [1]

3a can knock electrons from atoms, [1] this ionisation damages cell (**or** kills cell **or** affects genes in cell which can be passed on if cell generates more cells) [1]

b (place Geiger tube in a holder so it can be moved horizontally,) move tube so end close to source and Geiger counter detects radiation from source, [1] move tube gradually away from source until count rate decreases significantly, [1] distance from end of tube to source is range of α radiation from source [1]

4 very little γ radiation absorbed by foil, it would all pass straight through [1] so thickness of foil would not affect detector reading [1]

P7.5

1a average time for no. nuclei in sample of isotope to halve [1]

b 190 cpm [1]

2a i 4 milligrams (= 8 mg/2) [1]

ii 1 milligram (= 8 mg/2^3) [1]

b 5% of 8 mg = 0.4 mg [1] so mass < 0.5 mg (= 8 mg/2^4) after 4 half-lives, [1] time taken ∴ just over 4 half-lives → about 65 hours [1]

3a i 160 million atoms [1]

ii 1/32 (= 1/2^5) [1]

iii number remaining = 320 million/2^5 [1] = 10 million atoms [1]

b after 4 half-lives, count rate = initial count rate of 320 cpm/24 = < 37.5 cpm [1] so time taken to drop to 40 cpm from start < 180 minutes (4 half-lives) [1]

4 after 2 half-lives count rate due to wood = 25% of initial count rate, [1] ∴ the wood is 11 200 years old (= 2 × 5600 yrs) [1]

P8.1

1a size of quantity [1]

b scalar has magnitude only, vector has direction too [1]

2 between 20 and 21 km [1]

3 scale diagram with ratio B : A = 1.25 : 1 (= 15 N ÷ 12 N, arrow for B ∴ be 1.25 times the length of the arrow for A. [1]

4a depends on 48 N arrow length: e.g., 60 mm arrow → scale 10 mm ≡ 8.0 N [1]

b ratio B : A = 0.75 : 1 (= 36 N ÷ 48 N), arrow for B points downwards from object along dashed line, arrow ∴ 0.75 times length of arrow for A [1]

P8.2

1a decelerates [1]

b force equal and opposite to force road exerts on each tyre [1]

2a 50 N upwards [1]

b 200 N [1]

3a forces equal in magnitude to each other and opposite in direction [1] because book presses on table and table exerts equal and opposite force on book [1]

b forces vertically downwards but force of table on floor > force of book on floor [1] because floor supports weight of table **and** book, table only supports book [1]

4a 500 N downwards [1]

b 500 N upwards [1]

c 500N upwards [1]

P8.3

1 glider makes contact with track and stops moving along it, friction between glider and track no longer absent when glider makes contact with track so glider stops because friction opposes its motion [2]

2a opposite in direction to velocity [1]

b zero [1]

3a force of mud on car > force on car from tractor [1]

b 300 N [1]

Answers

4a weight vector downward vertical arrow with non-arrow end on car mid-way between wheels [1]

b support force vectors upward and vertical from point of contact of each wheel on road [1]

P8.4

1a and **c** centre of mass is where two diagonal lines from corners cross [2]

b centre of mass found by drawing two diametric lines at right angles, centre of mass is where the two lines cross [1]

2 centre of mass of child then directly below midpoint M of points of suspension of swing, [1] at this position, moment of child about M = 0 [1]

3 (see P8.6, Figure 4) make hole in one corner of card and suspend from rod, use plumb line to draw vertical line on card from rod, [1] repeat, hanging card from different corner, point where two lines meet is centre of mass [1]

4 in **a** resultant force = 0 because basket at rest, [1] **b** magnitude of resultant force is non-zero and acts towards wall in direction perpendicular to line between centre of mass and point of suspension [1]

P8.5

1a 50 N vertically upwards [1]

b 500 N up the slope [1]

2a 5.0 N at 37° to 4.0 N force [2]

b 6.1 N at 26° to 4.0 N force [2]

c 6.5 N at 28° to 4.0 N force [2]

3 5400 N (to 2 s.f.) correct diagram [1] correct answer [1]

4a diagram shows vertical line intersected at same point P by 2 upward straight lines at 70° to vertical line [1]

b i weight vector as downward vertical arrow from P, scale shown and arrow labelled 'weight' [1]

ii resultant of two tension arrows is equal and opposite to weight vector, resultant arrow ∴ vertically upwards from P and same length as weight arrow, [1] completing parallelogram of forces gives length of the two tension arrows, [1] using scale should then give 2.9 N for each tension [1]

P8.6

1 690 N correct diagram [1] correct answer [1]

2a 130 N (to 2 s.f.) correct diagram [1] correct answer [1]

b friction on bearings of trolley wheels makes trolley harder to push **or** force exerted by student may not be parallel to slope [1]

3 not enough friction on ladder at floor [1] so weight pulls ladder down [1]

4a correct diagram [1] with parallel component = 25 N [1], perpendicular component = 43 N [1]

b friction on box equal and opposite to parallel component of weight (25 N) [1]

P9.1

1a i does not change [1]

ii constant gradient [1]

b i $\dfrac{30\,000\,\text{m}}{1000\,\text{s}}$ [1] = 30 m/s [1]

ii 500 s [1]

iii $\dfrac{20\,000\,\text{m}}{1500\,\text{s}}$ [1] = 13.3 m/s [1]

2a $\dfrac{1800\,\text{m}}{60\,\text{s}}$ [1] = 30 m/s [1]

b 30 m/s × 3000 s [1] = 9000 m [1]

c $\dfrac{3300\,\text{m}}{30\,\text{ms}}$ [1] = 110 s [1]

3 distance = 7560 m, [1] speed = 18 m/s [1]

4a $\dfrac{360\,000\,\text{m}}{160 \times 60\,\text{s}}$ [1] = 37.5 m/s [1]

b $\dfrac{180\,000\,\text{m}}{40\,\text{m/s}}$ [1] = 4500 s = 75 minutes [1]

P9.2

1a speed is distance travelled ÷ time taken regardless of direction, velocity is speed in a given direction [1]

b distance apart = (30 m/s − 20 m/s) × 300 s [1] = 2400 m [1]

2 $\dfrac{28\,\text{m/s} - 8\,\text{m/s}}{16\,\text{s}}$ [1] = 1.25 m/s² [1]

3a i as it left motorway [1]

ii when travelling at constant velocity [1]

b $a = \dfrac{v-u}{t}$ gives $2.0 = \dfrac{v-7}{10}$ [1] $v - 7 = 2.0 \times 10 = 20$ [1]

∴ v = 27 m/s [1]

4a $\dfrac{9.2\,\text{m/s} - 0}{3.1\,\text{s}}$ [1] = 2.97 m/s² [1]

b $\dfrac{100\,\text{m}}{10.4\,\text{s}}$ [1] = 9.6 m/s [1]

P9.3

1 i B

ii A

iii D

iv C (all correct = [2] any 3 correct = 1])

2a i A [1]

ii C [1]

b B [1]

3a 8 × 20 = 160 m [1]

b $\dfrac{1}{2} \times 8 \times 20 = 80$ m [1]

4a $\dfrac{1}{2} \times 4\,\text{m/s} \times 20\,\text{s}$ [1] = 40 m [1]

b $\dfrac{1}{2} \times 6\,\text{m/s} \times 20\,\text{s}$ [1] = 60 m [1] difference = 160 m − 60 m = 100 m [1]

P9.4

1a $\dfrac{120\,\text{m}}{8\,\text{s}}$ [1] = 15 m/s [1]

b increases gradually [1] from 0 at start [1]

2a constant acceleration from rest to 8 m/s for 40 s [1] then constant deceleration for last 20 s [1]

b i $a = \dfrac{8\,\text{m/s} - 0\,\text{m/s}}{40\,\text{s}}$ [1] = 0.20 m/s² [1] $s = \dfrac{1}{2} \times 8\,\text{m/s} \times 40\,\text{s}$ [1] = 160 m [1]

ii $a = \dfrac{0\,\text{m/s} - 8\,\text{m/s}}{20\,\text{s}}$ [1] = −0.40 m/s² [1] $s = \dfrac{1}{2} \times 8\,\text{m/s} \times 20\,\text{s}$ [1] = 80 m [1]

c $\dfrac{(160 + 80)\,\text{m}}{60\,\text{s}}$ [1] = 4.0 m/s [1]

3a suitable scales [1] correctly plotted [1] best fit line drawn [1]

b $\dfrac{40\,\text{m/s} - 0\,\text{m/s}}{20\,\text{s}}$ [1] = 2.0 m/s² [1]

c i $\dfrac{1}{2} \times 40\,\text{m/s} \times 20\,\text{s}$ [1] = 400 m [1]

ii 40 m/s × 10 s [1] = 400 m [1]

4 $v^2 = 0 + (2 \times 2.0\,\text{m/s}^2 \times 1000\,\text{m}) = 4000\,\text{m}^2/\text{s}^2$ [1] $v = 63$ m/s [1]

P10.1

1a 640 N [1]

b 4.0 m/s² [1]

2a 16 N [1]

b 40 kg [1]

c 12 m/s² [1]

173

Answers

  d 2.4 N [1]
  e 25 000 kg [1]
3a 1500 kg × 2 m/s² [1] = 3000 N [1]
  b i 600 N [1]
    ii 3000 N − 600 N [1] = 2400 N [1]
4a total mass greater in 2nd case [1] and force same so acceleration is less [1]
  b $F = 0.60m = 0.48(m + 0.5)$ [1] gives $m = 2.0$ kg [1]

P10.2
1a initial resultant force = weight [1]
  b frictional force < weight [1]
  c zero [1]
  d zero [1]
2a 500 N [1]
  b 80 N [1]
  c mass = 300 N/10 N/kg = 30 kg [1] weight on Moon = 30 kg × 1.6 N/kg = 48 N [1]
3a resultant force = weight − frictional force [1] frictional force due to parachute increases with speed [1] so resultant force on parachutist decreases, [1] when frictional force = weight, resultant force = 0 and parachutist moves at terminal velocity [1]
  b i 900 N [1]
    ii 900 N upwards [1]
4a gradient measured at 0.10 s [1] = 5.2 m/s² [1]
  b for mass m, resultant force at 0.10 s = m × acceleration a, $a = 5.2$ m/s² = $0.52g$. Because resultant force = weight − drag force, drag force = $mg - ma$ [1] = $mg - 0.52mg$ [1] = $0.48mg$ ≈ half its weight [1]

P10.3
1a braking distance [1]
  b thinking distance [1]
  c braking distance [1]
2a i 6.0 m [1]
    ii 24.0 m [1]
    iii 30.0 m [1]
  b (30 m/s × 0.8 s) − (15 m/s × 0.8 s) [1] = 12 m [1]
3a i thinking distance proportional to speed [1] as reaction time is constant [1]
    ii when speed doubled and braking force constant, braking time greater [1] so braking distance more than doubles (think about area under velocity–time graph) [1]
  b braking distance divided by v^2 same for all three speeds [1] so braking distance proportional to v^2 [1] so claim is valid [1]
4a 312/150 [1] = 6.4 m/s² [1]
  b 1500 kg × 6.4 m/s² [1] = 9600 N [1]

P10.4
1a momentum = mass × velocity, kg m/s [1]
  b 40 kg × 6 m/s [1] = 240 kg m/s [1]
2a 80 kg × 5 m/s [1] = 400 kg m/s [1]
  b 400 kg m/s ÷ 80 kg [1] = 0.5 m/s [1]
  c 400 kg m/s ÷ 0.40 kg [1] = 1000 m/s
3a equal and opposite forces [1]
  b equal and opposite momentum [1]
  c v 80 kg skater = three-quarters v 60 kg skater [1] in opposite direction [1]
  d total momentum = 0 [1]

4a 120 kg m/s [1]
  b $80v = 60 × 2.0$ kg m/s [1] $\therefore v = 60 × 2.0/80$ [1] = 1.5 m/s [1]

P10.5
1a limit beyond which tension no longer proportional to extension [1]
  b force per unit extension as long as limit of proportionality not reached [1]
  c increase in length from its original unstretched length [1]
2a does not return to original length when released [1]
  b rubber band returns to original length when released whereas polythene strip does not [1]
3a i 80 mm [1]
    ii 54 mm [1]
    iii 10 mm [1]
  b i 60 mm [1]
    ii 3.0 N/0.060 m [1] = 50 N/m [1]
4a extension of spring directly proportional to force applied as long as limit of proportionality not exceeded [1]
  b i 25 N/m × 0.10 m [1] = 2.5 N [1]
    ii 5.0 N/25 N/m [1] = 0.20 m [1]

P11.1
1a oscillations perpendicular to direction of energy transfer in transverse wave but parallel in a longitudinal wave [1]
  b i electromagnetic wave **or** waves on stretched string / wire [1]
    ii sound waves [1]
  c particles displaced so closer together [1]
2a transverse [1]
  b i along rope from one end to the other [1]
    ii oscillates in a direction perpendicular to energy transfer [1]
3 stretch slinky out, move one end at right angles to slinky for transverse waves or parallel to slinky for longitudinal waves [1]
4 ball moves up and down repeatedly on surface [1] because waves consist of successive crests and troughs moving across surface, [1] each crest pushes ball up and each trough allows it to move down [1]

P11.2
1 the number crests passing a point in one second **or** the number of cycles of waves that pass a point in one second [1]
2a i horizontally from P to next crest [1]
    ii vertically from P to midpoint [1]
  b P moves vertically [1] down to a minimum then back to point P [1]
3a 2.0 Hz × 3.0 m [1] = 6.0 m/s [1]
  b i $\dfrac{6.0\text{ m/s}}{1.0\text{ Hz}}$ [1] = 6.0 m [1]
    ii 6.0 m/s × 60 s [1] = 360 m [1]
4a 340 m/s × 5.0 s [1] = 1700 m [1]
  b $\dfrac{340\text{ m/s}}{3000\text{ Hz}}$ [1] = 0.11 m to 2 s.f. [1]

P11.3
1 incident = reflected angle [1]
2 see P12.3 Figures 2 and 3: correct refraction, [1] correct directions, [1] refracted wavelength < incident wavelength [1]
3a slopes prevent reflection at sides of tank [1]
  b reflected waves make it hard to see incident waves [1]
4 any four from: place sunglasses on white paper at fixed distance from light source in darkened room directly facing light source, [1] place light meter behind each lens in turn with meter as close as possible to lens without touching it, [1] mark position of

Answers

meter at each lens on the paper, record each meter reading, [1] remove sunglasses without moving paper and record reading when meter at each marked position for each lens, [1] second reading – first reading for each lens → effect of lens on light: the bigger the difference the less light transmitted [1]

P11.4

1 340 m/s × 4.0 s [1] = 1360 m [1]

2a 20 000 Hz [1]

b time delay = 0.24 s (= 2.4 s /10) [1] distance to wall and back = speed × time = 340 m/s × 0.24 s = 82 m, $s = 0.5 \times 82$ m = 41 m [1]

3a cliff face reflects sound from horn creating echo, [1] indicating cliffs nearby [1]

b distance = 340 m/s × 5.0 s/2 [1] = 850 m [1]

P12.1

1a radio waves [1]

b same for all electromagnetic waves [1]

c X-rays [1]

d microwaves [1]

2a radio, infrared, X-rays and gamma rays [1]

b microwaves, visible light, ultraviolet [1]

c radio, microwaves, infrared, visible light, ultraviolet X-rays, gamma rays [2]

3a $\dfrac{300\,000\,000 \text{ m/s}}{600\,000\,000 \text{ Hz}}$ [1] = 0.50 m [1]

b $\dfrac{300\,000\,000 \text{ m/s}}{0.30 \text{ m}}$ [1] = 1000 MHz [1]

4 all electromagnetic waves travel at same speed in space, [1] gamma rays and visible light travel same distance and emitted at same time so reach Earth at same time [1]

P12.2

1a i radio waves [1]

  ii light [1]

b i microwaves [1]

  ii radio waves [1]

2a handset signals would interfere with mobile phone signals so calls less clear [1]

b other signals might 'mask' emergency services signals [1] making vital conversations difficult to listen to [1]

3 $\dfrac{300\,000\,000 \text{ m/s}}{2400\,000\,000 \text{ Hz}}$ [1] = 0.125 m [1]

4a reflects microwaves from transmitter into receiver [1]

b i place receiver directly in front of transmitter and measure signal detected, [1] place metal plate between receiver and transmitter and record meter reading [1]

  ii replace metal plate by cardboard and record reading again, [1] if reading not zero, microwaves can pass through [1]

P12.3

1a visible light, infrared [1]

b signals totally internally reflected so cannot escape from fibre except at receiver end, [1] radio signals travel through air so detected by any radio detector in their path [1]

2a child's skull is thinner than adult [1] so more radiation passes through more easily (and causes a greater heating effect) [1]

b light waves have a much higher frequency, [1] carry more pulses per second [1]

3 atmosphere absorbs microwaves less than radio waves [1] microwaves spread out less so suitable for satellite TV, [1]

radio waves diffract more so better reception in hilly areas for terrestrial TV [1]

4a $\dfrac{300\,000\,000 \text{ m/s}}{105\,000\,000 \text{ Hz}}$ [1] = 2.8 m [1]

b lower frequencies not absorbed so much by atmosphere [1] → longer range so suitable for national broadcasts [1]

P12.4

1a X-rays pass through crack but not through surrounding metal, [1] X-rays passing through crack darken photographic film, [1] crack appears as break in metal object shadow [1]

b yes [1]

c metal case stops low-energy X-rays but plastic does not [1] plastic allows X-rays to reach film inside case, giving more realistic account of exposure [1]

2a penetrate skin → skin cancer, [1] damage eyes → sight defects or blindness [1]

b i absorbs most ultraviolet radiation from Sun [1]

  ii ultraviolet radiation from Sun causes sunburn and skin cancer, [1] suncreams absorb UV that passes through ozone layer [1] to stop UV reaching skin [1]

3a X-rays and gamma rays [1]

b lead [1]

4a ionisation is process of making uncharged atoms become ions which are charged atoms [1] occurs when X-rays or gamma radiation pass through substances, [1] as X-rays and gamma radiation knock electrons out of uncharged atoms [1]

b i X-rays and gamma rays [1]

  ii ultraviolet radiation, X-rays and gamma rays [1]

P12.5

1a absorbs X-rays, [1] otherwise X-rays pass through stomach so no details of stomach seen on X-ray film [1]

b used to destroy cancerous tissue [1]

2a dense materials such as bone absorb X-rays and stop them reaching film, [1] X-rays that do not pass through dense material darken film, [1] when film developed, clear images of bones and other absorbing materials seen as X-rays did not reach these areas [1]

b light from room would darken film [1]

c X-rays ionise substances they pass through, [1] ionisation can damage or kill cells [1] or cause cell mutation and cancerous growth, [1] shielding prevents X-rays reaching and damaging cells in parts of patient not under investigation [1]

3a X-rays used for therapy have much shorter wavelengths/greater energy [1]

b not enough energy to destroy cancerous tumours [1]

4a a measure of the damage caused by ionising radiation to a person [1]

b about 0.3 millisieverts (≈ 13% of 2 mSv) [1]

P13.1

1a i N

  ii S [1]

b N-pole, [1] P repels X because it has same polarity [1]

2a i N [1]

  ii S [1]

  iii unmagnetised [1]

175

Answers

  b pole of compass nearest tip of nail induces magnetism in nail with opposite pole at tip [1] so tip of nail always attracts end of plotting compass nearest it because they have unlike poles [1]
3a X = N, Y = S [1]
  b needle would turn (anticlockwise) as N-pole end of compass follows Y [1] until X attracts the S-pole more than Y attracts the N-pole, [1] S-pole then turns towards X until adjacent to X when magnet completes the 180° rotation [1]
4 draw two straight lines crossing at middle, place plotting compass directly above where lines meet, turn paper so plotting compass points along one line, [1] place bar magnets equidistant on opposite sides of plotting compass, [1] move one magnet along the line so plotting compass points directly along the perpendicular line, magnet that is further from plotting compass must be stronger than other magnet, [1] because its effect cancels out effect of other magnet at a greater distance [1] (**or** valid alternative methods described correctly [2] and explained [2])

P13.2

1a see P15.2, Figure 1: concentric circles round wire, [1] lines of force in correct direction [1]
  b plotting compass points in same direction as nearest field line [1]
2a reverses direction plotting compass points [1]
  b gradually moves towards North, [1] magnetic field of current-carrying wire becomes weaker further from wire [1] so Earth's magnetic field has greater effect [1]
3a see P15.2, Figure 3: field lines are loops which pass through solenoid [1] and loop round outside, [1] lines in solenoid are parallel to solenoid axis [1]
  b i plotting compass points parallel to the axis [1] in a direction consistent with current direction in solenoid [1]
  ii plotting compass points turns more and more towards North [1] because field of solenoid becomes weaker so Earth's magnetic field has more effect [1]
4 similarities: field lines are continuous loops, [1] field lines reverse direction when current reverses (**or** both fields can be switched off by switching the current off) [1] differences: field lines around wire are circles whereas field lines inside solenoid are straight and parallel to solenoid axis, [1] field inside solenoid is uniform whereas field near wire is not [1]

P13.3

1 any three from: when current passes through coil of motor, a force acts on each side of coil due to magnetic field of magnet in motor, [1] force on each side has turning effect on coil and because current on each side in opposite directions, forces also in opposite directions so motor turns, [1] each time coil passes position where coil perpendicular to magnetic field, split-ring commutator reverses connections to battery so current round coil reverses direction, [1] without split-ring commutator, forces would reverse and coil would turn back, vibrating, [1] action of split-ring commutator allows forces to continue to turn coil in one direction [1]
2a current in opposite direction [1] so force on each side in opposite direction, coil ∴ rotates in opposite direction [1]
  b i faster (coil lighter) [1]
   ii faster (field much stronger due to iron) [1]

3 force decreases [1] → zero when wire perpendicular to field lines, [1] direction of force does not change [1]
4 $\dfrac{0.024\,\text{N}}{1.8\,\text{A} \times 0.035\,\text{m}}$ [1] = 0.38 T [1]

MS1

1a ratio = 5.6 g : 25.2 g = 1 : 4.5 [1]
  b width of strip = width of card / 4.5 [1] = 210 mm / 4.5 = 47 mm [1]
2a $\dfrac{30}{24}$ = 1.25, [1] ∴ ratio of car speed to coach speed = 1.25 : 1 [1]
  b for the same time, $\dfrac{\text{distance travelled by car}}{\text{distance travelled by coach}}$ = 1.25 [1]
  ∴ distance travelled by car = 1.36 × distance travelled by coach = 1.25 × 12 km = 16 km [1]

MS2

1a 1.679 s = 1.68 to 3 s.f. [1]
  b 1.66 s [1]
  c 1.61 s and 1.65 s [1]
2a 1 [1]
  b 3 [1]
  c 3 [1]
  d 4 [1]
  e 3 [1]
  f 3 [1]
3a gas was hardly used in 1990 whereas in 2010 it was used to generate about 40% of UK electricity, [1] coal was used to generate about two-thirds of UK electricity in 1990 but in 2010 this reduced to about one third of UK electricity, [1] oil generated < 10% of UK electricity in 2010 but this is much more than in 1990, [1] nuclear power stations provided just under 20% of UK electricity in both 2010 and in 1990 [1]
  b i renewable energy sources in 2010 were used to generate less than 10% of UK electricity whereas the comparable figure for fossil fuels was about 70%, [1] comparable figures for 1990 were about 5% for renewable energy and 75% for fossil fuels. [1]
   ii since 1990, fossil fuel use as a percentage of total UK electricity generation down by about 5% [1] and renewable energy use up by about same amount [1]
4 speed ~ 0.1 m/s, [1] distance in 1 minute ~ 6 m [1]

MS3

1a i m [1]
   ii m^3 [1]
   iii kg [1]
   iv N [1]
  b i 7.2×10^{-2} m [1]
   ii 1.6×10^{-5} m [1]
   iii 3.85×10^{8} m [1]
   iv 5.6×10^{4} [1]
2a the circumference of the Earth is much less than the circumference of the Sun [1]
  b atmospheric pressure is proportional to altitude [1]
  c 4.5 kJ is about the same as 4.61 kJ [1]
3a $k = \dfrac{F}{e}$ [1]
  b unit of k is the unit of force (N) divided by the unit of distance (m) = N/m [1]
4a $e = \sqrt{\dfrac{2E}{k}}$ [1]
  b $\sqrt{(\text{J} \div \text{N/m})}$ = m [1]

5a $S = \dfrac{v^2 - u^2}{2a}$ [1]
b 69 m [1]

MS4

1a i gradient [1]
   ii y-intercept [1]
b i positive gradient straight line [1] through origin [1]
   ii straight line below A with lower gradient and lower y-intercept [1]
2 $y \rightarrow F$, $x \rightarrow e$, $m \rightarrow k$ and $c \rightarrow y$-intercept [2]
3 $y \rightarrow v$, $x \rightarrow t$, $m \rightarrow a$ and $c \rightarrow u$ [2]
4 gradient of tangent at 4s [1] determined from gradient triangle [1] = 7.5 m/s (7.3 to 7.7 m/s acceptable) [1]

MS5

1a 4.4 m² [1]
b 0.21 m² [1] (both to 2 sf)
2a 3.4 m³ [1]
b 14 m² [1] (both to 2 sf)
3a area of each coloured triangle is same, taking base of each triangle as 1.6 m, height of each triangle is half width of kite = 0.575 m (= 1.15 m/2), [1] area of each triangle = $\dfrac{1}{2}$ × height × base = 0.5 × 0.575 m × 1.60 m = 0.46 m² [1] so area of kite = area of both triangles = 2 × 0.46 m² = 0.92 m² [1]

Index

absorption 141
acceleration 114–116, 118–119, 122–125
accuracy 201–202
acid rain 38
activity 92–93
air resistance 125
algebra 187–190
alpha radiation 84–85, 88, 90–91
alternating current 58–59
aluminium foil 28
ammeters 46
amperes 47
amplitude 138
angles 196
anomalies 205
appliances 18–21, 66–67
area 197
area under graphs 117, 119, 194
arithmetic computation 174–180
atomic numbers 88
atoms 84–93
automatic thickness monitoring 90–91
averages 182, 184, 203

balanced forces 98–111
bar charts 182–183, 203
bar magnets 158
Becquerels 92
beta radiation 84, 88–91
biofuels 32
Bohr's model of the atom 87
boiling points 74–75, 79
braking 14–15, 102, 116–117, 126–127
braking distance 126–127
Brownian motion 81
building insulation 25, 28
bulbs 50–51
bungee jumping 7

cables 48–49, 60–61, 63, 160–161
cancer 153, 155
capital costs of power stations 40–41
carbon capture and storage 38
carbon-neutral energy 32, 34–41
carrier waves 150–151
cars 126–127
categoric variables 182, 199
causal relationships 185

cavity wall insulation 28
cells 46, 52
centre of mass 104–105
changes of state 74–75
charge 46–47, 64, 87
charge-coupled devices 154
chemical stores of energy 4–5
clockwork radios 19
collisions 128–129
commutators 163
components of electric circuits 46, 50–51
compression 131
conclusions 203–205
conduction, thermal 24–25
conservation of energy 6–7
conservation of mass 72
conservation of momentum 128–129
constant speed 112–113, 118
contact forces 100–101
continuous variables 182, 199
contrast medium 154
control groups 201
controlled explosions 129
conversion, units 190
copper 61
corkscrew rule 160
correlation 185
costs of power stations 40–41
coulombs 47, 64–65
count rates 92
cuboids 197–198
current 46–47, 52–55, 58–59, 62–65, 160–163
current–potential difference graphs 49
curved graphs 193–194

dangers of radioactivity 91
data 181–186, 191, 203–205
deceleration 115–117, 123, 126–127
decimal form 174
density 70–71
dependent variables 200
diodes 46–47, 51
direct current 58
directly proportional 130–131, 204
discrete variables 182
displacement 98, 114
dissipation of energy 14–17

distance–time graphs 112–113, 118
doses of radiation 154–155
double-glazed windows 28
drag forces 124–125

earthing 58, 60–61
earth wires 60–61
echoes 143
echo sounding 143
efficiency 16–19, 21, 66–67
elasticity 4–5, 13, 130–131
elastic potential energy 4–5, 13
electrical appliances 18–21, 66–67
electric circuits 46–65, 160–163
electric current 46–47, 52–55, 58–59, 62–65, 160–163
electric fields 162–163
electricity 4, 18–21, 46–65, 160–161
electricity demand 32, 40
electricity generation 29, 32–41
electricity in the home 58–69
electric motors 163
electric shocks 61
electromagnetic spectrum 146–149, 152–153
electromagnetic waves 136–141, 146–157
electromagnetism 158–165
electrons 46–49
emission 88–89
energy
    amplitude and frequency 138, 147
    changes of state 74–75, 78–79
    internal 76–77
    potential 4–7, 10–13
    power 20–21, 62–63, 66–67
    work done 8–9
energy conservation 6–7
energy demand 32, 40
energy dissipation 14–17
energy efficiency 16–19, 21
energy resources 32–43
energy transfers 5–21, 24–31, 62–65, 78–79
equal and opposite forces 100–101
equations 187–189, 214
equilibria 104, 109
errors 202–203
estimates 179–180, 205

178

Index

evaluation 205
evaporation 75
evidence 204
extension 130–131

fair tests 201
faults in circuits 60–61
filament bulbs 50–51
fixed resistors 46, 55
Fleming's left-hand rule 162
fluids 71–73, 77, 124–125
flux density 162–163
forces
    acceleration 114–116, 118–119, 122–125
    in balance 98–111
    between objects 100–101
    braking 14–15, 102, 116–117, 126–127
    deceleration 115–117, 123, 126–127
    drag 124–125
    elasticity 4–5, 13, 130–131
    electric fields 162–163
    equilibrium 104, 109
    free-body diagrams 103
    friction 9, 14–15, 101–102, 124–125, 127
    momentum 128–129
    motion 102, 122–133
    parallelograms 106–107
    power 20–21, 62–63, 66–67
    pressure 80–81
    resolution 108–109
    resultant 102–103, 122–123, 126–127
    scale diagrams 99
    springs 13, 130–131
    unbalanced 102–103
    vectors and scalars 98–99
    vehicles 126–127
    weight 4–5, 10–11, 124
    work done 8–9
fossil fuels 32–33, 38
fractions 177
free-body force diagrams 103
freely suspended 104
freezing points 74
frequency 138, 146–147, 182–183
frequency tables 182–183
friction 9, 14–15, 101–102, 124–125, 127
fuses 46, 60–61, 63

gamma radiation 84, 89–91, 152–153
gases 72–73, 77, 80–81
gas pressure 80–81
generating electricity 32–41
geometry 196–198
geothermal energy 37
gradients 112–113, 118, 185
graphite 163
graphs 112–114, 116–119, 182–183, 185, 191–195, 203
gravitational potential energy 4–5, 10–11
gravity 4–5, 10–11, 124–125
greenhouse gases 38

half-life 92–93
handling data 181–186
hazards 200
heaters 46
heating 24–31
heating effect 63–64
Hooke's Law 13, 131
hydroelectric power 34–35
hypotheses 200

ice 76, 78
inclines 108–109
independent variables 200
indicators 46
induced magnetism 159
induction 159
inertia 123
infrared radiation 148
insulators 25, 28, 60–61
intercepts 193
internal energy 76–77
investigations 199–204
ionisation 91, 153
irregular-shaped objects 105
isotopes 88–89
issues, energy generation 40–41

joules 8, 10–13, 16, 20–21, 64–66

kilowatts 20–21, 66
kinetic energy 4–5, 12–13
kinetic theory of matter 73, 76–77

latent heat 75, 78–79
left-hand rule 162
light 148

see also electromagnetic waves; waves
light-dependent resistors 51
light-emitting diodes 46, 51
limit of proportionality 131
limits of efficiency 16–17
line of best fit 185
line graphs 203
liquids 71–73, 77
live wires 58, 60–61
loft insulation 25, 28
longitudinal waves 137, 142–143
loudspeakers 142

magnetic fields 158–163
magnetic flux density 162–163
magnetism 158–165
magnitude 98
mains cables 61
mains circuits 58–63, 66–67
mass 11–13, 70–72, 104–105, 123–124, 128–129
mass numbers 88
mathematical symbols 187
maths skills 174–198
matter 70–79, 124
mean 182, 203
measurement 74, 84, 202
mechanical waves 136, 142–143
median 184
medicine 153–155
mediums 136, 142–143
melting points 74–75, 78
metals, conduction 24, 46, 61, 160
metric prefixes 189
microwaves 149–151
millisieverts 155
mobile phones 150–151
mode 184
molecules 76–77
momentum 128–129
Moon 11
motion 102, 112–133
motive force 101
motor effect 162–163
muscles 21

National Grid 58–59
neutral wires 58, 60–61
neutrons 87–89
Newtons 8, 10–11, 16, 100

Index

Newton's First Law of motion 102
Newton's Second Law of motion 122–123
Newton's Third Law 100–101
non-contact forces 100
north poles 158
nuclear power 33, 38–39
nuclei 33, 85–89
numerical computation 174–180

object representations 196
objects in equilibrium 109
ohmic conductors 49
ohms 48–49
opposite and equal forces 100–101
optical fibres 151
orders of magnitude 20, 185–186, 189
oscillations 6, 136–137
oscilloscopes 59
output power 66–67
overall costs of power stations 41

parallel circuits 54–55
parallelogram of forces 106–107
particles 38–89
   electric circuits 46–57
   electricity in the home 58–69
   kinetic theory of matter 73, 76–77
   molecules and matter 70–83
   radioactivity 84–111
payback time 28–29
pendulums 6
penetrating power 90
percentages 178–179
photons 87
physical changes 72–79
plastic 60–61
plotting graphs 192
plugs 60–61, 63
plum pudding model 86–87
plutonium 33
potential difference 48–49, 52–55, 58–59, 61–64
potential energy 4–7, 10–13
power 20–21, 62–63, 66–67
power stations 32–41
precision 201–202
prediction 200
prefixes 189
pressure 80–81
properties of waves 138–139
protons 87

qualitative data 182
quantitative data 182
quantities 188–189

radiation 28, 84–85
radioactive decay 88–89, 92–93
radioactivity 84–95
radio waves 149–151
random errors 202
random motion 81
randomness 81, 93, 202
range 203
rates of change 193
ratios 176
reaction times 126–127
rectangles 197
reflection 140–141, 151
refraction 140–141
relationships between variables 200, 203–205
renewable energy 32, 34–41
repeatability 199–200
representing objects 196
reproducibility 199–200
resistance 48–53
resistance heating 63–64
resistors 46–47, 49, 52–53, 55, 64
resolution 202
resolution of forces 108–109
resultant forces 102–103, 122–123, 126–127
ripple tanks 138–139
risks 200

safety 200
scalars 98–99
scale diagrams 99
scatter graphs 185, 203
series circuits 52–53
short circuits 61
sieverts 155
signals 150–151
significant figures 181
SI system of units 188–189
slopes of graphs 193
smoke cells 81
sockets 60–61
solar heating 36
solar power 29, 36
solenoids 161
solids 70–73, 76
sound waves 139, 142–143

south poles 158
specific heat capacity 26–27
specific latent heat 78–79
specific latent heat of fusion 78
specific latent heat of vaporisation 79
speed 112–119, 122–127
   see also acceleration; deceleration; velocity
speed of sound 139
speed of waves 138–139, 146–147
springs 13, 130–131
stability of nuclei 85
standard form 174–175
start-up time 40
states of matter 72–79
step-up/-down transformers 58
stopping distances 126–127
storage heaters 27
stores of energy 4–5
straight line graphs 191–192
stretch tests 130
subject of an equation 187–188
supply and demand 40
suspended equilibrium 104
switches 46
symbols 187
symmetrical objects 105
systematic errors 203–204

tables 182–183, 203
tangents 118, 193–194
temperature
   gas pressure 80–81
   insulation 25, 28
   internal energy 76–77
   specific heat capacity 26–27
terminal velocity 124–125
thee-core cables 60–61
thermal energy 4–5, 9, 14–15, 24–31
thermistors 51
thinking distance 126–127
three-dimensional representations 196
three-pin plugs 61
thrust 102
tidal power 35
transfers of energy 5–31
transformers 58
transmission of light 141
transverse waves 137–141
triangles 197
trigonometry 196–198
turbines 32, 34–35, 37

Index

two-core cables 61
two-dimensional representations 196

ultraviolet waves 152
unbalanced forces 102–103
uncertainty 205
units 188–190
unstable nuclei 85
uranium 33
useful energy 14–19, 21

vaporisation 79
variable resistors 46–47
variables 199–201
vectors 98–99, 108–109
velocity 114–119, 122–133
velocity–time graphs 114, 116–119
visible light 148
voltage 58–59
voltmeters 46
volume 197–198

wasted energy 14–19, 21
water 79
watts 20–21, 62–63
wavelengths 138, 146–147, 150
wave power 34
waves
   absorption 141
   electromagnetic 136–141, 146–157
   longitudinal 137
   materials 141
   mechanical 136, 142–143
   mediums 136, 142–143
   properties 136–139
   reflection 140–141, 151
   refraction 140–141
   signals 150–151
   sound 142–143
   transmission 141
   transverse 137–141
wave speed 138–139, 146–147
weight 4–5, 10–11, 124–125
white light 148

wind power 34
wires 48–49, 60–61, 63, 160–161
work done 8–9

X-rays 91, 152–155